LATIN AMERICAN AMERICAN
INDIGENOUS WARFARE
AND RITUAL VIOLENCE

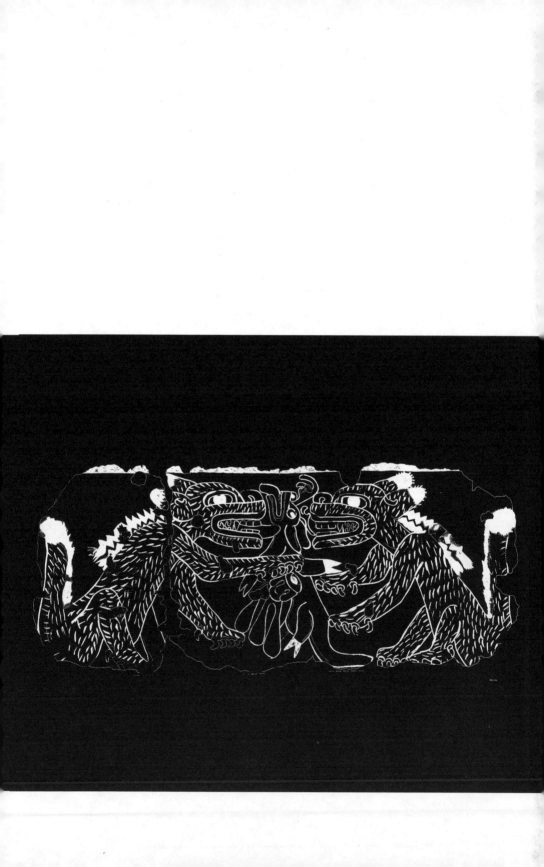

LATIN AMERICAN

INDIGENOUS WARFARE
AND RITUAL VIOLENCE

Edited by Richard J. Chacon and Rubén G. Mendoza

The University of Arizona Press   Tucson

The University of Arizona Press
© 2007 The Arizona Board of Regents
All rights reserved

Library of Congress Cataloging-in-Publication Data

Latin American indigenous warfare and ritual violence / edited
by Richard J. Chacon and Rubén G. Mendoza.
p. cm.
Includes bibliographical references and index.
ISBN-13: 978-0-8165-2527-0 (hardcover : alk. paper)
ISBN-10: 0-8165-2527-7 (hardcover : alk. paper)
1. Indians—Warfare. 2. Indians—Rites and ceremonies.
3. Violence—Latin America. 4. Human sacrifice—Latin America.
5. Territorial expansion—Latin America. 6. Social archaeology—
Latin America. 7. Violence in art. 8. Latin America—Antiquities.
I. Chacon, Richard J., 1959– II. Mendoza, Ruben G.
E59.W3L37 2007
980'.00498—dc22   2006038419

Manufactured in the United States of America on acid-free, archival-quality paper
containing a minimum of 50% post-consumer waste and processed chlorine free.

12 11 10 09 08 07   6 5 4 3 2 1

CONTENTS

Acknowledgments

I wish to thank my good friend Rubén Mendoza for the pleasure of working together on this volume. Much appreciation goes to Don McVicker, who aided in organizing the "Problems in Paradise" symposium on Amerindian violence at the 2003 American Anthropological Association meeting in Chicago. I am most appreciative of the many scholars who entrusted me with their work in this endeavor. I am also deeply indebted to my friend and colleague David Whitely, who played an instrumental role in the genesis and implementation of both the session and this edited volume. In addition, I would like to thank the two anonymous reviewers who provided valuable critiques.

I am grateful to all the people at Winthrop University who were supportive of this project, especially the dean of the College of Arts and Sciences, Debra Boyd, who generously provided financial assistance to defray the expenses associated with the manuscript's publication. I also wish to acknowledge Douglas Eckberg, chair of Winthrop's Department of Sociology and Anthropology, and Jonathan Marx, interim chair, for their continued backing of my research. This project benefited greatly from the diligent efforts of Douglas Short, Carrie Volk, and the entire Inter-Library Loan (ILL) staff of Winthrop University's Dacus Library, who succeeded at securing some of the most obscure documents ever published. I also received indispensable computer technical support from Campus Information Technology personnel, particularly Taylor Glass and Joseph Martin.

I wish to thank Patricio Moncayo (Pontifica Universidad Catolica de Ecuador) for years of friendship and collaboration. Also, much gratitude is extended toward Steve Nelson and his wife, Dorothy, for their gracious hospitality while I was in Ecuador. Lastly, I would like to thank my lovely wife, Yamilette Chacon, for her indefatigable support (academic, technical, and emotional). Without her assistance, this project would have never come to fruition.

Richard J. Chacon

I would like to acknowledge the many scholars and students who have informed my perspective on the question of indigenous ritual violence and conflict in the Americas. I am particularly indebted to my good friend Richard Chacon, whose diligence and determination to see through both the "Problems in Paradise" symposium and the creation of this volume proved both an inspiration and the beginning of a long-term collaboration. Moreover, I am particularly indebted to the many scholars who contributed significant new findings and research for the "Problems in Paradise" symposium. I also wish to thank the dean of the College of Arts and Sciences at Winthrop University, Debra Boyd, for her provision of a publication subvention when California State University–Monterey Bay was not in a position to fund my editorial treatment of the manuscript prior to submission to the University of Arizona Press.

At California State University–Monterey Bay, Lilly Martinez continues to provide critical clerical and administrative support, and department chair George Baldwin remains extraordinarily committed to creating a collegial and scholarly research and teaching environment for the faculty of the Social and Behavioral Sciences. Donaldo Urioste of CSU–Monterey Bay and Charlie Cambridge of the Office of Federal Acknowledgment provided invaluable feedback on many of the ideas presented in my chapter on Neo-Mexica revisionism, as well as offering suggestions pertaining to the introductory and concluding chapters of this volume. Longtime friends Hector Campoy and Glory Tacheenie have made their beautiful home a welcome respite for several of my "writing retreats" to the Sonoran Desert, and it is there and in Tucson that the resources of the University of Arizona Library have permitted me to bring to fruition this and related projects. Eddy Hogan and the staff of the CSU–Monterey Bay Library are to be commended for their extraordinary efforts on behalf of this and related projects via Interlibrary Loan requests and other research support. I also wish to acknowledge CSU–Monterey Bay student Genetta Butler, who assisted with word processing and related typescript revisions necessary to the completion of the introductory and concluding portions of the manuscript.

Finally, I acknowledge my wife and companion, Linda Marie Mendoza, and daughters, Natalie Dawn Marie and Maya Nicole Mendoza, for their generous understanding, ongoing support, and the many personal sacrifices made in support of my many research and writing projects.

Rubén G. Mendoza

LATIN AMERICAN
AMERICAN
INDIGENOUS WARFARE
AND RITUAL VIOLENCE

INTRODUCTION

Richard J. Chacon and Rubén G. Mendoza

The goal of this volume is to explore those uniquely human motivations and environmental variables that have led the native peoples of Latin America to engage in warfare and ritual human sacrifice since remote antiquity. Both popular lore and scholarly misrepresentations dominate a contrasting body of public perceptions regarding Amerindian warfare and ritual violence. As such, both Amerindian and Western preconceptions regarding those phenomena threaten to hinder further progress in our understanding of this dimension of the human experience. In sum, a sort of cognitive dissonance now echoes throughout academia. On one side of this divide stand those who dogmatically adhere to the endemic cultural "reality" of Amerindian warfare and ritual violence; on the other are revisionists who seek to co-opt the argument altogether. For those attempting an impartial, or reasonably impartial, assessment of Amerindian conflict in Latin America, we believe that a new and fundamental challenge has been presented in an increasingly contentious and highly politicized landscape of competing social, cultural, and nationalistic interests.

In an effort to address these challenges, the co-editors of this volume convened a distinguished group of scholars. Our prime objective was to review the archaeological, ethnohistorical, ethnographic, and forensic evidence for warfare and ritual violence in aboriginal Latin America. The present volume ventures well beyond those fundamental questions and revisionist arguments that today challenge the idea that Amerindians engaged in significant levels of armed conflict and ritual violence prior to the arrival of European invaders. Contributors to this volume individually and collectively explore the multifaceted world of causes and consequences that underpin indigenous conflict in the Americas, both past and present. Although warfare has been defined in a multitude of ways, we adopt the definition of warfare as "socially organized armed combat between members of different territorial units (communities or aggregates of communities)" (Ember and Ember 1994, 190). To accommodate the broader theme of armed conflict and ritual violence in the Americas, we have chosen to expand the aforementioned definition to include cultural, religious, ideological, political, and economic motivations in the fray as well.

Our collective analysis of the data presented here clearly indicates the great antiquity of indigenous warfare and ritual violence in Latin America. Moreover, armed conflict appears to have been prevalent, as every major culture area of Latin America reviewed here has produced archaeological, ethnohistorical, osteological, and/or ethnographic evidence for warfare and related patterns of conflict interaction.

Clearly, it would be unreasonable and naïve to attempt in this context to propose a singular or primary cause or set of variables that underlie warfare and ritual violence in aboriginal Latin America. Theoretical discussions concerned with armed combat and ritual violence in the Americas necessarily require consideration of the region's tremendous ecological and cultural diversity. Similarly, we must acknowledge that human motivations for going to war in any one context may vary dramatically and change through time.

Rather than conjure, and thereby promote, any one singular or monolithic explanation for warfare, we collectively interrogate the evidence for those patterns that belie the root causes of intergroup conflict by considering the evidence for warfare and ritual violence in each culture area on a case-by-case basis. This approach not only serves to illuminate the causes and consequences of conflict for those case studies so scrutinized but also will foster further research through theory building and the quest for those causal variables that underlie indigenous warfare and ritual violence in Latin America.

Since warfare and ritual violence are phenomena found continent-wide, we have attempted to be as exhaustive and inclusive as possible by presenting at least one scholarly contribution reflecting current research from each major cultural area of Latin America. This consideration was at the heart of our efforts to bring together a distinguished cohort of scholars for a symposium on that theme. Papers produced by invitation of the senior editor were presented before the 2003 annual meetings of the American Anthropological Association in Chicago. Results were delivered within the context of an interdisciplinary symposium titled "Problems in Paradise." Our prime objective at that time was to present data that inform the question of warfare and ritual violence in aboriginal America. Ultimately, so successful was our call for papers on this theme that the whole of the day-long symposium had to be divided into North American and Latin American sections solely for editorial considerations. Those insights and observations first presented within the context of the "Problems in Paradise" symposium have been assembled here to facilitate further examination of the evidence and, concomitantly, to challenge prevailing revisionist views such as that of Russell Means and Marvin Wolf (1995, 16), who assert, "Before the whites came, our conflicts were brief and almost bloodless, resembling far more a professional football game than the lethal annihilations of European conquest."

In chapter 1, Matt O'Mansky and Arthur Demarest document the antiquity and variability of Maya warfare by first establishing its origins in the Preclassic. They follow by reporting on the motivations for organized conflict and its change through time. They hold that the regional intensification of conflict in the seventh and eighth centuries AD derived in large part from interelite competition for positions of prestige, access to status-reinforcing exotic trade goods, and tribute. They cite as their evidence for conflict an increase in the number of fortifications, iconographic representations, and references to warfare and conflict in the Mayan glyphic texts. Their respective arguments challenge prevailing views that contend that organized conflict and the collapse of Classic period Maya civilization were largely attributable to environmental degradation or desiccation. With the end of the Classic Maya *k'uhul ajaw* system (ca. late eighth through early tenth centuries AD), they further contend that the aim of warfare shifted from constituting a mechanism for competing with and eliminating rivals (during the Classic era) to a political-economic strategy for securing interregional trade routes and resources such as salt and cacao.

In chapter 2, Rubén G. Mendoza critically reviews revisionist arguments that ethnohistorical accounts reporting Aztec ritual violence are to be dismissed as colonialist propaganda. He then proceeds to examine key archaeological, osteological, and forensic evidence and approaches bearing on precontact Mexica Aztec ritual violence recovered from the Templo Mayor as well as from the earlier Preclassic through Postclassic sites of Tlatelcomila, Electra, Tlatelolco, and Cantona. These locations throughout the Mexican highlands clearly provide context-specific findings necessary to corroborate firsthand accounts by sixteenth-century Europeans of Mesoamerican warfare, ritual human sacrifice, and cannibalism.

In chapter 3, Charles S. Spencer argues that military statecraft and territorial expansion originating with Monte Albán, Oaxaca, gave rise to the first state-level society in Mesoamerica circa 300 BC. The early Zapotec state was the epicenter of the development in question. Spencer cites the evolution of the palace compound, the multiroom temple, and a four-tiered settlement hierarchy as prima facie evidence for the presence of state-level social organization in the Valley of Oaxaca. Manifest patterns of military statecraft and the use of coercive force are interpreted from the iconography of Monte Albán and the archaeological record of regions that were targeted by the expansionist Zapotec state. The Building J complex of conquest (slab) inscriptions at Monte Albán and archaeological evidence from Cañada de Cuicatlán, the Sola Valley, Pacific coastal zone, and adjacent areas are cited as relevant in this regard. The evidence from the Cañada included burned and abandoned villages, intrusive fortifications, and the oldest *tzompantli* "skull rack" excavated in the region to date.

In chapter 4, Donald McVicker reviews Mesoamerican highland and lowland mural art from Teotihuacán, Cacaxtla, Bonampak, and Chichén Itzá. He considers how past scholars, seeking to promote the myth of the peaceful Classic Maya, have attempted to explain away battle murals and the iconography of captive sacrifice as "ritual battles" or representations of mythological events. McVicker then reviews the lack of evidence for images of armed conflict in the murals of Teotihuacán and concludes that the paucity of such imagery should not be uncritically accepted as evidence for Teotihuacán's reticence to engage in organized conflict. In fact, archaeological and forensic evidence clearly indicates that mass human sacrifice was practiced within and beyond the confines of the ancient metropolis. Although McVicker recognizes that art may reveal much about life in the precontact indigenous world, he warns against formulating preconceptions about the scale of social conflict based on the mere presence or absence of iconographic depictions of violence in murals and art-related forms alone.

In chapter 5, Elsa M. Redmond examines the earliest accounts of warfare among the Arawakan Taino at first contact (1492–97) by Christopher Columbus and other Europeans. These early accounts document the use of smoke signals for the purposes of intervillage communication, the presence of war councils, large numbers of armed combatants, the burning and destruction of enemy sanctuaries, formal defensive features, the seizing of war captives, and protracted and bitter rivalries between chiefs on the island of Hispaniola. Redmond then examines a pre-Columbian Arawakan archaeological site (ca. AD 600) located in the western Llanos region of Venezuela. There she and Charles Spencer recovered monumental architecture and massive causeways that served to identify this site as the center of a centralized and ranked society. Like the Taino chiefdoms of Hispaniola, this pre-Hispanic chiefly center had engaged in well-organized, large-scale, intense, and sustained organized conflict. Internecine warfare is manifest in the ubiquitous presence of defensive earthworks and palisades, disarticulated and other modified human remains, and the wholesale destruction of targeted settlements.

In chapter 6, John Verano reviews extant osteological and forensic evidence for armed conflict on the northern coast of Peru. He examines the evidence for mass burials from three archaeological sites, including one dating to the Early Intermediate period and two dating to the Late Intermediate period. In one case, captives were executed, with some having been mutilated and dismembered. Verano notes that these findings are consistent with pre-Hispanic iconographic representations of indigenous combat, capture, and the ritual human sacrifice of captives. Significantly, Verano's findings conclude that Moche artists depicted highly specialized forms of ritual violence corroborated by extant forensic evidence.

In chapter 7, Richard J. Chacon, Yamilette Chacon, and Angel Guandinango document patterns of ritual fighting and killing that occur during Catholic feast days in the Cotacachi and Otavalo Andean highland communities of San Juan, San Pedro, San Pablo, and Santa Lucia, Ecuador. The authors identify a direct association between those feast days devoted to the Inca Inti Raymi solstice celebration and those of the Pachamama cult. The inevitable bloodshed and killing that takes place during these events clearly serves to propitiate pre-Hispanic supernaturals controlling agricultural fertility. The authors acknowledge that the public display of bellicose behavior functions as a means for declaring ethnic identity as well as for asserting political rights. Ethnohistorical accounts of bloody and sometimes lethal Andean ritualized combats are corroborated in this study. Significantly, neither territorial encroachment nor resource acquisition is the objective of these often-fatal engagements.

In chapter 8, Stephen Beckerman and James Yost assess the nature and extent of armed conflict within the upper Amazon through an ethnohistorical context. Their analysis reveals that Europeans did not introduce armed conflict and organized violence into this region of the Americas. In addition, they acknowledge that documented differences in the nature and extent of armed conflict reported—particularly small-scale raids versus large-scale military mobilizations—covary with differing sociopolitical and economic formations. The authors provide an in-depth assessment of Waorani small-scale raiding and tribal warfare that had significant demographic consequences for local populations. The most pronounced and proximate motivations for conflict stemmed from the quest for revenge. Whereas some raiders sought the acquisition of Western goods, most Waorani intertribal raids cannot be attributed to the desire for European trade items circulating in the Tribal Zone per se (Ferguson and Whitehead 1992). Instead, Beckerman and Yost argue that the basic motivations for such conflict are rooted in evolutionary, biological, and psychological sources that provide the ultimate explanation for Waorani intertribal war and conflict.

In chapter 9, William Balée examines sixteenth-century ethnohistorical accounts together with secondary sources and concludes that certain Tupinambá groups of coastal Brazil were complex societies, in the sense of displaying institutions above the rank of the local settlement, with their complexity evinced in warfare patterns involving social substitution that were extant before first contact with Europeans. He argues that in late prehistoric and early colonial times, these Tupinambá societies exhibited structured patterns of internecine warfare as well as the implementation of truces, mobilized mass military engagements, and the usurpation of territory. Balée finds that conquest and ownership of the resource-rich albeit circumscribed Atlantic coastal habitat, rather than psychological motivations alone, helped fuel Tupinambá military ambitions.

In chapter 10, Marcela Mendoza cites sixteenth-century ethnohistorical sources to illustrate that raiding for scalps, human trophies, war booty, and captives by the hunter-gatherers of the western Gran Chaco derived from a precontact pattern that continued well into the 1920s. Her analysis of historical conflict in the region reveals that it was exacerbated by European settlers and nonlocal indigenous groups, such as the Chiriguano, who encroached into Chacoan territory. These incursions hindered efforts by hunter-gatherer groups, such as the Toba, to complete their traditional seasonal subsistence rounds. Chacoans in turn intruded on other tribal territories and engaged in raids against white settlements for essential resources. Such encroachments or raids invariably resulted in retaliatory strikes against those involved. Mendoza acknowledges that those who were successful in acquiring human trophies, such as decapitated heads, enjoyed great prestige. Apparently, decapitated human heads were thought to impart supernatural powers to those who acquired them in battles against the enemy. In this instance, patterns of indigenous warfare were transformed as a direct result of the emergence of the Tribal Zone (Ferguson and Whitehead 1992).

In chapter 11, Alfredo Prieto and Rodrigo Cárdenas draw on archaeological, ethnohistorical, ethnographic, and osteological evidence documenting the antiquity and forms of armed conflict in the Tierra del Fuego–Patagonian area. Whereas warfare was primarily incited by revenge, fighting and conflict often arose in response to the defense of territorial claims. In such contexts, both women and children were taken as captives wherever possible. The authors conclude that violent behavior on the part of their subjects is a complex phenomenon affected by a variety of variables, including those pertaining to environment, gender, and ideology. They do, however, argue that the ultimate origins of violent and aggressive behaviors are most profitably sought by way of arguments advanced within the realm of evolutionary psychology.

In chapter 12, Richard J. Chacon and Rubén G. Mendoza explore the ethical issues that are raised when evidence for Amerindian warfare and ritual violence is published. Conversely, we discuss those ramifications that stem from the reticence of or refusal by some scholars to report indigenous armed conflict, ritual human sacrifice, or cannibalism. Additionally, we summarize key findings regarding aboriginal warfare and ritual violence advanced by the contributors to this volume. As editors, we hope that the following chapters provide insight into and serve as a stimulus for further research on Amerindian warfare and ritual violence in Latin America.

1 STATUS RIVALRY AND WARFARE IN THE DEVELOPMENT AND COLLAPSE OF CLASSIC MAYA CIVILIZATION

Matt O'Mansky and Arthur A. Demarest

As Carl von Clausewitz wrote nearly two centuries ago, "war is not merely a political act but a real political instrument, a continuation of political intercourse, a carrying out of the same by other means" (Clausewitz [1832] 1943, 16). In other words, warfare does not exist as a discrete category of human action. Rather, it is a label for those aspects of politics that involve violence between organized groups. The logical difficulties in analyzing warfare among the ancient Maya, therefore, result primarily from our weak understanding of ancient Maya politics. Because of the ambiguities in the archaeological and textual record, we remain uncertain as to the size of individual Maya kingdoms, the nature and importance of wider multikingdom alliances or hegemonies, and the actual meaning of political authority within any Maya kingdom (e.g., Demarest 1992; Fox et al. 1996; Marcus 1993). Our still-vague understanding of ancient Maya political institutions and activities makes it difficult to specify why, when, and how such activities turned to organized violence.

Study and analysis of Maya warfare has also been hampered by a thirty-year concern with an outdated dialectic on the presence and intensity of Maya warfare. Most publications on Maya warfare focus at least in part on attacking the so-called "traditional model" of the peaceful Maya in which the Classic Maya are viewed as a dispersed series of nonurban ceremonial centers ruled by peaceful, priestly leaders and sustained by simple slash-and-burn maize agriculture (Morley 1946; Thompson 1954). Only then do authors move on to assert that the Maya were not wholly peaceful, that they did have warfare, and that their warfare was important in shaping Classic period (ca. AD 300–900) Maya civilization.

In fact, the idea of the peaceful Maya was never universally accepted by archaeologists, and even the earliest projects in the Maya Lowlands included debate on issues of population density, urbanism, and intensive agriculture (e.g., Lundell 1933; Ricketson and Ricketson 1937). The traditional model became dominant only after the publication of J. Eric Thompson's *The Rise and Fall of Maya Civilization* in 1954. Thompson was such an elegant writer, as well as a scholar of great credentials, that much of the public and many archaeologists were seduced by his romantic presentation of the scholarly, devout priestly rulers of the Classic Maya ceremonial centers. Yet this perspective never completely dominated scholarly thought and began to be challenged by epigraphic, iconographic, and archaeological studies within a decade of its ascendancy (e.g., Armillas 1951; Proskouriakoff 1960; Rands 1952). The focus on further criticizing the long-outdated views of the late Dr. Thompson has only been an impediment to discussion. The growing body of evidence on warfare demonstrated long ago that warfare was a critical element in ancient Maya society.

However, the relative paucity of research and evidence on Maya warfare has done far more than intellectual oppression from an outdated model to prevent informed generalization. Until the 1980s, knowledge of Maya warfare was based on the excavation of only a few earthworks predating the Postclassic period, circa AD 1000–1542 (e.g., Armillas 1951; Demarest 1978; Webster 1976, 1978), as well as some studies of Maya epigraphy and iconography (e.g., Graham 1967; Rands 1952). Even this very limited perspective on Maya warfare was sufficient to demonstrate that Maya wars were as varied in form and nature in the Preclassic and Classic periods as the political systems of which they were a part. Some earthworks, such as those at Becan (fig. 1.1), were massive siege defenses (Webster 1976), others were more extensive palisade systems (e.g., Demarest et al. 1997), and yet other evidence suggests violence and destruction with ritual motives (e.g., Freidel 1986). These are not contradictory perspectives but the beginnings of plotting the variability in Maya warfare over time and space.

Our current challenge in studying Maya warfare is this variable nature in time and space. Rather than a debate on its presence or absence or general degree of intensity, a more fruitful approach to Maya warfare is the plotting of its nature and variations. We can now begin to wrestle with the more difficult issues of why, when, and how ancient Maya politics and ritual utilized violence to achieve desired ends. Fortunately, recent and ongoing research and publications are beginning to address such issues (cf. Brown and Stanton 2003; Trejo 2000).

EVIDENCE FOR WARFARE AMONG THE ANCIENT MAYA

Another reason for the lingering influence of the traditional model is the long-perceived absence of clear evidence for warfare or violence among the Classic Maya. Many depictions of captives are known from carved stelae and altars, but these were explained away as the aftermath of small-scale raids or as occasional offerings to the gods (Ruppert, Thompson, and Proskouriakoff 1955; Thompson 1954). However, this view began to face serious challenges when Lacandon Maya led Giles Healey to the remote site of Bonampak in 1946. There, spectacular murals depict a battle and its aftermath, including the torture

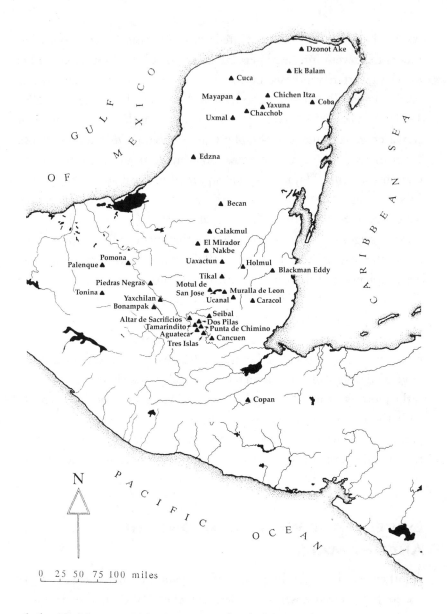

1.1 The Maya area, with sites mentioned in the text.

of captives (fig. 1.2a; Miller 1986). Subsequent research and advances over the past six decades—particularly the decipherment of most of the Classic Maya script—has revealed that warfare was an important aspect of Maya civilization, as with all other complex societies past and present throughout the world. Although specific interpretations vary on what, exactly, the evidence represents, there can no longer be arguments on whether or not warfare was important.

Evidence for warfare and violence among the Classic Maya comes from several types of sources, including iconography, ethnohistory, the Popol Vuh (a Maya creation myth), archaeology, and the epigraphic record. The most prevalent evidence comes from depictions in art, particularly carved stone stelae, altars, and panels. Monuments at numerous sites depict bound captives (fig. 1.2b), often beneath the feet of rulers. Other depictions of warfare and its aftermath recorded in wood or other perishable media have certainly been eroded away over the past millennium by the humidity and rains of the southern lowlands jungle.

Archaeological evidence for Maya warfare and conflict has increased exponentially since the first systematic studies of defensive features in the 1970s by David Webster (1976, 1978). Whereas walls had been noticed previously at a number of sites, such as Mayapán (Shook 1952) and Tikal (Puleston and Callendar 1967), Webster's research focused not only on the presence of walls but also on the implications of such constructions. Although walls may serve functions other than defensive—such as demarcating property boundaries, separating ritual from nonritual space or elite from nonelite space, or a combination of functions—several projects have convincingly demonstrated that at many sites walls were primarily for defensive purposes (e.g., Demarest 1978; Demarest et al. 1997; Webster 1976, 1978).

Prior to the Postclassic period, only a few Maya sites had large permanent walls. Rather, most walls were low mounds of earth and rubble that served as footings for wooden palisades. Such walls often leave faint traces. The fact that these low walls supported perishable superstructures has been confirmed at Punta de Chimino in the Petexbatun region, where archaeologists discovered a line of postholes in a low wall above a massive moat, and at the nearby site of Quim Chi Hilan, where impressions of a palisade and a probable wooden gate were preserved in burned clay impressions (Demarest et al. 1997). Such perishable defenses were likely much more prevalent than is known today, since areas with deeper soil would not require stone bases. Instead, palisades could be pushed deep into the earth and securely lashed together.

Other archaeological manifestations of warfare include deposits

a

b

1.2A A battle scene from the Bonampak murals. (Reconstruction painting by Heather Hurst and Leonard Ashby; © Bonampak Documentation Project)

1.2B A step from Dos Pilas Hieroglyphic Stairway 3, showing a bound lord from Yaxchilán. (From Demarest et al. 1991, fig. 3.11; courtesy of Vanderbilt University Press)

of stone bifaces and other implements that could have been used as weapons, evidence of burning and destruction, caches of skulls and/or skeletons of young men, and bodies left unburied, apparently where they fell. While such finds are not exclusively indicative of warfare, in combination with other types of evidence these things speak to the frequency and intensity of ancient Maya conflict.

Finally, the ancient Maya tell us of their wars in their own words, in the permanent stone record they left. Stelae, altars, and panels at numerous centers record battles waged and captives taken. Although these monuments are the records of the rulers and were carved at their command, the statements are increasingly corroborated by the archaeological evidence.

The types of available evidence thus suggest that we are underrepresenting rather than overstating the frequency and intensity of ancient Maya warfare, as archaeologists have recently been accused of doing (e.g., Castañeda 1996; Montejo 1999b). Direct evidence of warfare is limited to the archaeological and epigraphic records described above, and as noted, the problems of preservation have certainly erased many traces of battles, while smaller-scale engagements may leave no record at all.

CLASSIC MAYA POLITICAL ORGANIZATION AND ELITE STATUS RIVALRY

Just as warfare took various forms, so too was the Classic Maya state highly variable in political form; no unified, panregional centralized state ever arose. At the center of Classic period Maya political organization, though, was always the *k'uhul ajaw,* the divine or holy lord. This form of rulership was multiple in its functions and regionally varied. The power of the k'uhul ajaw was very heavily ritual and ideological but was also involved in control over prestige goods and in directing warfare. In general, rulers had a limited role in the management of the infrastructure of their states, and their power was based on personal performance in ritual and warfare. Polities were not clearly defined entities but rather were dependent on the charisma and influence of their rulers—and their connections to rulers at neighboring centers (Demarest 1992, 2004b; Freidel 1992).

There is no reason to believe that the Classic period k'uhul ajaw system of rulership did not evolve from a similarly manifold and complex Preclassic form of chiefdom in which ideology and religion were dominant forces but warfare was also a factor in status rivalry, along with external economic sources and control over other aspects of the economy. As in the Classic period, the various aspects of these systems likely varied from region to region. In other words, the complex and regionally variable k'uhul ajaw system of Maya kingship evolved from a similarly complex and regionally variable landscape of chiefdoms.

The k'uhul ajaws employed a variety of strategies to enhance their personal prestige and to compete with other rulers, whether direct or indirect competitors. These strategies included control and display of exotic and foreign goods that were rare or nonexistent in the lowland jungles (such as jade, pyrite, obsidian, quetzal feathers, and jaguar pelts), large-scale construction projects, commission of artwork that aggrandized the ruler, and warfare and sacrifice. Even at centers where rulers and elites had more control of local infrastructure, such as Calakmul (Folan et al. 1995), Cancuen (Demarest 2004b, 228–31), Caracol (Chase and Chase 1987), and Edzna (Matheny 1987), the basic k'uhul ajaw form of rulership and its attendant status rivalry is clearly manifested in the archaeological and iconographic record. Although the specific form of Classic Maya political organization was variable, the basic tenets of the k'uhul ajaw form of rulership were common across the Maya world.

WARFARE IN THE PRECLASSIC AND THE ORIGINS OF THE MAYA STATE

The timetable for the evolution of the Maya state varied from region to region, but its origins are considerably earlier than the evidence that has sometimes been cited for warfare as a prime mover (e.g., Carneiro 1970; Webster 1977). There is ambiguous evidence for warfare in the Middle Preclassic (ca. 1000–400 BC) at Blackman Eddy in the Belize River valley, where apparent conflict-related destruction and burning occurred around 650 BC (Brown and Garber 2003). However, the first evidence of fortifications appears at only a few sites at the very end of the Preclassic and beginning of the Early Classic period (Late Preclassic is ca. 400 BC–AD 300, Early Classic is ca. AD 300–600).

As Clausewitz noted, variability in the form of warfare corresponded to the particular forum of political action in which organized violence, or the potential for violence, played a part. In the Late Preclassic period, rulers beginning to assert their authority may have resorted to warfare to define their realms versus competing leaders and to eliminate competitors for rule. Note that such competition was almost certainly not over territory and access to limited land, as was once asserted (e.g., Carneiro 1970; Fried 1961; Webster 1977). There is little direct evidence of population stress, and in any case, defenses cited as evidence for early warfare date at least several centuries too late to have played a role in the rise of Maya civilization—several centuries after urbanism, state formation, and related institutions were in place at sites such as Nakbe and El Mirador (Dahlin 1984; Hansen 2001; Matheny 1987). More cogent are analyses that emphasize the role of warfare in giving leaders access to external resources and to its role in competition between leaders, or "status rivalry" (e.g., Freidel, Reece-Taylor, and Mora-Marín 2002; Webster 1978).

Most of the early fortifications in the Maya world appear to have been built toward the end of the Late Preclassic or beginning of the Early Classic and are possibly related to interaction with Mexican polities, especially the great metropolis of Teotihuacán. At the site of Becan, for example, a major fortification system was built at the end of the Preclassic with ramparts up to 5 meters high and a ditch 2.5 meters deep and averaging 16 meters across surrounding the site epicenter (Webster 1976). Teotihuacán-style vases and figurines and central Mexican Pachuca obsidian indicate connections—direct or indirect—to that distant center (Ball 1974). At El Mirador, only part of the site is fortified, and these walls appear to date to the very end of the Late Preclassic (Dahlin 1984). The northern earthworks at Tikal, first noted by Dennis Puleston and Donald Callendar (1967), have an ambiguous dating and are a fairly weak defensive system. In fact, the earthworks were probably part of an early warning system rather than siege defenses. This ditch and rampart wall system is located 4.5 kilometers north of the site center, directly between central Tikal and its Early Classic rival Uaxactún. Ongoing research suggests that the Tikal earthworks may encircle the city, comprising a total length of some 50 kilometers (Webster et al. 2004).

Two other sites with fortifications that have been cited as Preclassic, Muralla de León and Punta de Chimino, in fact date to the Terminal Classic (ca. AD 800–1000; Demarest, Escobedo, and O'Mansky 1996; Rice and Rice 1981). In the case of Punta de Chimino, there is a significant Preclassic component at the site. Most of the architecture and occupation, however, including all of the tested massive fortifications and protected field systems, date to the Terminal Classic (see below).

Warfare in the Late Preclassic and Early Classic often may have consisted of small-scale raids, the taking of captives, and other potentially prestige-enhancing actions. Such status-rivalry warfare also served to increase the realms of some kingdoms and added the economic benefits of tribute. The issue of tribute, which has been raised by recent epigraphic decipherments (Stuart 1995), needs clarification. Rulers, of course, were not providing their own sustenance. Rather, they were provided with food and goods through one or a combination of several means. Today, the term *tribute* has connotations of war booty. Yet any goods given to the ruler would be tribute, regardless of the reasons for his sovereignty over those citizens. The results of tribute were probably limited in the Late Preclassic. We do know, however, that at least one state in the Late Classic (ca. AD 600–900), Dos Pilas, was a predatory (i.e., war tribute–based) state (Demarest 2006; Dunning and Beach 2007; Dunning, Beach, and Rue 1997).

Our knowledge of the specifics of Maya warfare—weapons, tactics, the size of armies, and so on—is largely speculative. Reconstructions primarily come from representations in art and monuments, but, as noted above, these depict what the rulers wished to portray and are not necessarily accurate characterizations of methods, actions, or participants. The hard evidence from archaeology is perhaps more reliable, and it indicates that spears and atlatls were the major weapons of choice. Siege warfare was probably rare in the Preclassic and Early Classic—not only are there just a handful of known fortifications, but also most sites and even site epicenters were largely indefensible in layout and design. That is, they were not located on high ground or similarly defensible areas, and/or they were dispersed across the terrain. It is worth noting, however, that the dispersed settlement pattern of Maya centers would have made surprise raiding extremely difficult. During the Classic period, some major centers had well-defined peripheral defenses or warning systems, such as the *bajos* (low-lying seasonal wetlands) and walls around Tikal (Puleston and Callendar 1967; Webster et al. 2004) and the canal systems at Calakmul (Folan et al. 1995) and

Edzna (Matheny 1987). Whether or not the primary intended function of such features was military, they nonetheless would also have served a defensive function.

Warfare appears to have played a more prominent role in Early Classic political intrigue through affiliations with central Mexico. Influence from the militaristic center of Teotihuacán was apparent throughout much of the Maya world by the third through fifth centuries AD. In the fourth century, the ruler of Tikal took the throne, claiming an affiliation with Teotihuacán. Although the exact nature of these events is unclear, recent decipherments indicate that a war leader or agent from that distant Mexican center was involved in wars and dynastic upheaval at Tikal and the nearby center of Uaxactún (Braswell 2003; Martin and Grube 2000). Similar Teotihuacán-influenced political events took place elsewhere, including Copán (Sharer 2003) and Tres Islas (Graham 1965). In all of these cases, the new dynasties celebrated their Teotihuacán affiliations in monuments and artifacts.

INTERREGIONAL WARFARE IN THE LATE FOURTH THROUGH SEVENTH CENTURIES AD

Iconographic and especially epigraphic evidence indicates that beginning in the late fourth century, the scale and intensity of warfare increased, with conflicts between competing "international" alliances and hegemonies (Martin and Grube 2000; Stuart 1995). The intrusion of Teotihuacán into the Maya Lowlands—whether invited or as a conquering force—began this trend. By the middle of the sixth century, the sacking and destruction of site centers may have become part of the grammar of warfare. In that period, conflict throughout much of the southern lowlands was guided or influenced by the great rival superpowers Tikal and Calakmul, each of which may have attempted to form a larger unified "empire." Many of the wars recorded on monuments and which were once viewed in local terms—such as Tikal versus Dos Pilas and Tikal versus Caracol—must be put into an interregional perspective. Both Tikal and Calakmul formed alliances with other kingdoms that, in turn, battled other centers, often at the instigation or with the support of their more powerful allies (e.g., Chase, Grube, and Chase 1991; Martin and Grube 2000).

Rulers probably had specific motivations in conducting wars, but the fact that wars were in any degree tied to interregional schemes could have increased their intensity and duration. The involvement of distant proxy powers extends the duration and intensity of conflict well beyond what would have been necessary to solve local and regional problems. There are examples throughout history, including modern conflicts such as Vietnam, Cambodia, and Somalia. In all of these cases, regional conflicts, as between communists and noncommunists in Vietnam or between subgroups in Ethiopia and Somalia, had already existed. In twentieth-century Korea, the war and standoff continues today. In Vietnam, French and later U.S. involvement prolonged for two decades a war that might have been resolved in a few years. In Somalia, the involvement of foreign powers caused a massive flow of arms into the region and spiraling conflict and political disintegration. In these and other proxy wars, the involvement of distant foreign powers has two effects: the level of conflict and the resources invested in the wars increase, and the duration of wars is extended beyond any period that would have been necessary to resolve local or regional conflicts.

WARFARE AND STATUS RIVALRY IN THE LATE SEVENTH AND EIGHTH CENTURIES AND THE MAYA COLLAPSE

In the same way, it is probable that throughout the Maya world, the period of interregional warfare led to a general intensification of conflict in the seventh and eighth centuries. Another cause for the intensification of Late Classic warfare may have been increased status rivalry. Proliferation of the nobility through elite polygyny, in conjunction with the loose structure of inheritance of the k'uhul ajaw title, led to increased competition for royal and elite positions (Demarest 2004b, 243–60; Demarest, Rice, and Rice 2004). Such competition was manifested in numerous ways, including architectural construction and display, the establishment and extension of patronage networks in exotic goods and fine artifacts, and ritual displays at periodic events. Warfare was merely the most violent form of this increased competition. There is no need to continue the debate as to whether wars were astronomical or ritual versus "meaningful" political and economic wars. Classic Maya warfare was all of these things at once. It was involved in the elimination of rivals, the seizure of tribute, and the taking of captives for ritual events, which were also another form of status rivalry (see Cowgill 1979 for an early and prophetic discussion of the role of basic human ambition and greed—definitely elements in status rivalry—in Late Classic [post-Teotihuacán] Maya warfare).

Much of our knowledge of Late and Terminal Classic warfare comes from recent epigraphic decipherments (e.g., Martin and Grube 2000; Schele and Miller 1986). Many such texts come from sites in the western Maya world along the Usumacinta River, where monuments record continuous conflicts in the Late Classic. Much of this warfare may have been instigated to gain control of the lucrative Pasión/Usumacinta river system route that extends from the base of the highlands in Guatemala to the Gulf of Mexico. This route of trade and communication was of critical importance to the entire western and central Maya world. The goods that flowed along this trade artery—including obsidian, jade, pyrite, and quetzal feathers—were critical elements of the k'uhul ajaw system and of elite status rivalry, both as part of the regal attire and in reinforcing patronage networks (Demarest 2004b; Freidel, Reece-Taylor, and Mora-Marín 2002). For this reason, the river system was, from at least the beginning of the Classic period, a target of control by the major powers of the Maya world, including Tikal and Calakmul.

For this period of warfare, the most clear and abundant evidence comes from the 1989–97 Vanderbilt Petexbatun project, a regional, multidisciplinary study of Maya war that has yielded the most evidence to date on Maya warfare, its antecedents, and its ecological and political contexts (Demarest 1997, 2004b, 2006). The research design did not focus on a major center and its hinterland or a geographically defined basin or valley. Instead, war was studied from the varying evidence and perspectives of all sides in the conflict, including the various warring major centers, the satellite centers, villages, and rural landscape caught in these conflicts.

The history of warfare in the Petexbatun (fig. 1.3a) begins in AD 632, when a royal lineage from Tikal arrived at the site of Dos Pilas, establishing a new ruling dynasty (Demarest and Fahsen 2003). This lineage was likely sent from a weakened Tikal, in decline after being defeated by Caracol in AD 562—probably at the instigation of Calakmul (Martin and Grube 2000)—to establish a base from which they could attempt to assert control over the Pasión/Usumacinta river system trade route and defend it from Calakmul's expanding hegemony, thereby controlling the status-reinforcing goods critical to the k'uhul ajaw system. Unfortunately for Tikal's strategic designs, in 652 Calakmul conquered Dos Pilas and turned the now-vassal center into its ally and agent—including pitting Dos Pilas directly against Tikal (Demarest and Fahsen 2003; Martin and Grube 2000).

Over the course of the next century, the predatory Dos Pilas tribute state employed a strategy of military conquest and strategic alliances to expand its control to an area of 1,500 square kilometers, including most of the Pasión River trade route. According to epigraphic evidence, this expansion first occurred under the aegis of Calakmul. Yet after the defeat of that powerful rival by Tikal in 695, the subsequent Dos Pilas rulers reasserted and expanded this hegemony while wealth flowed into the kingdom, as evidenced by large-scale construction projects, monuments, and abundant rich offerings (Brady et al. 1997; Demarest 2004b, 2006).

The goals of the Dos Pilas hegemony's expansion were varied. In addition to the standard eighth-century status rivalry, the Dos Pilas kingdoms may have been unusually dependent on warfare. The initial impetus may have been to secure tribute, especially in foodstuffs. Dos Pilas was established in an area that could not support itself—the soil in and around Dos Pilas could not have maintained more than a fraction of the site's population (Dunning and Beach 2007; Dunning, Beach, and Rue 1997). Thus, it lived on tribute. Perhaps this dependence—and subsequent need for an expanding tribute base—led to overreach in the case of the Petexbatun hegemony.

Another of the goals of the Dos Pilas hegemony was control of the lucrative Pasión River trade route. Long-distance exchange in food and commodities was probably of minor importance in the general Maya economy, but elite control of highland exotic prestige goods was absolutely critical to the political economy of Maya kingdoms. This can be seen at the kingdom of Cancuen, which was allied with Dos Pilas after the early eighth-century marriage of the ruler of Dos Pilas to a princess from Cancuen (Demarest 2006). Cancuen sits at the head of navigation of the Pasión River at the base of the highlands and thus controlled the importation of highland exotics along this major trade artery through the western Maya world. Recent research there has discovered workshops for the processing of obsidian, jade, and pyrite surrounding the site's palace (Demarest 2004b, 228–31, 249–50).

The Late Classic florescence of the Petexbatun hegemony came to an abrupt end in the middle of the eighth century. After a century of rapid expansion, the overextended kingdom dramatically collapsed in 761, when the nearby center of Tamarindito rebelled against Dos Pilas, defeating and exiling K'awiil Chan K'inich (Ruler 4), the last known ruler of Dos Pilas (Valdés 1997). The region then descended into a spiral of endemic warfare. By AD 830, the Petexbatun was almost completely abandoned (Demarest 2004a; O'Mansky and Dunning 2004).

The archaeological manifestations of warfare in the region are most clearly evident at Dos Pilas, where defensive walls of stone footings and wooden palisades were rapidly constructed at both the West Plaza Group and El Duende (fig. 1.3b; Demarest et al. 1997). At the West Plaza Group, a pair of concentric walls totaling more than a kilometer in length were rapidly built between and across existing structures using stone torn from existing nearby structures, including palaces, hieroglyphic stairways, a ball court, and even the funerary shrine of Ruler 2.

Extensive excavations of the West Plaza group walls yielded baffle gateways, killing alleys, and a cache of heads of young adult males, presumably captured warriors (Demarest et al. 1997). Ceramics encountered in these excavations date the walls to the end of the Late Classic, coinciding with the date of the fall of Dos Pilas based on epigraphic decipherments. Mapping and excavations within the plaza area enclosed by the walls revealed a dense grouping of low platforms for thatch huts (Palka 1997). Ceramics from associated middens date this "squatters' village" in the ceremonial heart of Dos Pilas securely to just after the capture of Ruler 4.

After the defeat of Ruler 4, ceremonial construction and the erection of monuments at Dos Pilas ceased and the city was largely aban-

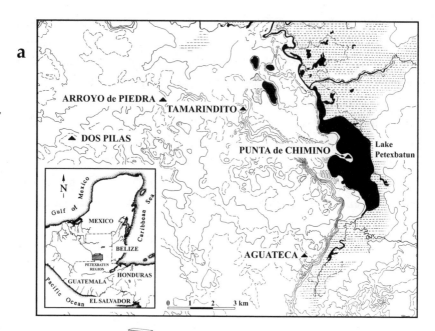

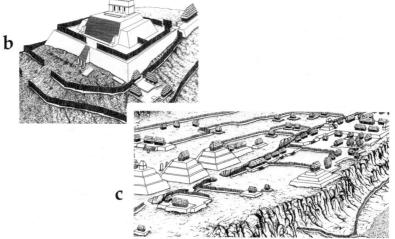

1.3A The Petexbatun region, showing major sites. (Courtesy of Vanderbilt University)

1.3B Eighth-century defensive systems around El Duende complex, Dos Pilas. (Drawn by L. F. Luin; from Demarest 2004b, fig. 10.6; courtesy of Vanderbilt University Press)

1.3C A portion of the fortification system at Aguateca. (Drawn by L. F. Luin; from Demarest 2004b, fig. 10.7; courtesy of Vanderbilt University Press) doned. The remaining royal family may have then relocated to the more defensible site of Aguateca, located high on a steep eroded fragment of the Petexbatun escarpment (fig. 1.3c). To further secure the city, over five kilometers of stone-footed wooden palisades were constructed in and around it. Despite this extensive, well-planned defensive system, Aguateca fell by about AD 810. The last known monuments there date to 790, and recent research has discovered evidence for burning and rapid abandonment in the site center (Inomata 2003, 2006).

Regional settlement pattern research discovered further evidence for warfare in intersite zones (O'Mansky and Dunning 2004; Van Tuerenhout 1996). West of Aguateca, in an area with extremely thin soils and a lack of convenient water sources, several dense clusters of small walled settlements—some tiny villages—are perched atop karst towers (O'Mansky and Dunning 2004). Thus, by the end of the Late Classic period in the Petexbatun, endemic warfare had caused a significant shift in settlement strategies, even among the rural peasant population. No longer were the usual factors for settlement location—fertile soils, water, and so forth—important. Instead, a single factor, defensibility, determined where people lived. Yet by the middle of the ninth century, even these intersite zones had been completely abandoned.

The last remaining center of population in the Petexbatun was at the small site of Punta de Chimino. There, the naturally defensible peninsula on which the site is located was fortified through the construction of three moats, the largest of which was perhaps twelve meters deep. The other two moats protected the arable land between the mainland and the tip of the peninsula. This neck of land was used for intensive agriculture, including stone box gardens (Demarest 2004b, 255). The construction of the moats effectively cut the site off from the mainland and, with the erection of palisade walls, made Punta de Chimino an island fortress.

The Petexbatun project examined all aspects of paleoecological (Dunning and Beach 2007; Dunning, Beach, and Rue 1997), osteological (Wright 2006), and paleozoological evidence (Emery 2008) to assess the correlation, or lack thereof, between environment, subsistence, and diet before, during, and after wars. Surprisingly, the Petexbatun subprojects determined that there was no significant environmental degradation, desiccation, or evidence of nutritional stress. Other commonly cited potential causes for the "Classic Maya collapse," such as foreign invasion (e.g., Sabloff and Willey 1967) and economic factors (e.g., Rathje 1973), similarly are inapplicable to the Petexbatun.

For the underlying causes of warfare and collapse in the Petexbatun and across the Maya Lowlands more generally, we must again look to the political and economic stresses created by the demands of the k'uhul ajaw system. These demands were exacerbated in the seventh and eighth centuries by increasing interelite status rivalry, the growing proportion of elites in the population attributable to elite polygyny, and the consequent increase in interelite competition for limited positions of royal power and for status-reinforcing exotic goods. This cycle led first to intercenter warfare and rapidly devolved into more-widespread conflict as the basic infrastructure of the region was disrupted (Demarest 2004a; O'Mansky and Dunning 2004).

The siege at Dos Pilas and subsequent endemic warfare in the Petexbatun should not be seen as a unique historical event. Rather, it is a clear example of processes that may have been taking place throughout the west and perhaps other areas of the Maya world at the end of the Classic period.

TERMINAL CLASSIC REFUGEES AND ENCLAVE FORMATION

The most damaging aspect of conflict in both ancient and modern warfare is often the displacement of populations, rather than direct deaths and destruction (e.g., Cohen and Deng 1998; Hakovirta 1986). The impact of events in the Petexbatun surely was felt up and down the Pasión River trade route, which had been disrupted by the endemic warfare of the region, as well as by the probable movement of thousands of refugees.

At Cancuen, a large influx of population occurred during the Terminal Classic period. More than two hundred structures have been identified in the area immediately south of the site's epicenter in a zone of rich agricultural land that previously was unoccupied. Extensive excavations have dated this occupation to the Terminal Classic, and the ceramics recovered demonstrate clear western Petén affiliations (Demarest and Fahsen 2003). The occupants may have been refugees from the Petexbatun region seeking shelter and sustenance from their relatives and allies. Yet even this distant center at the base of the southern highlands appears to have soon been swept up in conflict. At about AD 800, the Cancuen lords began to construct defensive walls around their massive palace and around their vital strategic portage. Shortly afterward, however, the king, the queen, and forty nobles at the site were massacred and the city was abandoned with its defensive systems left unfinished, with new construction of an even larger palace left half completed, with a royal tomb chamber left empty, and with bodies left unburied where they fell. Epigraphic evidence suggests that the seat of power was moved inland during the ninth century to the site of Machaquila—a move east, away from the wars along the Pasión River (Demarest and Fahsen 2003).

Meanwhile, closer to the Petexbatun, the early ninth-century florescence at Seibal rose from the wreckage of the Petexbatun kingdom. This florescence occurred under the guidance of an agent from distant Ucanal, apparently with the support of Tikal, Calakmul, Motul de San José, Lakamtun, and possibly Chichén Itzá (Tourtellot and Sabloff 2004). These centers may have been attempting to reopen the Pasión/ Usumacinta route to regain access to the status reinforcing goods that were essential to the k'uhul ajaw system. Furthermore, the Seibal construction program in monumental art and architecture at that time— once attributed to foreign invasion (Sabloff and Willey 1967)—might have been part of the strategy of the site's elites to politically maintain diverse remnant populations from other western centers. There is evidence for similar enclaves at Punta de Chimino (Demarest 2004a; Demarest, Escobedo, and O'Mansky 1996) and Altar de Sacrificios (Willey 1973). Such militaristic enclaves at sites along the Pasión and Usumacinta rivers would have continued to disrupt that important trade route. Thus, in addition to the direct impact of Late Classic warfare, the decline in the western Petén is attributable in part to the disruption and closure of the Pasión-Usumacinta trade route, along which most major centers were portages. Farther north on the Usumacinta, the collapse of other centers in the early ninth century, such as Yaxchilán and Piedras

Negras, were a consequence of recorded military defeats, just as elsewhere in the Maya world (Martin and Grube 2000).

The depopulation of the Petexbatun and the sites along the Pasión and Usumacinta rivers and the subsequent migrations of refugee populations may have exacerbated problems in other regions. Elsewhere in the Petén, population shifts and increases in the late eighth and ninth centuries were sometimes accompanied by political fragmentation (Demarest, Rice, and Rice 2004; Rice and Rice 2004). In northeastern Petén and northern Belize, the picture is complex; whereas some sites witnessed great population increases, others declined or were abandoned (e.g., Adams et al. 2004). Still, the general late-eighth and early-ninth-century picture throughout the Petén and to the north in the Puuc zone appears to reflect population increases, but in an irregular pattern, accompanied by political disruptions and re-entrenchment.

THE TERMINAL CLASSIC PERIOD IN THE NORTHERN LOWLANDS

While much of the southern lowlands was in decline during the Terminal Classic period, the northern lowlands experienced its greatest florescence. This was accompanied by cultural transformation and population growth but also by an intensification of warfare between competing regional polities. In the Puuc region, great cities arose beginning in the late eighth century in what was previously a sparsely populated zone. The organization of Puuc society was similar to that of the southern lowlands (Dunning 1992), and the florescence of the Puuc region may be directly connected to the collapse of the southern lowlands, though slightly later. By the late ninth century, the city of Uxmal had come to dominate the region. Exactly how this occurred is unclear, and there is little direct evidence of warfare. However, carved monuments—a key source of evidence for warfare in the southern lowlands—are relatively rare in the north. A low wall does surround Uxmal, but this may be indicative of conflict with Chichén Itzá to the east rather than with other Puuc polities. In fact, expansion of the Puuc realm eastward led to conflict with the expanding Chichén polity. While the reason for the fall of Uxmal is not entirely clear, Chichén may have played a key role, and by the middle of the tenth century, Uxmal had been largely abandoned. Shortly thereafter, the other Puuc sites also collapsed (Carmean, Dunning, and Kowalski 2004).

To the east, across the Yucatán Peninsula, Coba was the largest polity in the Late Classic period. A massive city with strong ties to the southern lowlands throughout its history, Coba controlled an extensive polity through numerous sites connected by causeways. The longest of these causeways extended one hundred kilometers west to Yaxuna. Researchers at that site have noted several periods with signs of warfare, including desecratory termination deposits and a fifth-century mass grave, beginning in the Early Classic. In the late ninth century, a hastily constructed defensive wall was built around the site center. Despite the fortifications, Yaxuna fell to Chichén Itzá in the mid tenth century (Ambrosino, Ardren, and Stanton 2003; Suhler et al. 2004).

Numerous sites throughout the northern lowlands, in addition to Uxmal and Yaxuna, were fortified in the Terminal Classic period. These include Ek Balam, Chacchob, Dzonot Ake, and Cuca. At all of these centers, low defensive walls encircle the site epicenter, just as in the Petexbatun a century earlier. These walls are, of course, indicative of the political situation in the northern lowlands during the Terminal Classic period. The political climate of warfare was in large part a result of the expansion of the powerful Chichén Itzá polity, which dominated much of the northern lowlands from about AD 900 until 1050 (Cobos Palma 2004). The militarism of the period appears in the iconography of Chichén in murals, carved stone panels, and a stone *tzompantli* (skull rack).

Note that we are not arguing that warfare caused the collapse of Classic Maya civilization, but rather making the point that it was symptomatic in many regions of the collapse. The factors that led to more violent forms of political action by rulers included elite overpopulation, the resulting increased burden on the economy, and the resulting increase in status rivalry, which further exacerbated other economic and ecological stresses. These factors, ultimately, led to the breakdown of the political systems to a point at which violent group political action (i.e., war) was no longer controlled by the state. Such a breakdown appears to have occurred in the Petexbatun, where in the Terminal Classic the landscape included small fortified villages. War was no longer controlled by the state but by kinship groups and/or small communities, indicating the total breakdown of the state political system.

POSTCLASSIC WARFARE

By the Postclassic period, the nature of warfare had changed. But per the rationale of Clausewitz, such changes in warfare merely marked major changes in the political system. War was less about leaders competing for prestige and image enhancement and more about economic and coercive power between competing interregional groups. War also reflected the new economic and political order of which it was a part. The k'uhul ajaw system and its attendant status rivalry had collapsed, and Postclassic states became more secular, with a focus on trade and other economic concerns (e.g., Sabloff and Rathje 1975). In the Postclassic, there was a great focus on interregional trade in commodities, such as cacao and salt, throughout Mesoamerica. This led to direct economic functions of warfare in the coercive extension of such interregional economic systems.

THE ROLE OF WARFARE IN THE HISTORICAL DEVELOPMENT OF MAYA CIVILIZATION

Warfare was always an aspect of Maya political life, even going back to the Preclassic period. Its role and importance not only changed over time but also varied regionally. In general, warfare is best regarded as an aspect of status rivalry between leaders of comparable polities, as well as status rivalry within a given polity. In most polities, warfare was probably secondary to rulers' functions as religious leaders and distributors of exotics to establish, extend, and affirm patronage networks. Therefore, we should not try to analyze warfare as a separate institution from Maya politics, since it is simply a more violent aspect of elite competition and alliance. Beginning in the Late Classic in the Petexbatun and then in other regions, warfare appears to have even intensified to a point at which it was no longer controlled by the state but manifested as violent organized action at all levels of society. This is different not only quantitatively, in terms of intensity and frequency, but also qualitatively, in the lack of centralized control and ordered outcomes. The political violence during this period in the Petexbatun and other regions was no longer merely Clausewitz's instrument of a political system—rather, it had become a symptom of the disintegration of the political system itself.

The data on Maya warfare are very complex. The manifestations of Maya warfare were extremely variable in time and space. Motivations for warfare were always multiple, with shifts in emphasis from region to region and from period to period. An appreciation for the variability and complexity of warfare in ancient Maya civilization must now be developed hand in hand with our growing understanding of the variability of all other aspects of this ancient society.

2 AZTEC MILITARISM AND BLOOD SACRIFICE
THE ARCHAEOLOGY AND IDEOLOGY OF RITUAL VIOLENCE

Rubén G. Mendoza

New and controversial perspectives on Mesoamerican militarism and blood sacrifice have emerged in the wake of archaeological discoveries at a number of Mexican sites that extend this culture of violence into remote antiquity (Boone 1984; Neiderberger 1987; Pijoan Aguadé and Mansilla Lory 1997; Williams and López Reyes 2006). Recent investigations at Teotihuacán (Sugiyama 1995, 2005), Cacaxtla and Xochicalco (Mendoza 1992), Tecuaque/Calpulalpan (Bremer 2006; Rodriguez 2006), Alta Vista (Pickering 1985), Casas Grandes (DiPeso 1974), and the Classic

Maya sites of Bonampak in Mexico (Miller 1986) and Tikal and Dos Pilas in Guatemala (Demarest, Rice, and Rice 2004) affirm the Classic and Epiclassic affinities of a pan-Mesoamerican complex of war and sacrifice once thought a predominantly Postclassic (ca. AD 900–1521) pattern centered on Toltec and Mexica Aztec military statecraft (Diehl and Berlo 1989). Despite compelling evidence and interpretations forthcoming from the Proyecto Templo Mayor (López Luján 1994), a revisionist denial-based movement is afoot, the primary orientation of which is the dismantling of centuries of scholarship concerned with Aztec and, by extension, Mesoamerican religious violence (Mendoza 2001b).

In an effort to address the prevalence of human sacrifice in Mesoamerica, I have examined both traditional (ethnohistorical) sources and primary archaeological or forensic findings relevant to the question at hand. The basis for recent perspectives (including postprocessual, postmodern, and radical revisionist) regarding Mesoamerican religious violence can be weighed through three questions. First, what analytical approaches and interpretive critiques do both traditionalists and revisionists advance to support or refute claims for Mesoamerican blood sacrifice? Second, what primary sources effectively document the Aztec and pre-Aztec antiquity of blood sacrifice and human heart excision in central highland Mesoamerica? Finally, what specific contextual and diagnostic indicators exist to support a formal analysis of the archaeological and forensic evidence for human sacrifice in Mesoamerica? Devotees of the "denial" movement and radical revisionist camps have coalesced into formidable lobbies in recent years, questioning the merits of existing scholarship on the prevalence and antiquity of religious violence in Mesoamerica—and indeed, much remains undefined within this body of scholarship. Fortunately, new forensic applications and archaeological strategies promise to radically alter prevailing methodologies for the analysis and interpretation of sacrificial remains in Mesoamerica and beyond.

PRECEPTS OF THE IMPONDERABLE

If, as noted by Chicano/a studies scholar Daniel Cooper Alarcón (1997: xv), "Transculturation . . . implies a cultural interaction that forces us to consider the important role played by marginal or colonized peoples in the production of discourses about them," then clearly, this assessment necessarily devolves from an attempt to frame a transcultural analysis that invites into the fray the contested discourses of the historically marginalized and the scientifically marginal, the culturally dispossessed and the academically suspect.

As an archaeologist with a long-standing scholarly interest in ancient and modern Mesoamerica, I have often been challenged to address the reliability and veracity of sixteenth-century colonial accounts attributing human sacrifice, cannibalism, and religious violence to Aztec and other Mesoamerican peoples. For some Chicana/o university students and Mexican and Amerindian nationalists alike, that corpus of scholarly discourse that documents the prominent and disproportionate role played by religious violence in Mesoamerican empires is taken to represent a Eurocentric, hegemonic, and colonialist paradigm. One need not go far to find contrarian claims that human sacrifice was a fabrication of the Spanish colonial propaganda machine. The writings of University of Zurich ethnologist Peter Hassler (1992a, 1992b, 1992c), for example, now fuel a Neo-Mexica (revisionist) discourse contending that the majority of evidence for pre-Hispanic blood sacrifice is suspect. Hassler (1992a) argues that such works are the products of a long-standing pattern of political fiction intent on perpetuating the denigration of Amerindian communities.

Hassler (1992b) contends that "after careful and systematic study of the sources, I find no sign of evidence of institutionalized mass human sacrifice among the Aztecs. The phenomenon to be studied, therefore, may be not these supposed sacrifices but the deeply rooted belief that they occurred." This has prompted the emergence of a Neo-Mexica school of thought (see Mendoza 2001b) arguing that "the idea that our ancestors practiced human sacrifice is not only absurd, it is a calculated lie which was carried out and promoted by the Spanish propaganda machine" (Tlapoyawa 2003, 1). The Neo-Mexica now promulgate their beliefs within transnational and inter-American venues via Azteca dance groups, social clubs, online discussion forums, blogs, and public workshops and lectures led by self-proclaimed Amerindian "elders" from Mexico City and beyond (e.g., Mexica Movement 2005 [www.mexica-movement.org]; www.mexika.org/ZemanSac.htm; or for an alternative perspective, www.runestone.org/wotvstez.html).

While most anthropologists find little value in addressing the claims espoused by the denial movement, such radical-revisionist perspectives are rapidly gaining ground on college campuses across the United States, Latin America, and Europe. Our respective failure to address this emerging discourse is akin to early efforts to dismiss the work of Michael Harner (1977) regarding the ecocultural basis of Aztec cannibalism. Harner's thesis ultimately found a broad and diverse following in the world of international popular culture and cultural materialist studies. I therefore frame the balance of this discussion against the backdrop of those revisionist challenges that vex prevailing interpretations regarding the place of human sacrifice in Aztec society. As a flashpoint of competing epistemological constructs, a measured assessment of the revisionist perspective encourages critical consideration of those dimensions of transculturation and popular culture that bring into question both the evidence and the scholarly assumptions that have long been argued to document religious violence in the Americas.

DISSECTING THE DIATRIBE

Much of the revisionist perspective draws on the problematic nature of eyewitness testimony from the period of the Spanish conquest. Revisionist claims necessarily rely on the accounts of Hernán Cortés (1967), Bernal Díaz del Castillo (1982), and Diego de Landa (1978), among others. The revisionists dismiss such accounts as untenable. First, whereas Cortés and Díaz del Castillo document the sacrifice of their companions in the initial rout of the Spanish invaders by the Aztec, claims that the bodies underwent human heart excision are questioned, as such observations were made from a point some eight kilometers distant. Their testimony is therefore impeached, thereby advancing arguments that the accounts of Díaz del Castillo (1982) and Cortés (1967) are based on hearsay. Díaz del Castillo's accounts are further undermined because his memoirs were written some five decades after key incidents were allegedly observed. Finally, Landa's (1978) reputation for desecrating and destroying Maya texts and idols is used to impeach his testimony as wholly biased against any and all "pagan" practice.

In addressing the unreliability of colonial sources, the revisionists posit that any and all reference to Aztec blood sacrifice necessarily devolve from the writings of the aforementioned Spanish chroniclers. While this may well be the case for the writings of William H. Prescott (Prescott and Kirk 1873) and related secondary accounts, the revisionists fail to acknowledge other period documents, such as those of Francisco López de Gómara (López de Gómara and Ramírez Cabañas 1943 [1519–40]), Fernando Alvarado Tezozómoc (1944 [1598]), and other sixteenth-century chroniclers. They contend that all subsequent accounts are secondary and, as such, of limited value to the question of Mesoamerican blood sacrifice.

AN EPISTEMOLOGY OF THE ABSURD

In a position paper on human sacrifice, the Centro de Cultura Pre Americana states that representatives are regularly dispatched to canvass Mexican heritage sites (see fig. 2.1) in an effort to question museum narratives that equate specific monuments with blood sacrifice (Centro de Cultura Pre Americana 2003). Their mandate then is to challenge purported evidence for human sacrifice by ancestral peoples. Their strategy lies with advancing those questions that undermine extant traditionalist models that belie Eurocentric, and racist, perspectives emanating from within the academy. One point of departure has been to assess whether archaeologists have taken to critically employing scientific, physical anthropological, and forensic approaches in their efforts to interrogate the evidence for blood sacrifice in Mesoamerican contexts.

HUMAN HEART EXTRACTION

One argument employed by revisionists to discredit extant views on Mesoamerican religious violence entails the manipulation of archaeology and the physical sciences to examine and undermine existing anthropological discourse. Néstor Martínez (2003, 3), for example, questions the feasibility of extracting the human heart from the chest cavity following a blow from a "flint" axe or knife blade. Though Francis Robicsek

2.1 The purported burial ground of the last Aztec emperor, Cuauhtémoc, drew members of the Centro de Cultura Pre Americana to Ichcateopan, Guerrero, Mexico. Because the Centro and other related Neo-Mexica groups in the United States seek the revitalization of Mexica Aztec thought and culture, Cuauhtémoc signifies a direct link to this culture of resistance and renewal. (Photo © Rubén G. Mendoza, 1979)

and Donald Hales (1984) contend that bilateral transverse thoracotomy (i.e., parting the sternum and opening both pleural cavities) is the most effective method for heart extraction, their results remain open to question. The revisionists draw on such assumptions to dispute the technical feasibility of human heart excision through the use of stone tools. Said investigators reviewed the limitations of differing methods, including (a) midline axial sternotomy, (b) the left anterior intercostal approach, (c) bilateral transverse thoracotomy, and (d) the transdiaphragmatic approach. Their comparative assessment provided the basis for the Martínez (2003) critique. As such, Martínez argues that bilateral transverse thoracotomy requires recourse to a "circular saw" or a chisel and hammer, thereby implying that Stone Age people would not have had the technical skills necessary for the procedure.

Twenty Seconds to Immortality

An experimental simulation of human heart excision conducted for a Discovery Channel production titled *Unsolved History: Aztec Temple of Blood* (2002) invalidated the effectiveness of bilateral transverse thoracotomy with stone tools. Through the use of a synthetically accurate human torso, the transdiaphragmatic approach was determined to constitute the most effective means for human heart excision. The latter approach would necessarily permit a skilled surgeon or ritual specialist to excise a still-beating human heart—via an incision located just below the sternum—within a time frame of seventeen to twenty seconds.

On April 19, 2004, using said findings as a pretext for discussion on the question of human sacrifice in Mesoamerica, I posted a message to the Aztlan-L discussion forum. Aztlan-L explicitly asks that participants refrain from discussions concerned with Mesoamerican blood sacrifice. The rationale posted by the list-owner is that the topic of blood sacrifice generally elicits a barrage of emotionally charged e-mail. Because this research centers on the question of Mesoamerican human sacrifice, I nevertheless acted on the belief that Aztlan-L remains a necessary and appropriate venue for such discourse. Responses ranged from those that utterly dismissed the relevance of the topic to the perennially popular ecocultural challenge about how the purported scale of human sacrifice would have disturbed the delicate ecology of the Basin of Mexico. One respondent alleged racism on my part for my focus on Amerindian blood sacrifice. Another self-identified as a high-ranking member of the Neo-Mexica (*danzante*) movement but nevertheless expressed appreciation for my concerns with the outlandish claims, denials, and revisionism of the more radical elements of the *movimiento*.

Heart Excision by Analogy

If the Matamoros, Mexico, cult killings of 1985 through 1989 are any indication, then the act of excising the beating heart of a living victim can in fact be accomplished by a single individual with only the most basic surgical instruments. Journalist Edward Humes (1991) documented the phenomenal evolution and violent demise of the Matamoros cult and its leader, Adolfo Constanzo. In this instance, human heart excision, cannibalism, and the acquisition of human trophies were all undertaken for the purpose of invoking supernatural protection for the cult's trafficking of drugs across the U.S.–Mexico border. These killings were the product of the cult's pathological obsession with witchcraft and the Palo Mayombe variant of Santeria, which resulted in the death and mass burial of some twenty-five victims and the disappearance of many more who remain unaccounted for.

The cult leader convinced his followers that only those sacrificial victims who died under the most horrific and frightening conditions were suitable as supernatural guardians. According to Humes (1991, 1), "It was important that the offering die in confusion and pain and, most of all, in fear. A soul taken in violence and terror could be captured and used by the priest, turned into a powerful, angry servant that would wreak horrible revenge on the priest's enemies." Ironically, the Matamoros cult would initiate its own demise with the torture, heart excision, and dismemberment of a drug lord who failed to scream before having his blood drained into one of four cauldrons of blood and human body parts maintained by the cult for the purposes of conjuring supernatural forces. This failure led to the torture and sacrifice of an American whose death was more vigorously investigated and prosecuted, thereby exposing the cult and its altar of blood and gore. Although this latter human sacrifice took place on March 13, 1989, the religious executioner in question conducted himself without the assistance of those others deemed necessary by revisionists to assist in the extraction of the human heart.

CALCULATING THE TOTALITY OF THE HOLOCAUST

Hernán Cortés (1967) documented the execution of some 4,000 captives per annum in his efforts to calculate the number of sacrificial victims dispatched at Tenochtitlán in any given year. Despite other similar evidence from the period of the conquest, scholars and skeptics alike question recent estimates of this number. The magnitude of ritual killings identified with the consecration of the Templo Mayor is often cited where discussions of body counts come into play (Carrasco 1999). While recounting the ritual execution of 20,000 to 60,000 (or 80,400) Huastec war captives (López Luján 1994, 283), Kurly Tlapoyawa (2003,

4) asserts that "this means that roughly one person was sacrificed every six seconds, nonstop for 96 hours straight" by a single team of executioners. The implication is that this would have been a logistical impossibility, and such scenarios only serve to impeach Spanish accounts regarding the ritual slaughter at the Templo Mayor. This massive act of blood sacrifice entailed twenty individual groups of executioners dispatched throughout the civic-ceremonial precincts of México-Tenochtitlán. However, a careful reading of Leonardo López Luján's analysis (1994, 283) reveals that on the first day of the festival of Tlacaxipehualiztli in the year 1487, the consecration of the Templo Mayor entailed the simultaneous deployment of not one but some twenty individual teams of executioners, including the Huey Tlatoani Ahuitzotl and the Lords Tlacaelel, Nezahualpilli, and Totoquihuatzin. Tlapoyawa (2002) disregards this ethnohistorical detail in an effort to promote the logistical impossibility of conducting such a feat during the four-day period cited from firsthand accounts.

While many of the aforementioned revisionist arguments are readily dismissed within academic and professional circles, what constitutes that primary evidence necessary for dissecting the diatribe in question? And given what select special interests construe as an outright distortion of the Amerindian past by academics, what then should be our point of departure for arriving at that evidence necessary to substantiate mass human sacrifice in Mesoamerica?

Those who actively challenge revisionist claims tend to view them as largely sentimental, romanticized, misinformed, and politicized cultural fictions unworthy of response (Rosenberg 1997). Our failure to address such popular misconceptions has fueled the growth of such perspectives at home and abroad. How, then, do we reconcile extant evidence for social and religious violence within a culture that created an otherwise uniquely civil society that produced brilliant works of art, poetry, philosophy, technology, and statecraft? What role did religion, or the Aztec elite, play in the origin and perpetuation of the ritualized violence in question? And by what yardstick do we measure and assess evidence that has long framed our perspectives on Aztec ceremonialism and human sacrifice?

Though I profess no illusions regarding the prospects of ever nailing down the visceral roots and shoots of that family tree that spawned the sacrificial complex of war and blood sacrifice that eloquently framed the Aztec ritual cycle, I do believe that we stand at the threshold of a body of archaeological and forensic strategies that hold considerable promise. Forensic archaeology now permits investigators to more precisely identify and assess the evidence for key elements of that complex ultimately woven together into a crimson tapestry of violence and bloodshed that serves as the measure for this analysis.

REVISITING THE ARCHAEOLOGICAL EVIDENCE

Why, after some five hundred years, does the question of human sacrifice, cannibalism, and warfare among the Aztec continue to engender much contention and, in turn, come into question from a panoply of diametrically opposed points of view? Despite what appears to constitute an otherwise formidable body of evidence, our failure to address the variability of the archaeological and cultural contexts for ritual human sacrifice necessarily provides a vexing point of departure for those who continue to question the available data and the interpretations derived from those data. Ultimately, scholarly discussion regarding Mesoamerican sacrifice and militarism remains shrouded in nationalistic, and culturally relative, frameworks of analysis that continue to hinder further exploration of the sort advocated here.

Despite years of scientific study devolving from the recovery of human trophies exhumed from the Templo Mayor, from within and beyond the central precincts of the Zocalo in Mexico City, and from Aztec sites in and beyond the Valley of Mexico, the most problematic questions remain. In fact, little has been done to operationalize that fundamental body of forensic criteria that necessarily constitutes prima facie evidence for ritual human sacrifice. Among an earlier generation of politically charged arguments remains the question of what ultimately became of the physical remains of the many sacrificial victims. Where are the mass burial grounds, bone beds, and recycled by-products of the horrific experience in question? And what effect, if any, would such a massive scale of carnage have had on the putatively delicate ecology of the Basin of Mexico?

SEROLOGICAL ANALYSIS

I am first drawn to revisionist claims regarding the paucity of specialized forensic studies concerned with Aztec blood sacrifice. Indeed, blood serum or serological studies specific to those offerings, cult objects, and architectural features recovered from the Templo Mayor remain problematic. Despite an ability to detect human blood serum from archaeological contexts dating back some 90,000 years, little to no such work has been conducted on human blood let in Aztec ritual contexts.

Located within the Templo Mayor complex, the Templo de las Aguilas recently produced positive indications for residual human blood serum recovered from a thick dark organic material coating two elaborate ceramic braziers identified with the deity Mictlantecuhtli (López Luján and Mercado 1996). Nevertheless, blood residues from such contexts may represent autosacrificial bloodletting by individual penitents as opposed to sacrificial victims. Some detractors argue that all such serological evidence recovered from architectural features at the Templo Mayor may constitute that (Aztec) blood drawn by the weapons of the Spanish *conquistadores* in 1521. Once again, we are left to ponder the potential benefits and limitations of such an approach.

Clearly, serological analysis of Aztec-era materials should be limited to those contexts and specimen types most specifically identified with Mexica rites of ritual human sacrifice. To that end, I propose that four specialized categories of cult materials and objects hold the greatest potential for eliciting serological results consonant with indications for ritual human sacrifice:

1. Those sacrificial altar stones upon which human victims were purportedly splayed during the rites of human heart excision (Matos Moctezuma 1984, 141, fig. 6);
2. Obsidian and chert knives, or *tecpatl*, deposited by the hundreds in dedicatory caches recovered from the substructures of the Templo Mayor (López Luján 1994);
3. Cuauhxicalli "Eagle Vessel" cauldrons allegedly employed as repositories for human hearts and blood (Orozco y Berra 1877); and
4. Monolithic basalt and andesite representations of the primary

deities of the Aztec pantheon of gods and supernaturals upon whom the blood and hearts of sacrificial captives were smeared.

One other source for the recovery of viable serological samples lies within the architectural facings of Aztec monuments; the extent to which such monuments retain their original stuccoed surfaces clearly plays a role in the recovery of relevant trace evidence. Where architectural features test positive for human blood proteins, the investigator is left to question whether such traces derived from human sacrifice or autosacrificial rites and practices. Ultimately, cult objects such as those recovered from ethnohistorically documented sacrificial contexts hold the greatest potential for retaining their original serological patina or signature. Such evidence provides an undisputed, and contextually relevant, ritual identification with the practice of human sacrifice, heart excision, and/or decapitation.

Substantive assessment of the evidence for ritual human sacrifice must consider both contextual (ritual) and forensic (trace element) criteria. Clearly, one cannot override the other insofar as such an analysis is concerned. Serological evidence without a concomitant consideration of associated ritual features, artifacts, and archaeological deposits remains unreliable as an indicator of human sacrifice. By contrast, in situ forensic evidence—particularly that identified with the osteological or taphonomic analysis of cut marks, "pot polish," blunt force trauma, flayed limbs, impaled heads, and other modifications to human bone—holds the greatest promise for resolving such questions. To that end, John Verano (2001a) and colleagues have advanced a significant framework of analysis.

IDENTIFYING RITUAL HUMAN SACRIFICE

In a recent anthology devoted to ritual sacrifice in ancient Peru (Benson and Cook 2001), Verano suggested an analytical framework for the interpretation of forensic evidence from those sites deemed to contain sacrificial offerings. Verano's study and those of Steve Bourget and Donald Proulx (Benson and Cook 2001:chaps. 5 and 6) document findings from the Peruvian archaeological sites of Huaca de la Luna on the northern coast of Peru and the lower Río Grande de Nasca valley. Each considers evidence from sites that contain a significantly better record of preservation than that typically characteristic of archaeological sites and deposits from Mesoamerica.

FORENSIC ANALYSIS

Verano's (2001a) analysis of the evidence for ritual sacrifice in Peru provides yet another new, and potentially powerful, means by which to assess the primary data and discourse for ritual sacrifice in Meso-america. Verano (2001a, 167) begins with the question "how is human sacrifice identified archaeologically?" He goes on to acknowledge that "preconceived notions can lead to distinctly different interpretations of archaeological data." Verano (2001a, 167) then argues, "Human sacrifice implies the intentional offering of human life . . . distinguishing between natural and induced death in archaeological remains is often difficult." He advances a forensic framework for just such an analysis and thereby articulates the potentials and limitations of the methodology proposed.

That body of forensic and contextual evidence deemed necessary to demonstrate the presence or absence of human sacrifice necessarily subsumes a number of key indicators. Verano distinguishes between natural and induced death as indicated from remains recovered from archaeological contexts and acknowledges that "the way in which sacrificial victims are dispatched may leave recognizable skeletal or soft-tissue evidence, but this is not always the case" (Verano 2001a, 167). Complicating factors such as postburial disturbance may elucidate or cloud determinations of whether those remains examined are pertinent to primary versus secondary offerings, or human sacrifice versus postmortem trophy collection and/or modification. Careful consideration of the contexts within which human remains are recovered are key to assessing their primary versus secondary status, in situ or postburial disturbance, and ritual or nonritual associations. The superimposed layering of human remains and their prolonged exposure to the elements (see fig. 2.2) may in turn be correlated with projectile point and blunt force trauma, dismemberment, decapitation, cannibalism, isolated limbs and articulated elements, trophy taking, and perimortem or postmortem mutilation.

2.2 Ritual deposits at the Epiclassic through Postclassic site of Cholula, Puebla, Mexico, included these two young sacrificial victims. Note evidence for a puncture wound on the skull of the adolescent on the left and the particularly weathered and fragmentary conditions of both skeletons, exposed to the elements long after recovery. (Photo © Rubén G. Mendoza, 1983)

MESOAMERICAN CANNIBALISM

The forensic analysis and interpretation of cannibalism from human remains from ritual contexts has been undertaken in Mesoamerica. Drawing on the forensic analysis of three Mesoamerican site collections, Carmen María Pijoan Aguadé and Josefina Mansilla Lory (1997) have determined that (a) Tlatelcomila, Tetelpan, D.F. (500–300 BC), (b) Electra, Villa de Reyes, San Luis Potosí (AD 350–800), and (c) Tlatelolco (AD 1337–1521), Mexico City, D.F., all contain collections of human remains bearing primary evidence for perimortem violence and cannibalism, human sacrifice (in the form of defleshed, dismembered, and butchered human remains), and indications of a concomitant ritual specialization. Pijoan Aguadé and Mansilla Lory (1997, 236–37) conclude, "from these three samples, we can propose that human sacrifice and cannibalism were interrelated to each other, both dating to deep antiquity in México." They further acknowledge that "based on the archaeological evidence, the distribution of human bones, and the indications of violence left on them, there can be little doubt that cannibalism and human sacrifice were long prevalent in ancient societies in México." Patterned cut marks on long bones and disarticulated remains from mass burials remain a primary point of departure for studies that similarly conclude that evidence for cannibalism is in order (Guilliem Arroyo 1999; Ojeda Díaz 1990; Pijoan Aguadé, Mansilla, and Pastrana 1995).

BUTCHERING PATTERNS   Patterned cut marks specific to the cutting of muscle attachments for the defleshing of bodies has been documented from the site of Tlatelolco (Pijoan Aguadé and Mansilla Lory 1997; Pijoan Aguadé, Mansilla, and Pastrana 1995; Pijoan Aguadé, Pastrana, and Maquivar 1989). Investigators interpret the evidence as representing ritual cannibalism at the heart of the Aztec Empire. When Verano (2001a) encountered similar remains at both Plaza 3A and 3B at Huaca de la Luna, Peru, he arrived at a similar conclusion. Recent investigations at the Epiclassic (ca. AD 600–900) site of Cantona in Puebla, Mexico, indicate a pattern of human bone modification similar to that identified at Tlatelolco, with the exception that a sizeable sample of human bone (N = 200) from Cantona provides indications of boiling sans "pot polish" (Talavera, Rojas, and García 2001, 37). Pot polish is thought to result from the prolonged mixing or stirring of fleshed bones in ceramic vessels, as identified by Tim White (1992) from prehistoric remains recovered from the American Southwest.

According to investigators (Talavera, Rojas, and García 2001:37), of the 505 individual human and nonhuman bones examined at Cantona, specimens include 27 human crania with cut marks, 3 human mandibles with cut marks at muscle attachments, 23 long bones with cut marks at muscle attachments, 200 human bones subjected to boiling, 111 carbonized or calcified human bones, 58 percussion-fractured human bones (i.e., bone marrow extraction), and 83 animal bones with cut marks from mixed deposits. Investigators concluded that "all of this leaves us to suppose that the most probable interpretation that can be given for all of the different cultural treatments observed in the osteological materials is that it concerns the dispatch of sacrificed victims, the cadavers having been intentionally dismembered as a prelude to the ritual ingestion of human flesh" (Talavera, Rojas, and Garcia 2001, 37, translation by Mendoza). Investigators also noted a distinct pattern in the interment of remains bearing the aforementioned indications, including but not limited to being subsequently buried as fill in structures, deposited as offerings in civic-ceremonial areas, or strewn throughout domestic trash dumps in one limited sector of the large portion of the site that has thus far been subjected to archaeological investigation. Angel García Cook (1994, 65) concluded that ritual and religion at Cantona are clearly manifest in the evidence from decapitation, mutilation, and dismemberment. Significantly, Epiclassic Cantona encompasses some twenty-five to thirty square kilometers of relatively contiguous occupation debris. Much work therefore remains to be done at Cantona to achieve a comprehensive archaeological understanding of the civic-ceremonial core and its hinterland.

BONE MODIFICATION   Cut marks, fractures, and related indicators of perimortem and postmortem bone modification and/or trauma, perimortem injuries, and postmortem treatment are critical to the analysis and interpretations noted (López Alonso, Lagunas Rodríguez, and Serrano Sánchez 2002; Sánchez Saldaña 1972). The presence or absence of articulated upper cervical vertebrae are in turn taken to constitute primary indices of whether a deposit of human crania constitutes the dispatch of "freshly decapitated individuals" (Browne, Silverman, and García 1993; Verano 2001a, 168). Cut marks to the anterior surfaces and transverse processes of the first through fourth cervical vertebrae may indicate the slashing of the throat versus complete decapitation (Verano 2001a, 178). Concomitantly, such trauma to the throat rarely produces cut marks on the intervertebral joints and spinous processes, as is generally the case in instances of decapitation (Verano 2001a, 181). While manual strangulation may result in the fracture of the hyoid bone, Douglas Ubelaker (1992) acknowledges that strangulation with ligatures seldom results in such damage.

Associated artifacts—such as ligatures (Uhle 1903), projectile points, bifacial knives, prismatic blades, and wooden clubs (Bourget 2001:figure 5.18—provide corroborating evidence for human sacrifice. Collections at Cantona (Talavera, Rojas, and García 2001) and other Mesoamerican sites (Pijoan Aguadé and Mansilla Lory 1997) have undergone experimental studies centered on stone tool use and taphonomy in an effort to ascertain the significance of cut marks, striations, and other modifications to human bone recovered from such sites. By examining microscopic indicators of lithics usewear and cut marks resulting from actions consonant with the butchering of animal or human bone with stone tools, specialists have more effectively begun to identify the specific tool types and behaviors that produce specific cut marks or striation patterns as butchering activities (Talavera, Rojas, and García 2001).

In their study of the *tzompantli*, or skull rack, of Tlatelolco, Pijoan Aguadé and Mansilla Lory (1997) published the results of an analysis of some 170 human crania retrieved from the remains of said structure. All such crania bore 5.0- to 8.5-centimeter-wide bilateral perforations through each aspect centered on the parietal and temporal areas (Mendoza 2004, 5; Mendoza 2007). Microscopic analysis of cut marks indicate that each skull had been decapitated in its perimortem state and was flayed and perforated with stone tools to open the cranial vault for the insertion of wooden *varas*, or beams, for suspension (Sánchez Saldaña 1972). Significantly, virtually all 170 such crania recovered from the controlled excavation of the tzompantli of Tlatelolco exhibit patterns of defleshing and modification commensurate with period descriptions relating Aztec practices for the display and preparation of human crania destined for such structures at México-Tenochtitlán and Tlatelolco. Finally, the presence of human antiserum or blood protein on the aforementioned tools recovered in direct association with modified or disarticulated human remains provided corroborating evidence for the interpretations in question. This finding is similar to Steve Bourget's (2001, 110) recovery of a wooden mace from Tomb 1 at Huaca de la Luna. Subsequent immunological analysis of a thick black substance that completely coated the mace was found to react to the presence of human antiserum or blood residue.

MASS INTERMENTS   Multiple burials in which disarticulated human remains are recovered in primary contexts, coupled with sampling patterns that indicate age- or sex-based selection or massing, are essential to documenting the presence or absence of intentional or ritual killings. The biometric measurement of human skeletal remains may in turn provide a point of departure for assessing ethnic and regional differences between those killed and those within whose territory the remains were recovered. Perhaps a more reliable indicator of regional differences in skeletal populations is that evidence that centers on the isotopic analysis of bone collagen in efforts to determine dietary, and thereby geographical, differences from skeletal remains (Verano and DeNiro 1993). One recent study succeeded in tracing the nonlocal origins of a single Maya lord ("18 Rabbit" or "18 Images of the War Serpent"; see Van Cleve 2003) from Copan, Honduras, to Mexico's Yucatán Peninsula. This latter approach promises significant new revelations if applied to skeletal remains from ritual and civic-ceremonial contexts in México-Tenochtitlán and Tlatelolco, in particular.

MUTILATION AND EXPOSURE   Postmortem mutilation or prolonged exposure to the elements (and thereby, the absence of formal mortuary rituals) is cited as evidence that victims were sacrificial offerings, particularly given that the remains are generally those of individuals or groups not deemed to merit proper care in their treatment upon death (Verano 2001a, 171). Verano (2001a, 173) cites the "surface weathering" of human remains and the presence of scavenging insects from a mass burial of approximately fourteen individuals from the defensive trench at Pacatnamú, Peru, dated to circa AD 1100–1400. He also cites the "sun bleaching" of human bone at Huaca de la Luna, Peru. In Mesoamerica, Angel García Cook (1976, 1994) and Beatriz Leonor Merino Carrión (1989) have similarly identified several such mass interments in Epiclassic- and Postclassic-era deposits recovered from sites located along the "Teotihuacán Corridor" of Tlaxcala, Mexico (Mendoza 1992, 1994).

Finally, interpretations drawn from the ethnohistoric, iconographic, or text-based evidence for ritual human sacrifice must ultimately be correlated with the archaeological record. The iconography and ethnohistory necessarily serve as secondary resources for corroborating past human practices and at the same time infuse such studies with a parsimonious balance of interpretation and firsthand corroboration for interrogating the evidence at hand. In this latter regard, the firsthand accounts of Spanish soldiers, missionaries, and native informants hold particular relevance, despite the probable political or cultural biases that may accrue in any number of cases so documented (Mendoza 2003: 228).

FUTURE RESEARCH AND KEY QUESTIONS

This exploration of the primary and secondary evidence for ritual human sacrifice in Mesoamerica clearly raised many more questions than it sought to resolve. Although the realm of forensic science promises to bring some degree of clarity to our interpretation and assessment of the evidence for early human conflict and violence in the Americas, lingering questions regarding epistemological and methodological constructs and criteria, as well as nationalistic and revisionist agendas, will necessarily shadow much of the writing, analysis, and interpretation to come. Key questions for consideration and debate include the following:

◆ Does prima facie forensic evidence exist to contest recent claims by the revisionists that all firsthand accounts of Mesoamerican blood sacrifice are mere fabrications of the Spanish invaders?

◆ If we are to demonstrate that blood sacrifice was a matter of fact among such groups as the Aztec, do scholars have ready access to that body of osteological and forensic evidence necessary to specify those systems of blood sacrifice that may best account for the data (e.g., human heart excision, decapitation, etc.)?

◆ Given revisionist claims that human sacrifice was merely a radical form of autosacrifice, can antiserum, DNA, or bone collagen studies definitively settle the matter of who specifically was selected for such an auto-da-fé? And finally,

◆ Given revisionist claims that the practice of surgically excising the human heart is not technically or surgically feasible with stone tools, how might the Matamoros cult killings of the 1980s or recent efforts in experimental archaeology provide that corpus of "ethnographic" analogs needed for ultimately rendering this portion of the debate null and void?

The archaeological and osteological evidence presented here corroborates available ethnohistorical descriptions of ritual violence and anthropophagy in Mesoamerica and challenges revisionist claims that no hard evidence exists to document these practices. However, this chapter is by no means intended to constitute the definitive treatment for considerations of Mexica ritual violence and bloodshed, much less the broader question of human sacrifice and/or cannibalism in precontact Mesoamerica. Rather, my intention remains to move the debate away from the simplistic question of whether Amerindians engaged in religious violence and cannibalism to the deeper question of why any human group would have adopted ritual human sacrifice and anthropophagy on a monumental scale. Continued inquiry along these lines will require a far greater scrutiny and examination of the available evidence and will be revisited by the editors in a forthcoming publication.

Given the many questions that remain unanswered and the many assumptions about blood sacrifice made about virtually every pre-Columbian platform mound and artifact recovered on the Mesoamerican landscape, how can we begin to fruitfully and effectively interrogate that evidence and those questions that continue to vex Amerindian communities and Americanist scholars alike? Ultimately, I contend that irrespective of the forum within which arguments are framed for or against the evidence for ritual human sacrifice in the Americas, both the emergence of a forensic approach to the archaeological evidence and the coincident growth of the Neo-Mexica denial movement promise to push the envelope of discovery and discourse identified with this seemingly endless and often dark and tragic exploration into the depths of the human spirit (Mendoza 2001a).

ACKNOWLEDGMENTS

California State University–Monterey Bay student Genetta Butler assisted with word processing and related revisions. Lilly Martinez provided critical clerical and administrative support. Benjamin F. Hernandez offered new leads to some of the more radical elements of the revisionist movement. I gratefully acknowledge each of these contributions. Finally, I express my heartfelt gratitude to my loving wife and companion, Linda Marie Mendoza, and my daughters, Natalie Dawn Marie and Maya Nicole Mendoza, for their understanding, support, and the many personal sacrifices made so that I might complete this and other related project efforts.

3 TERRITORIAL EXPANSION AND PRIMARY STATE FORMATION IN OAXACA, MEXICO

Charles S. Spencer

The three major branches of the Oaxaca Valley (Etla, Tlacolula, and Ocotlán-Zimatlán) converge in a broad central zone, in the middle of which lies the hilltop city of Monte Albán (fig. 3.1). Although Monte Albán was founded at the beginning of the Early Albán I phase (500–300 BC) (Blanton 1978; Marcus and Flannery 1996), the earliest signs of state organization in Oaxaca date to the following Late Monte Albán I phase (300–100 BC); key evidence includes a regional settlement hierarchy of four tiers and the appearance of key institutional building types such as the palace and multiroom temple (Flannery 1998; Kowalewski et al. 1989, 125–38; Marcus and Flannery 1996, 162–64; Spencer and Redmond 2001a, 2003, 2004a). By the Monte Albán II phase (100 BC–AD 200), Monte Albán had become the capital of a fully developed state that dominated the entire Oaxaca Valley and several other surrounding regions (Flannery and Marcus 1983, 1990; Marcus and Flannery 1996, 206–7). The Monte Albán state (probably founded by Zapotec speakers) is currently Mesoamerica's best candidate for a first-generation or primary state (Spencer and Redmond 2004b).

In a classic paper, Henry Wright (1977) defined the state as a society with a centralized and also internally specialized administrative organization. He contrasted the state with the chiefdom, which he defined as a society with a centralized but not internally specialized administration. Although not all chiefdoms evolve into states, several scholars have argued that all primary states evolved from preexisting chiefdoms (Carneiro 1981; Earle 1987; Flannery 1972; Spencer 1990).

It has been suggested that predatory expansion may play a key role in the formation of a primary state (Algaze 1993; Carneiro 1970; Flannery 1999; Marcus and Flannery 1996, 157; Spencer 1990, 2003). Elsewhere, I developed a mathematical model that shows how a strategy involving territorial expansion through the conquest of polities in other regions, coupled with regularized tribute exaction, could bring about a transition from chiefdom to state (Spencer 1998b). According to this model, for such a strategy to succeed (especially when the conquered polities lie more than a half-day's trip away), the leadership will have to dispatch components of administration to the conquered polities, not only to carry out the subjugation but also to maintain long-term control and manage the mobilization and transfer of tribute. Because such a strategy requires that central authority be delegated to these dispatched functionaries, the central leadership should promote internal administrative specialization (and thus bureaucratic proliferation) as a way of narrowing the breadth of authority, and the potential for independent action, possessed by the dispatched functionaries and other officials. At the same time, the success of the conquest strategy would make new resources available to defray the costs of the administrative transformation. The expansionist model would have us look for evidence that

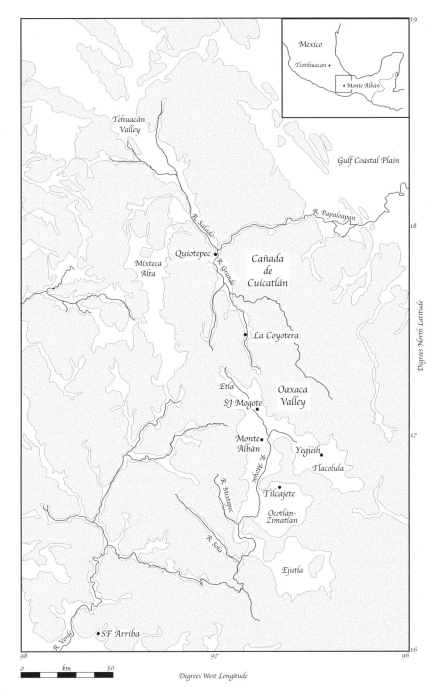

3.1 The location of the Oaxaca Valley, its major subregions, and other surrounding regions. Key archaeological sites are also indicated.

long-distance territorial conquest was an integral part of the process of primary state formation.

Monument 3 at San José Mogote dates to the Rosario phase (700–500 BC) and is Oaxaca's earliest known stone with writing; shown on the monument is a named, sacrificed individual who probably represents a casualty of intervillage raiding (Flannery and Marcus 2003). Although there is evidence of intervillage raiding as soon as sedentary villages first appeared, in the Tierras Largas phase (1500–1100 BC), such raiding had intensified greatly by the Rosario phase (Flannery and Marcus 2003). At this time, the three branches of the Oaxaca Valley appear to have been occupied by three independent chiefdoms, separated by a sparsely occupied buffer zone in the central zone (Marcus and Flannery 1996, 124–25). San José Mogote was the chiefly center of a polity in the Etla branch (fig. 3.1). Its rival in the Ocotlán-Zimatlán branch was the Rosario phase occupation of the El Mogote site at Tilcajete, while the site of Yegüih was the probable center of the contemporaneous Tlacolula chiefdom (Marcus and Flannery 1996, 123–26).

When Monte Albán was founded around 500 BC, there was a nearly complete abandonment of San José Mogote, a coincidence that Joyce Marcus and Kent Flannery (1996, 139–40) have explained by proposing that the leadership of the Etla polity decided to shift its political center to the middle of the previous buffer zone. The initial phase of occupation at Monte Albán (Early Monte Albán I) is associated with the famous Danzantes inscriptions, of which the most widely accepted interpretation is that they represent slain and mutilated captives (Coe 1962, 95; Marcus 1976, 126–27). Marcus has drawn attention to the potential propaganda value of the Danzantes, attributing special significance to the fact that they were evidently all carved very early in Monte Albán's history, when "the rulers of Monte Albán would have felt the greatest need to legitimize their power and sanctify their position. Perhaps by creating a large gallery of prisoners, they were able to convince both their enemies and their own population of their power, although it was not yet institutionalized or completely effective" (Marcus 1974, 90).

Marcus's interpretation of the Danzantes is consistent with what Elsa Redmond and I have called the "rival polity model," which sees Monte Albán's political domain during both the Early and Late

Monte Albán I phases *not* extending into the Tlacolula and Ocotlán-Zimatlán branches (Spencer and Redmond 2001a). During the Early Monte Albán I phase, the territory controlled by Monte Albán probably included the central zone, the Etla branch, and a small portion of the mountainous area north of the Etla branch where Robert Drennan (1989, 376) reported an Early Monte Albán I occupation that he interpreted as an "expansion of Etla Valley population northward into the mountains."

While the Danzantes can reasonably be interpreted as depicting captives taken in raids and skirmishes, the "conquest slab" inscriptions on Monte Albán's Building J seem to be referring to a different form of warfare: true conquest, that is, the taking and holding of territory. Joyce Marcus (1976, 128) noted that the more than forty conquest slabs were first identified as such by Alfonso Caso (1947), who pointed out that they typically include four elements: (1) an upside-down human head; (2) above the upside-down head, a "hill" sign that signifies "place"; (3) a glyph or combination of glyphs that probably represent the specific name of the place, usually situated above the "hill" glyph; and (4) sometimes an accompanying hieroglyphic text. Marcus (1976) sought to carry the analysis further by proposing several places to which the conquest inscriptions might be referring. One of her proposed places was the Cañada de Cuicatlán, a canyon traditionally inhabited by Cuicatec speakers, situated about eighty kilometers north of Monte Albán (fig. 3.1). In making this reading, she noted the close resemblance between the toponym on a particular inscribed conquest slab (Lápida 47) and the glyph that refers to Cuicatlán as the "Place of Song" in the Codex Mendoza, a sixteenth-century Aztec document recording places that were paying tribute to the Aztec (Marcus 1980, 1983). Yet she was careful to point out that "such a correlation between a 16th-century Aztec codex and Zapotec glyphs of Period II implies some 1,500 years of place-name continuity. Hence, my suggestion is no more than a hypothesis, subject to proof or disproof by future analysis" (Marcus 1980, 56).

Although many Oaxaca scholars have assumed that Building J and its inscriptions date to the Monte Albán II phase, Alfonso Caso (1938, 11) actually suggested that it was constructed in the preceding phase, a premise based on the presence of Monte Albán I phase ceramics in its walls. The building continued in use during the Monte Albán II phase (Acosta 1965). Drawing together Caso's and Marcus's interpretations, we can propose that the differences between the Danzantes and the conquest inscriptions reflect a shift in the predominant warfare strategy pursued by Monte Albán, from a raiding pattern in the Early Monte Albán I phase to outright territorial conquest by the Late Monte Albán I and Monte Albán II phases. Obviously, such proposition requires testing through an examination of the archaeological record.

In 1977–78, Elsa Redmond and I carried out a program of archaeological survey and excavations in the Cañada de Cuicatlán, a central goal of which was to test Marcus's interpretation of the Building J conquest slabs (Redmond 1983; Spencer 1982; Spencer and Redmond 1997). We recovered substantial evidence that the Cañada was, in fact, conquered by Monte Albán at the onset of the Lomas phase (ca. 300 BC) and remained in a subordinate, probably tributary, relationship until the end of that phase (ca. AD 200), a time span that corresponds to the Late Monte Albán I and Monte Albán II phases combined (Spencer and Redmond 2001b).

Prior to the Lomas phase, the Cañada was occupied by twelve Perdido phase (750–300 BC) villages, all located on high alluvial terraces or low piedmont spurs directly overlooking pockets of fertile low alluvium. The proximity to low alluvium and the lack of evidence of irrigation facilities associated with Perdido phase sites suggest that farming at this time used simple techniques of diversion dams and floodwater farming, both of which have been practiced in recent times in areas of low alluvium.

At the beginning of the Lomas phase (300 BC–AD 200), a major settlement-pattern disruption occurred in the Cañada; all the Perdido phase sites were abandoned and new sites were founded nearby. In the Quiotepec area at the northern end of the Cañada, the single small Perdido phase site was replaced by a forty-five-hectare complex of seven sites that sprawled across both sides of the natural pass into the Cañada from Tehuacán as well as occupying the strategic mountain peaks. Heavily fortified, the Quiotepec sites were undoubtedly a military frontier installation, designed to control movement through the northern frontier of the Cañada (Redmond 1983, 91–120). The Quiotepec installation also marks the northern limit of Lomas phase pottery, some of which is nearly identical to the pottery of the Late Monte Albán I and Monte Albán II phases. A radiocarbon sample (Beta-147535) associated with the Cerro de Quiotepec site yielded a date of 1910 ± 70 BP, with a 2-sigma calibrated range of 50 BC–AD 250 (Spencer and Redmond 2001b, table 1).

Our excavations at the site of Llano Perdido found that this Perdido phase village had been burned to the ground; we recovered densities of burned daub and adobe that were five times greater than Robert Drennan (1976) recorded at Fábrica San José, a contemporaneous village site in the Oaxaca Valley (Spencer 1982, 217–18). Upon the floor of a residence was the body of a woman who had evidently perished when the community had been destroyed (Spencer 1982, 212–20). At the onset of the Lomas phase, around 300 BC, settlement in the locality was shifted to an adjacent ridge (Loma de La Coyotera), where we excavated evidence of major changes in local economic, social, and politico-religious organization that persisted throughout the Lomas phase (Spencer 1982, 215–42). Economic activities became more narrowly focused on agricultural production, which was greatly intensified through the introduction of canal irrigation (Spencer 1982, 221–31). Residential patterns changed from the multifamily compounds of the Perdido phase to a single-family form that not only was more like the Zapotec pattern at that time but may also reflect a Zapotec policy of rupturing the traditional Cañada kin ties (Spencer 1982, 231–34). The rich ceremonial life of the Perdido phase disappeared in the Lomas phase, replaced by the fearsome presence of the Zapotec state, as attested by the skull rack that we excavated in front of the main Lomas phase mound (Spencer 1982, 234–42; Spencer and Redmond 1997, 520–24).

A series of radiocarbon samples recovered from Perdido and Lomas phase deposits indicates that the Zapotec conquest of the Cañada began around 300 BC (Spencer and Redmond 2001b, fig. 8), which corresponds to the onset of Late Monte Albán I in the Oaxaca Valley. Two overlapping radiocarbon dates from the Cañada, in particular, help us pinpoint this invasion in time (Spencer and Redmond 2001b, table 1). From the preinvasion site of Llano Perdido, the latest radiocarbon date (Beta-143347) was 2370 ± 100 BP, with a 2-sigma calibrated range of 790–195 BC. From the postinvasion site of Loma de La Coyotera, the earliest radiocarbon date (Beta-143349) was 2170 ± 70 BP, with a 2-sigma calibrated range of 390–40 BC. The midpoint of the overlap in these 2-sigma ranges is 293 BC—roughly 300 BC, the beginning of the Late Monte Albán I phase. The date from the Loma de La Coyotera skull rack falls somewhat later in time, though still within the Lomas phase. Beta-143344 was charcoal from a carbonized post mold associated with the skull rack; it yielded a radiocarbon date of 1960 ± 100 BP, with a 2-sigma calibrated range of 190 BC–AD 255 (Spencer and Redmond 2001b, table 1), making this the oldest known example of a skull rack in the Oaxaca area.

Our alignment of the beginning of the Lomas phase (and the Zapotec invasion of the Cañada) with the beginning of the Late Monte Albán I phase would be consistent with Caso's (1938, 11) suggestion of a pre–Monte Albán II construction date for Building J (and its conquest inscriptions) at Monte Albán. The alignment is also notable in view of the fact that the earliest convincing evidence of state formation in the Oaxaca Valley (in the form of a four-level settlement hierarchy and the appearance of the palace and the multiroom temple) dates to the Late Monte Albán I phase (Spencer and Redmond 2004b). Taken together, the data from the Cañada and the Oaxaca Valley support the view that aggressive territorial expansion played an important role very early in the process of Zapotec primary state formation (Spencer and Redmond 2001b, 2003, 2004b).

Bearing in mind that more than forty conquest inscriptions are associated with Building J, one can readily believe that the Cañada was probably not the only region that fell under Monte Albán's control at this time. One example is the Peñoles region, immediately west of the Oaxaca Valley. Here, Laura Finsten (1996) reported evidence of an intrusion from the Valley of Oaxaca during what she called the Late Formative (400 BC–AD 200), corresponding fairly closely to the Late Monte Albán I and Monte Albán II phases in my usage. Drawing attention to a line of sites in the northern part of her study region, she noted, "Both their pottery, which is visually indistinguishable from vessel fragments found at contemporary Valley of Oaxaca settlements, and their location suggest that Late Formative sites along the continental divide and in the northwest near the Nochixtlán Valley represent settlements along a communication corridor that must have been important to the Monte Albán state" (Finsten 1996, 84).

Although Monte Albán seems to have been expanding toward the Nochixtlán Valley in Late Monte Albán I, little evidence of a takeover has been found there or in any of the other valleys of the Mixteca Alta (Balkansky et al. 2000, 373). The hilltop site of Monte Negro (covering 78 ha) was founded at the beginning of the Ramos phase (corresponding to the Late Monte Albán I and Monte Albán II phases), and its foundation coincided with the abandonment of the previously occupied center of La Providencia and that center's dependent villages (Balkansky et al. 2000, 373). A reasonable hypothesis is that the new center was founded, in part, as a defensive response to the aggressions of the Monte Albán state: the people of La Providencia and its satellite villages sought to protect themselves by moving en masse to the hilltop site of Monte Negro.

Andrew Balkansky (2002) has argued that his survey data from the Sola Valley, about seventy-five kilometers southwest of Monte Albán, indicate that this region had been brought under Monte Albán's control by Late Monte Albán I. Whereas the Early Monte Albán I phase in Sola was a time of sparse occupation (a single small site), the Late Monte Albán I phase saw a major influx of settlement, associated with ceramics that closely resemble those of the Oaxaca Valley (Balkansky 2002, 37). Balkansky's analysis demonstrated that the distribution of Late Monte Albán I sites does not correspond to the distribution of the best-quality agricultural soils (Balkansky 2002, 42). Noting that several key sites are located along what would have been the major route between the Oaxaca Valley and the Pacific coast, he suggested that "Monte Albán's expansion into the Sola Valley seems intended to control this boundary region for its access to the coast" (Balkansky 2002, 84). He concluded that Sola continued to be dominated by Monte Albán through the Monte Albán II phase (Balkansky 2002, 95).

Drawing together the data collected by Spencer and Redmond (1997, 2001b), Finsten (1996), and Balkansky (2002), I propose that the territory dominated by Monte Albán during the Late Monte Albán I phase consisted of the Etla-Central "core" area of the Valley of Oaxaca, along with certain other regions to the north, west, and southwest (fig. 3.2). Other areas to the east and south, including Tlacolula and Ocotlán-Zimatlán, evidently resisted Monte Albán's aggressions and remained independent during Late Monte Albán I. The proposed expansion, therefore, did not proceed in a gradual, concentric fashion; instead, the territorial growth of the Monte Albán state was notably asymmetric.

It might seem paradoxical that Monte Albán was able to extend its control during Late Monte Albán I to territories that lay well beyond a half-day of foot travel from the capital but failed to bring the much closer Ocotlán-Zimatlán and Tlacolula branches of the valley under its domination. The reason may be that the Ocotlán-Zimatlán and Tlacolula polities were both more populous and greater military threats at the onset of the Late Monte Albán I phase than were those in the Cañada and Sola (Spencer and Redmond 2001a). Indeed, we have argued that the Ocotlán-Zimatlán polity went on to become a secondary state during the Late Monte Albán I phase, probably as part of its overall resistance strategy, which included shifting the main settlement to a more defensible location and constructing fortifications (Spencer and Redmond 2003, 2004a).

If, as Balkansky (2002) has suggested, Monte Albán expanded into Sola for the purpose of gaining access to the Pacific coast, then we might expect to find evidence of an intrusion by the Valley Zapotec in a nearby coastal region. Balkansky (2002, 95) has noted that "Sola fits squarely between Monte Albán and coastal-piedmont Tututepec," and it happens that Tututepec is one of the places that Marcus (1976, 1980, 1983) identified in the conquest slab inscriptions on Building J at Monte Albán. The slab in question is Lápida 57, and it depicts a bird sitting on what appear to be bound arrows, which she pointed out was similar to the glyph for "Tototepec" ("Hill of the Bird" in Nahuatl) in the Codex Mendoza, an alternative name for the Oaxacan coastal town of Tututepec (Marcus 1983).

Did the Tututepec area also fall under Monte Albán's control? Joyce Marcus and Kent Flannery (1996, 201) were uncertain "whether Monte Albán was claiming conquest of the Tututepec region, or merely political and diplomatic colonization." They drew attention, however, to the monograph by Gabriel DeCicco and Donald Brockington (1956), in

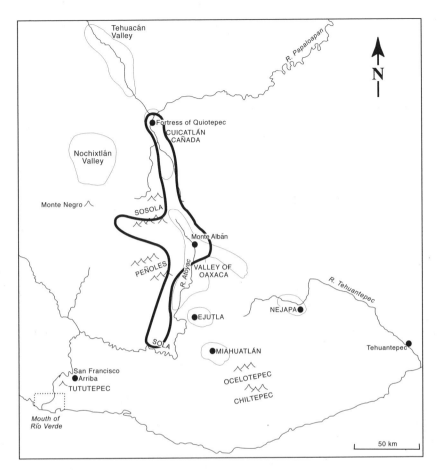

3.2 The proposed extent of the territory dominated by Monte Albán during the Late Monte Albán I phase (300–100 BC). (Base map redrawn, with modifications, from Marcus and Flannery 1996, fig. 242)

which pottery from the Tututepec region was reported to show a close relationship with Monte Albán I and Monte Albán II pottery (DeCicco and Brockington 1956, 59). These ceramic similarities were especially marked at the site of San Francisco Arriba (see fig. 3.1), situated on a hillslope about three kilometers north of the town of Tututepec.

Notable among the ceramics collected at San Francisco Arriba were fourteen sherds of *crema* ware (DeCicco and Brockington 1956, 56), which amounted to 11.97 percent of DeCicco and Brockington's total ceramic sample. When the analyzed sample was limited to rim sherds, the cremas comprised 14.29 percent of the total. Since the investigators were assisted in their ceramic analysis by John Paddock (DeCicco and Brockington 1956, 59), we can have much confidence in their statement that "this crema pottery fits perfectly in the classification of Monte Albán" (DeCicco and Brockington 1956, 55, translated by C. Spencer).

The crema ware is of special significance because the raw material used to make this distinctive ware is found only in the Atzompa locality near Monte Albán (Feinman 1982, 188–91; Flannery and Marcus 1994, 22). Redmond and I have suggested that the relative frequency of crema ware in a given Late Monte Albán I or Monte Albán II site can be used as one indicator of the relative intensity of interaction between that site and Monte Albán (Spencer and Redmond 2003). Three samples (two from excavations, one from surface survey) from the site of El Palenque (SMT-11b) near Tilcajete (in Ocotlán-Zimatlán) plus one excavated sample from the Cañada site of La Coyotera (Cs25), as shown in table 3.1, can be assigned to the Late Monte Albán I phase only. The ratio of cremas to total diagnostic sherds is much higher at La Coyotera than at El Palenque; this result is consistent with other lines of evidence indicating that the Cañada was conquered by Monte Albán in the Late Monte Albán I phase, while the Tilcajete area remained independent until the Monte Albán II phase (Spencer and Redmond 2001a, 2001b, 2003).

Table 3.1 also presents two other excavated samples from La Coyotera that can be attributed to the Late Monte Albán I and the Monte Albán II phases; these samples from La Coyotera likewise have higher ratios of cremas to total diagnostics than were observed in the three samples from El Palenque. In addition, table 3.1 reveals that the sample collected at San Francisco Arriba by Gabriel DeCicco and Donald Brockington exhibits a ratio of cremas to total diagnostics (rims only) of .1429, falling between the highest value noted for La Coyotera and the two lower values from that site. Notably, the San Francisco Arriba ratio of cremas to total diagnostics is much higher than those observed in the El Palenque samples. These results suggest that the relationship between San Francisco Arriba and Monte Albán was more like that between the Cañada de Cuicatlán and Monte Albán than that between

TABLE 3.1 Distributional Analysis of Crema Ceramics

Site	Sample	Cremas/total diagnostics[a]
Late Monte Albán I phase samples only		
El Palenque (SMT-11b)	Excavation (Feature 14)	.0077
El Palenque (SMT-11b)	Excavation (Areas B, G, I, P, W1, W2)	.0552
El Palenque (SMT-11b)	Surface survey (67 collections)	.0143
La Coyotera (Cs25)	Excavation (Level 9, Feature 4)	.2353
Late Monte Albán I and Monte Albán II phase samples		
La Coyotera (Cs25)	Excavation (Feature 4)	.0613
La Coyotera (Cs25)	Excavation (Lomas phase chronology sample)[b]	.0677
San Francisco Arriba[c]	Surface survey	.1429

Sources: El Palenque data were recovered during the 1993–2000 fieldwork directed by the authors at San Martín Tilcajete. La Coyotera data are from Spencer and Redmond 1997. San Francisco Arriba data are from DeCicco and Brockington 1956.

[a] Total diagnostics are rim sherds, base angles, decorated bodies, and special forms, except in the case of San Francisco Arriba, where "total diagnostics" are all rim sherds and "cremas" are crema rims only. The crema types are described in Caso, Bernal, and Acosta 1967.

[b] An explanation of the chronology sample from La Coyotera is presented in Spencer and Redmond 1997, chap. 4.

[c] A more recent study at San Francisco Arriba (Workinger 2002) does not present data on the frequencies of ceramic wares and cannot be used in this analysis.

El Palenque and Monte Albán. This outcome is consistent with Marcus's (1980, 1983) reading of Lápida 57 as representing a conquest of the Tututepec area and Lápida 47 as representing a conquest of Cuicatlán.

A different view of Tututepec's relationship to Monte Albán has been taken by Andrew Workinger (2002), who conducted survey and excavation at San Francisco Arriba and concluded that there was no evidence that the site and its locality had fallen under Monte Albán's control. Although his dissertation does not contain data tables with frequencies of ceramics according to ware, he reported that he found only one sherd of the "cream paste" during the course of his project (Workinger 2002, 355)—a paucity that strikes me as curious, given the substantial frequency of cremas reported by DeCicco and Brockington

(1956) based on John Paddock's analysis. This analytical discrepancy should be examined more closely by future researchers.

I think it is fair to say that Workinger (2002, 390–93) emphasized three lines of negative evidence in his rejection of the conquest hypothesis: (1) the lack of a major disruption in settlement patterns; (2) the lack of an unoccupied buffer zone between the San Francisco Arriba area and the lower Río Verde, said by Marcus and Flannery (1996, 201–2) to lie beyond the zone subject to Monte Albán; and (3) the lack of physical evidence of an attack. Throughout, he made much of what he saw as the differences between his data set and that from the Cañada de Cuicatlán (Spencer and Redmond 1997). As one of the coauthors of the latter study (which was based on the coauthors' doctoral dissertations), I feel obliged to say that we should not expect all the regions affected by Monte Albán's expansionistic designs to have had exactly the same experience as the Cañada's. As Marcus and Flannery (1996, 198–99) and Balkansky (2002, 95) have emphasized, Monte Albán is likely to have not only employed a variety of military and diplomatic tactics as it sought to extend its influence, but also encountered a variety of responses from the target regions. If a region capitulated to Monte Albán as a result of diplomatic or economic inducements or threats of force (rather than outright conquest), we would not expect the archaeological evidence to mimic what was recovered in the Cañada. Indeed, we should expect varying political relations to be associated with variation in the archaeological record.

In addition, the power of negative evidence rests heavily on the representativeness of the sample, and there is reason to suspect that Workinger's survey sample was less than representative. His survey was not a full-coverage regional survey but was limited to two transects (1 km wide and 2 km wide) with sites subjected only to "grab-bag" sampling (Workinger 2002, 78–79, 239). His excavated sample was also not extensive: three test pits in the 1997 season (Workinger 2002, 84–85), followed by eleven operations in the 1998–99 season, with exposures that ranged from 2 square meters to 32 square meters (Workinger 2002, 88). I do not wish to devalue Workinger's accomplishment; the Oaxaca coast is a difficult setting in which to carry out fieldwork, and I applaud him for doing it. Nevertheless, I must point out that Redmond's and my year of dissertation fieldwork in the Cañada was no picnic either, and it included a full-coverage survey of the study region that located 93 sites; topographic mapping and controlled, intensive surface collecting at 25 Formative and Classic period sites; and excavations at the Llano Perdido and Loma de La Coyotera components of the La Coyotera site. These excavations comprised twenty test pits and five areas of horizontal excavation with exposures of 1,200, 400, 162, 108, and 16 square meters, totaling about 1,900 square meters (Spencer and Redmond 1997). Moreover, it is worth noting that the conclusions of the Cañada research were based largely on positive discoveries, not negative evidence (Redmond 1983; Spencer 1982; Spencer and Redmond 1997, 2001b).

Arthur Joyce and his colleagues (Joyce 1991, 1994; Joyce, Winter, and Mueller 1998) have also stated that they found no evidence of violent intervention by the Valley Zapotec in their excavations at the sites of Cerro de la Cruz and Río Viejo in the lower Río Verde valley, some ten to fifteen kilometers west of San Francisco Arriba. Yet Balkansky (1998, 2001) has disputed their assessment, seeing evidence of a "possible massacre" in the fifty-nine human skeletons associated with Structure 1 and the MTS (retaining wall) in Zone A at Cerro de la Cruz (Joyce, Winter, and Mueller 1998, 71). Joyce and colleagues (2000, 623) have rejected Balkansky's interpretation, claiming that "the individuals were interred over a long period, probably at least several generations." That statement, however, seems inconsistent with one of the conclusions in their earlier work: "During the occupation of the structures constructed during this final phase, Structure 1, just as various other areas of Zone A, was the center of intensive funerary activity" (Joyce, Winter, and Mueller 1998, 71 [all quotations from this work translated by C. Spencer]). Elsewhere, Joyce and colleagues state, "There were 41 adults buried in the lower part or alongside Structure 1, all of them buried during the last two construction phases" (Joyce, Winter, and Mueller 1998, 65).

The assertion that the individuals interred in Structure 1 indicate that this structure was a locus of communal funerary ritual (Joyce 1998, 65) was challenged by Balkansky (2001, 560), who noted that "no grave goods were associated with the interments (an exceptional discovery), the body count is higher than expected for the structure's size and duration, and the age profile differs from that of formal cemeteries." In their excavation at the MTS, also within Zone A, Joyce and colleagues (1998, 65) recovered nine additional individuals "piled one atop another alongside a 2-m section." Such a deposit would seem to give additional support to Balkansky's suggestion of a mass interment.

The Cerro de la Cruz excavators did recognize the extraordinary nature of the entire sample of Zone A interments. They drew attention, for example, to the complete absence of grave goods: "The combined burials of Zone A consisted of 59 individuals and surprisingly none of the burials was accompanied by offerings" (Joyce, Winter, and Mueller 1998, 65). They also asserted, "This number of individuals is highly atypical in comparison to burial patterns in residences documented at other Formative sites" (Joyce, Winter, and Mueller 1998, 65). In addition, they noted that the age distribution of the Zone A burials (86 percent are adult) does not correspond to an expected mortality profile (Joyce, Winter, and Mueller 1998, 65). They drew a contrast between the Zone A interments and the eighteen burials associated with Structure 8 in Zone B; in the latter group, adults comprise 28 percent of the individuals, a pattern, as Joyce and colleagues (1998, 65) argued, that more closely matches expected mortality profiles. Moreover, three of the adults in the Structure 8 group did have grave goods (Joyce 1994, 164), which further underscores the difference between that group and the Zone A skeletons. For the present, while it may be difficult to conclude whether Balkansky's interpretation of the Zone A skeletons is more convincing than that of Joyce and his colleagues, I am inclined to favor Balkansky's view.

Balkansky's attack hypothesis is also supported by the fact that Structure 1 produced considerable evidence of burning. Joyce and colleagues (1998, 49) note that "within the building were found remains of two burned floors." Elsewhere, they state, "The horizontal excavations revealed deposits of burned clay upon the foundation stones of the west room of Structure 1-3a, including a burned adobe brick resting on a foundation stone" (Joyce, Winter, and Mueller 1998, 69). Several areas of charcoal are located as features on the plan of Structure 1; some appear much too large and irregular to have been simple hearths (Joyce, Winter, and Mueller 1998, fig. 3.3). One of these large charcoal concentrations is

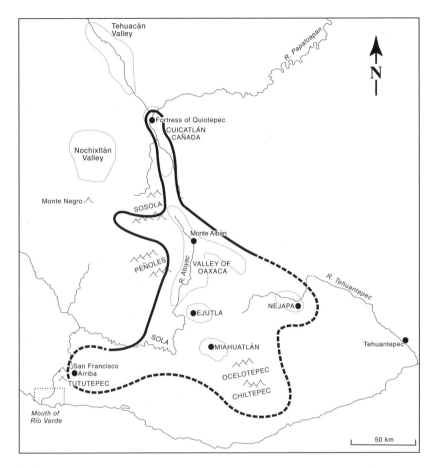

3.3 Proposed extent of the territory dominated by Monte Albán during the Monte Albán II phase (100 BC–AD 200). (Base map redrawn, with modifications, from Marcus and Flannery 1996, fig. 242)

Elemento 1; it covered 3.0 square meters and yielded a radiocarbon date (Beta-30490) of 120 BC ± 80 (Joyce, Winter, and Mueller 1998, 47), falling toward the end of what investigators defined as the Minizundo phase (400–100 BC)—corresponding to the end of the Late Monte Albán I phase—at which point Cerro de la Cruz was largely abandoned (Joyce, Winter, and Mueller 1998, 75). Summing up, I suggest that the data from Cerro de la Cruz should not lead us to reject a hypothesis of violent intervention toward the end of the Late Monte Albán I phase.

Marcus and Flannery (1996, 199–202) have argued that other regions, such as Ejutla (Feinman and Nicholas 1990), Nejapa, Miahuatlán (Brockington 1973; Markman 1981), and Ocelotepec, were brought into Monte Albán's sphere of influence by the Monte Albán II phase, though they point out that more research is needed to clarify these relationships. In view of these uncertainties, as well as the differing interpretations of the data from San Francisco Arriba and the lower Río Verde, I offer (in fig. 3.3) a tentative multiregional territory dominated by Monte Albán during the Monte Albán II phase, using dotted lines to indicate those boundaries that are poorly defined or have been incompletely researched.

During the Early Monte Albán I phase, the amount of territory controlled by Monte Albán probably reached no more than 35 kilometers from the capital, roughly the distance that could be traveled on foot in half of a twelve-hour day. In the Late Monte Albán I phase, Monte Albán succeeded in annexing previously independent regions to the north, west, and southwest, bringing under its control a territory whose farthest boundaries reached about 100 kilometers from the center (fig. 3.2). The Late Monte Albán I phase is also when state organization first appeared. During the Monte Albán II phase, the Monte Albán state continued to expand its political territory until the most distant boundaries lay some 140 kilometers from the center (fig. 3.3).

In sum, the Late Monte Albán I phase has yielded the earliest evidence of major interregional expansion as well as the earliest evidence of state organization in Oaxaca. This concurrence lends empirical support to the expansionist model of primary state formation.

Acknowledgments

I thank Elsa M. Redmond and Joyce Marcus for their comments on an earlier version of this chapter. Bridget Thomas McKnight prepared the illustrations.

4   IMAGES OF VIOLENCE IN MESOAMERICAN MURAL ART

Donald McVicker

The contrasts between the Mesoamerican cultural traditions of central highland Mexico and the Maya Lowlands to the southeast have provided a scholarly challenge for over a century. Early European and American explorers were awed by the art and architecture and scholarly accomplishments of the Classic Maya; in turn, scholars (usually of the armchair variety) were appalled and repelled by accounts of Aztec savage warfare and barbarous sacrifices. As the concept of the nonviolent Maya ruled by priest-kings developed during the first half of the twentieth century, it was extended to include other Classic cultures under the rubric of "theocratic societies," in opposition to the Postclassic "militaristic societies" (e.g., Pasztory 1997, 28).

Yet violence and military themes are presented on painted walls at the Late Classic southern Lowland Maya site of Bonampak as well as those of Middle Classic Teotihuacan, located just northeast of the Valley of Mexico. In the Terminal Classic, these themes continued in both cultural traditions, with paintings embellishing temples at Chichén Itzá in the arid northern lowlands of the Yucatán Peninsula and at the central Mexican highlands site of Cacaxtla (fig. 4.1). The parallel sets of paintings do not necessarily mean that both the Maya and their central Mexican contemporaries shared a common trajectory of ritual violence and warfare, however. The presence or absence of expression of violence in art reflects sets of aesthetic traditions and stylistic choices and therefore cannot be assumed to directly mirror a culture's aggressive actions or passive responses. Too often the orientations of the observers and their interpretations of the cultures they are analyzing lead them to evaluate artistic expressions of violence in their own terms and to use their evaluation to label cultures as aggressive or passive.

IMAGES OF VIOLENCE

Images of warfare, human sacrifice, and bloodletting rituals are infrequently encountered on the painted walls of ancient Mesoamerica. Although ethnohistoric accounts of the highland Aztec stress military might and sacrificial proclivities, these characteristics are only rarely seen in surviving Aztec mural art. Even the predecessors to the Aztecs, the mural artists of Teotihuacan, chose not to decorate their architecture with overt scenes of violence. In sharp contrast, the "peaceful" Classic Maya presented vivid illustrations of warfare and its aftermath.

Ross Hassig (1992, 88, 195–97) in his analysis of social structure has presented a proposition that contrasts "meritocratic systems" with "aristocratic systems." In Mesoamerica, he argues, meritocratic systems characterized the civilizations of the Mexican highlands. Within this type of society, successful bellicose expansion "inspires few depictions of militaristic subjects," because what is celebrated is the corporate nature of the society, not its aristocratic rulers. Clearly the Maya and their art represent the opposite, the aristocratic system.

For Hassig, the evidence of militarism is there in the art of meri-

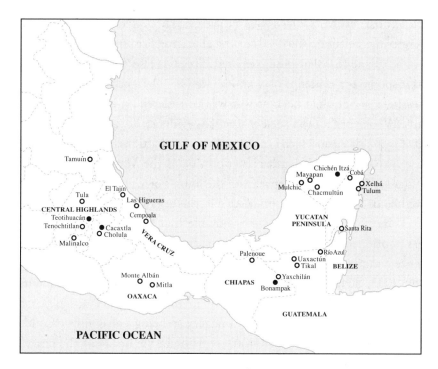

4.1 Mesoamerica, showing sites with surviving mural programs and major sites mentioned in the text. Solid circles designate the four sites whose murals are evaluated in this chapter. (Map drawn for the author by Kent Hadraba)

tocratic societies, but the devil is in the details, not the scenes. For example, if extensive depictions of weapons characterize the mural paintings of Teotihuacan, does this not indicate the prevalence of warfare? If the purpose of warfare is to obtain sacrificial victims, might the preference be to emphasize symbols of sacrifice rather than illustrations of battles? Saburo Sugiyama (2000, 120–21) suggests, "Like the Maya, who preferred to depict victory celebrations culminating in sacrificial rituals instead of the actual war scenes, the Teotihuacanos also may have stressed warfare-related rituals in visual presentation more than the wars that often preceded them."

Although the Maya might have preferred to paint sacrificial rituals and victory celebrations, they took equal pleasure in recording the bloody battles (M. Miller 1986). However, as Hassig reasons, these vivid renderings celebrate the deeds of the elite in an aristocratic system. Steven LeBlanc (LeBlanc and Register 2003, 64) also considers visual art as a source for evidence of war. He argues, "Demonstrating how successful a society had been at war was considered an important use of art." What, then, does a society accept as evidence of success in warfare? If it is the ritual and sacrifice that follows the battles, this would explain the virtual absence of battle scenes outside of the Maya area. As will be discussed below, the evidence from the murals of Cacaxtla in the central highlands is particularly provocative in this regard.

In all the cases above, it is notable that the authors are making assumptions regarding what is depicted and why. As research on violence and conflict has become more fashionable (e.g., Brown and Stanton 2003; Schmidt and Schroeder 2001) and as LeBlanc's arguments on the universality of warfare and the myth of the peaceful state have become more acceptable, visual imagery is being constantly reevaluated and reinterpreted. Previously, to maintain the image of the peaceful Maya, the bloody battles and sacrifices brilliantly depicted on the Bonampak murals were explained away as ritual local raids, and the warfare and raiding vividly depicted on the temple walls at Chichén Itzá were blamed on the Toltec invaders (Thompson 1966). The reverse was true at Teotihuacan. Laurette Sejourné (1978) defined Teotihuacan as the sacred city of Quetzalcoatl and in truly creative ways saw quetzal images and feathered serpents everywhere; others saw Tlalocs and priests performing agricultural fertility rites in the rain god's paradise.

When the evidence for the impact of Teotihuacan abroad mounted, it was often interpreted as evidence for the expansion of a "commercial empire." However, when the glyphic inscriptions at Tikal and elsewhere were deciphered, Teotihuacan appeared as a warlike expanding imperial state (Stuart 2000). If militarism can be read in the Classic Maya inscriptions, how are scholars to assess the mural evidence for militarism at Teotihuacan, where true hieroglyphic writing was absent and it appears that the image was the text?

Teotihuacan Murals

The murals of Teotihuacan are abundant and are the best known and studied (A. Miller 1973; de la Fuentes 1995). Paintings are most frequently found on the interior walls of the site's multiroom residential complexes. These images were both public and semiprivate and clearly intended to communicate the status of those who dwelt within and their claims to supernatural connections.

Residential complexes that once displayed complete mural programs are located throughout the city. This suggests a pattern of barrios (neighborhoods), each with its own resident elite and ritual center. However, several multiroom complexes adjacent to the city's main avenue (the Street of the Dead) display exceptionally well-painted interiors. These "palaces" appear to have served administrative and ritual functions as well as residential, and they may have been occupied by members of a ruling elite.

Curiously, little painting aside from polished red surfaces and simple geometric designs is known from the exterior walls of the monumental buildings located in the city's center. There is also little architectural sculpture. This suggests sharply different uses of public and private space: brilliant ritual performances took place in public spaces against monochromatic backdrops; these same performances, and the myths they communicated, were displayed on the interior walls of residences.

Unlike the Maya tradition, Teotihuacan mural themes are nondynastic and noncommemorative; they appear to be both corporate and impersonal and glorify neither events nor rulers (Hassig 1992, 88; Pasztory 1988, 45–46; 1997). Since the use of perspective and overlap is virtually absent and scenes are exceedingly rare, the effect is one of images unbound by time or space.

Reflecting the impersonal quality of Teotihuacan art, the painters appear to have had an aversion to depicting human beings unless formally presented as priests, deity impersonators, or possibly military leaders buried in abstract and symbolic costumes. The individual identity or social status of these figures is open to debate. For example, the processional figures depicted on Atetelco Portico 3 were once described as "gods dancing in the middle of a patio." Today René and Clara Millon, who are convinced that Teotihuacan became a military power, see them as dancing military figures carrying lances with hearts impaled upon them (C. Millon 1988, 214, fig. VI.32a).

However, there is only one mural known that depicts the sacrificial act of heart excision (fig. 4.2): two coyotes removing a heart from a deer (C. Millon 1988, 122, 218–21, fig. V.11). Clara Millon interprets this as "a symbolic representation of human heart sacrifice and a rare exception to an evident convention discouraging portrayals of explicitly violent scenes." Apparently, if you cannot find the explicit evidence for violence, you can blame it on an artistic convention that discourages its portrayal.

Plentiful evidence for violence in the form of dedicatory human sacrifice has been uncovered during excavations at the Feathered Serpent Pyramid. More than two hundred soldiers or soldier-priests were sacrificed and dedicated to the erection of the pyramid around 200 CE. It seemed to Sugiyama (1992, 225) that he was excavating the burial monument of a Teotihuacan "king." However, no royal tomb was found, and the mass sacrificial burials may have been an aberration. Similar evidence for warfare as a "fundamental feature" has not been recovered from other monumental structures.

In the case of the Pyramid of the Moon (Sugiyama and Cabrera 2003), the dedicatory sacrificial burials are associated with the initiation of building stages 4, 5, and 6. However, they are considerably less extensive than those excavated at the Feathered Serpent Pyramid, and there is no evidence that the victims' hearts had been removed. In fact, there is ample evidence of head sacrifice. This is also true of the Feathered Serpent Pyramid victims.

The iconography of the Teotihuacan murals is a fertile field for conflicting interpretations. For example, the butterflies flitting around the "dancing" figures in the Tlalocan murals at the palace of Tepantitla have been considered but part of a scene in the rain god's paradise; a paradise filled with abundant plants, flowers and flowing water. These murals are an exception to the abstract, conceptual, and possibly allegorical art of Teotihuacan. However, Annabeth Headrick (2003) in her exhaustive review of butterfly iconography at Teotihuacan links this image to warfare. Although butterflies (and fruit bats and hummingbirds) have long been linked to warriors, heart sacrifice, and the "souls"

4.2 Teotihuacan, probably Techinantitla, Metepec(?). Two coyotes remove the heart from a deer. (C. Millon 1988, fig. V.11; tracing by Saburo Sugiyama; courtesy of the Fine Arts Museum of San Francisco)

of the dead (McVicker 1988), Headrick goes beyond this interpretation. She makes the case that the ubiquitous appearance of the image in art and architecture is direct evidence of "a deeply engrained association with social concepts of [male] duty and gender." If the butterfly is seen as "an image of a heroic warrior enjoying the fruits of the exalted afterlife he earned through service to the state, then the image becomes propaganda, designed to manipulate the actions of the population into the act of war" (Headrick 2003, 169).

The identity of deities has been particularly contested. Images of the rain or storm god, known as Tlaloc among the Aztecs, are omnipresent on the wall of the residential compounds but are curiously absent from palaces and centrally placed temples. Hasso Von Winning (1987, 1:23–40) notes the absence of representations of death or skeletons in the Teotihuacan murals. He concludes that representations of Tlaloc as storm god with jaguar imagery are so common and so tied to warfare that there was no need for images of death gods.

Feathered serpent images abound on painted walls but again are most frequently found on interior walls marking doorways and dividing painted registers rather than displayed in public places. Despite Sejourné's (1978) reading of these images (and many others) as evidence that Teotihuacan was the sacred city of Quetzalcoatl, there is scant evidence that they are images of the legendary Aztec plumed serpent (Sug-iyama 1992). They may be more characteristic of the lightning serpents associated with the storm god, Tlaloc (Sugiyama and Cabrera 2003).

The single image that is distributed both in the residences and in palaces, and is even carved in stone, is that of a great goddess (Pasz-tory 1997, chap. 6). She is prominently featured on the upper wall of the "Tlaloc Paradise" murals referred to above. Following Peter Furst's (1974) identification of the goddess as a Teotihuacan version of Spider Woman, Annabeth Headrick (2003) pushes on and identifies a male "butterfly" side of the image to balance the female "spider" side. Again, the butterfly signifies warfare as the primary image of the male.

Is it possible that Teotihuacan's immense size, influence, and centuries of stability were based on peaceful commerce and that the priesthood of a female agricultural deity guided the life of the city? If this is so, then the great goddess's sodality may have directed a politi-cal economy that distributed power equally among corporate kin-based groups. Such a corporate cadre would indeed appear as depersonalized and eternal as the art itself. However, scholarly opinion, led by the Mil-lons, has discarded this view, at least for the later half of the occupation of the city. Esther Pasztory still maintains the uniqueness of Teotihua-can as "an experiment in living" and argues, "A reasonable perspective is as likely to be lost in the new view of the 'blood of Teotihuacan' as in the old hypothesis of the 'paradise of Tlaloc.'"

Metepec, the final phase at metropolitan Teotihuacan, is marked by a major shift in mural art. The palette becomes even more dominated by reds and the figure/ground contrast ever more subtle. Late murals display more glyphs and signs than do earlier murals, while new icons appear and others are painted less frequently. This has been interpreted as a change in the political and economic order symbolized by new dei-ties of war and sacrifice challenging the ancient gods of fertility. For example, Pasztory (1988, 75) has concluded that Metepec murals rep-resent a progressive erosion of the old corporate value system, a decen-tralization of authority, and "reflect the growth of secularism and the beginnings of dynastic pride." In analyzing murals from the "barrio of the looted murals," particularly from the Techinantitla compound, Rene Millon (1988, 105–8) concludes that this growth of secularism is clearly marked by the celebration of knightly orders and the frequency of weapon bearing warriors.

CLASSIC MAYA MURALS

As the analysis of Maya warfare and its expression in art and epigraphy has expanded rapidly over the past fifteen years, "The fog of war has descended on ancient Maya civilization . . . we now encounter patterns in evidence . . . subject to a bewildering array of contested interpretations" (Freidel, MacLeod, and Suhler 2003, 189). Out of this fog, at least two distinct scenarios have emerged. The first emphasizes the role of "Killer Kings" (Webster 1993, 433). This approach argues that war, at least through the eighth century, was motivated and conducted by divine kings for the capture of rival elites and their sacrifice. Others see wars as institutional and the product of ecological and social forces.

However, the use of art to support either scenario is problematic. Even David Webster (1993, 422) is concerned that art which is claimed to be related to warfare can actually be superficially militaristic but "merely metaphorical." (This point is discussed more fully below, in reference to the terminal Classic/Early Postclassic art of Chichén Itzá.)

Regardless of the emphasis placed on the forces driving warfare, all scholars agree that there were at least four conceptions of warfare among the Classic Maya, manifested in four glyphic verbal expressions: *chuc'ah*, capture; *hubi*, destruction (achieving specific goals and objectives); *ch'ak* (axe), decapitation or battle; and shell-star or star-war (Chase and Chase 2003, 172–77). Of all of these, star-war–designated events were the most catastrophic instances of warfare (Schele and Freidel 1990, 147, 443–44n45). The type and severity of wars appear to have shifted as the southern Maya lowland elites approached the "calamitous" ninth century. For example, Mary Miller (1993, 402) suspects that the Bonampak shell/star emblems record a massive battle.

The murals at Bonampak may be the only ones that survived in the humid tropical lowlands with their full program intact (de la Fuentes 1998, vols. 1 and 2). The three rooms of Structure 1 are filled with hundreds of brightly painted individuals; in true fresco, the painters recorded the rituals, battles, and sacrifices associated with the last major dynastic succession at Bonampak.

Mary Miller and Simon Martin (2004, 164) refer to this pattern of warfare as a "two-act play." The first act is "distant, unruly, chaotic, and set in places of tangible risk and subject to high emotions by all concerned." The second act returns events to the city, and "a scripted picture of order and control emerges, with emotion manifest only in the forms of tormented prisoners who become a special focus of war representation." Room 2 of Structure 1 portrays act one on its east, south, and west walls (fig. 4.3). The battle is presented as an intermingling of friend and foe, of heroic combat stressing individual actors in hand-to-hand combat, until small groups of victors "gang up" to capture an enemy alive. On the north wall, the captives are arraigned in a scene of beauty and brutality. The victorious lords stand on a platform while the bleeding tortured prisoners on the stairs below plead for their lives.

The concentration on the capture and dispatching of live opponents is a characteristic that appears to be shared by many Mesoamerican cultures. This concentration is interpreted by Miller and Martin (2004, 166, 168) as a reenactment of a mythic program ordained by the gods. Although it is well documented for the Aztecs and the Toltecs, it is not expressed in the mural art of Teotihuacan. However, the pattern of tying historical events to myth is carried to new heights in the murals of Cacaxtla.

TERMINAL CLASSIC MURALS

CACAXTLA

The themes of the Bonampak murals are dramatically developed at Cacaxtla, in the central highlands state of Tlaxcala (McVicker 1985; G. Stuart 1992). The murals were produced at the end of the Classic period, after the fall of Teotihuacan created a power vacuum in the highlands. They follow closely on the murals of Bonampak and demonstrate the persistence of aristocratic Maya concepts of war, even when extended into the central Mexican highlands. Although most likely painted by Maya artists in Late Classic Maya style, there is no

4.3 Bonampak, Structure 1, Room 2, south wall. Bonampak's ruler Chaan Muan captures and humiliates his adversary. (© 2002 Bonampak Documentation Project; reconstruction by Heather Hurst with Leonard Ashby; black-and-white photo enhancement by Kent Hadraba)

accompanying hieroglyphic text. Instead there is an eclectic collection of signs, glyphs, and numerals drawn from both highland and lowland traditions. This communication system well served the purposes of new linguistic groups moving into the already multilingual highlands.

The first set of murals flank a staircase opening onto a major patio; they depict an extensive ritual slaughter. Victors in jaguar skins are sacrificing dozens of men dressed mainly in elaborate bird helmets and a treasury of green stone jewelry (fig. 4.4). Both dress and physical type indicate that highland peoples were victorious over Maya-related peoples from the Gulf Coast. The victors may also have "captured" the art of their victims (M. Miller 1993, 409).

4.4 Cacaxtla, Structure B, east talud battle scene. (McVicker 1985, fig. 7; drawing by George McVicker)

In the "palace" above the battle-sacrifice scenes is the entrance to a room flanked by the "state portraits" of an eagle lord and a jaguar lord. The eagle lord is framed by a rampant feathered serpent, the jaguar lord by one dressed in the skin of the tiger. The doorjambs flanking the entrance to the "throne room" display a jaguar "acolyte" pouring water from a Teotihuacan Tlaloc vessel and a man from the sea holding a huge conch shell from which emerges a Maya deity.

These murals not only reveal much about the troubled times following the fall of Teotihuacan but also tell of the balance struck between highland and lowland competitors. The "state portraits" represent an apotheosis of the leaders of both sides depicted in the battle scene. They suggest dual rulership as well as complementary oppositions between the jaguar deities of the earth and feathered serpent deities of the sky (McVicker 1985). (This apotheosis and dualism is repeated in the mural from Chichén Itzá, discussed below.)

As excavations continued at Cacaxtla, new murals were revealed. On the stairwells leading to a section of the site dubbed the "Red Temple," fantastic scenes were uncovered showing a Maya merchant deity pausing on the road up from the Gulf Coast.

Within the temple, however, the theme switches from commerce to war. Painted on the floor of the entrance to the temple are bony captive figures and hieroglyphs naming conquered towns. Nearby is what may be a star-war chamber devoted to human sacrifice. The columns are decorated with a scorpion man and a scorpion woman wearing kilts decorated with large Venus symbols. The association of Venus with the star-war iconography and the blood of kings appeared first in the Maya area, spread to the highlands during the Late Classic period, and later was fated to become an aspect of Quetzalcoatl as the morning star.

CHICHÉN ITZÁ

The murals at Chichén Itzá lack hieroglyphic texts, and the illusionistic perspective and foreshortening of Classic Maya art is replaced by images that must speak for themselves. However, the violence portrayed equals that at Bonampak and Cacaxtla.

The first murals brought to the attention of the Western world were located in the Upper Temple of the Jaguars overlooking the great ball court (fig. 4.5). There were six narrative scenes on the walls of the inner room. They illustrated five fiercely fought battles that Linda Schele and Peter Mathews (1998, 240) conclude "document . . . Itza migrations and the conquests that they saw as legitimizing their right to rule." These scenes also include images of human heart sacrifice modeled on the death (and regeneration) of the Maize God (Schele and Mathews 1998, 241).

The conquering Itzá are associated with green plumed serpents, identifying them as followers of Quetzalcoatl (called Kukulcan in Yucatec Maya). Their opponents are associated with a solar disc, and the battle scenes have been interpreted by Clemency Coggins (1984) as a transformation of historical conquest events into cosmic solar/ Venus myths. This transformation of events has already been noted at Cacaxtla. The double portrait of Captain Serpent and Captain Solar Disc, victor and vanquished portrayed as equals, also is reminiscent of Cacaxtla imagery.

The painted walls uncovered by the Carnegie Institution at the Temple of the Warriors match the Upper Temple of the Jaguars murals. Murals on the portico and inner room of the temple also illustrate a

4.5 Chichén Itzá, Upper Temple of the Jaguars, southwest panel, battle scene. (Drawing by Adela Breton; courtesy of Bristol [U.K.] City Museum and Art Gallery)

narrative sequence of events. The inner-room mural shows a trading scene, and the portico shows a coastal settlement under attack by black-painted invaders. The vanquished are led off to be sacrificed, and a heart sacrifice is realistically drawn (A. Morris 1931, plates 139 and 145). Throughout these scenes, images of the feathered serpent and the jaguar appear in opposition.

Despite these mural scenes, overall in the art of Chichén Itzá there is a shift from depictions of nude prisoners and sacrificial victims to portraits of captives as near-equals. This may indicate the incipient reorganization of a society from an aristocratic model to an imperial model, stressing incorporation of the conquered into the state of the victor; such a process is clearly at work in the terminal Classic at Cacaxtla in the battle scenes and "state portraits."

If the conquered and vassals are depicted more generously at Chichén Itzá, then why are explicit scenes of sacrifice and its consequences so omnipresent at that site? Virginia Miller, directly addressing this apparent contradiction, suggests (2003, 400) that if we had to rely on only images to reconstruct the past, Chichén Itzá would appear to have practiced human sacrifice with more regularity than any other Mesoamerican city. She challenges this interpretation by arguing that the lords of Chichén were publicly presenting these images as part of their political rhetoric. The images were part of the sacred space surrounding staged events as representational strategies, a theater of terror. This strategy to keep the conquered in line was certainly practiced extensively by the later Aztecs.

However, it is notable that among the Aztecs, as among other Late Postclassic societies, the painted walls tell little of war. The symbolic, abstract, and geometric tradition established centuries earlier at Teotihuacan continued to dominate the highlands. Although artifacts and sculpture reveal patterns of war and sacrifice, overall the walls are silent.

PUBLIC IMAGES AND POLITICAL POWER

All of the evidence reviewed above illustrates the difficulty of defining societies as peaceful or warlike based on a single class of data. Reading militarism into figures carrying what appear to be weapons and implements of sacrifice has its pitfalls. Although the murals of Bonampak, Cacaxtla, and Chichén Itzá present battles as historical events, even these data are suspect. Public art is propaganda. Art created by the elite to be viewed by the masses is always didactic. It serves the ends of those for whom it is produced. A primary goal of such art is to convince the populace of the legitimacy, strength, and daring of rulers who claim connections with divinity. Even the veracity of elite hieroglyphic texts must be challenged. How is the reality of their bellicose claims to be judged?

As Bettina Schmidt and Ingo Schroeder (2001, 9) assert, "The symbolic meaning of prior wars is reenacted and reinterpreted in the present, and present violence generates symbolic value to be employed in future confrontations. Wars are fought from memory, and they are often fought over memory, over the power to establish one group's view of the past as the legitimate one." Maya literacy gave their kings a special tie to memories of the past.

A final variable that should be considered is the times and cultural milieus of the scholars evaluating images of violence. Who is to say that many of the current interpretations stressing war and violence in the past are not affected by the world in which the scholars live? Peace seems out of reach in our times; how could it have been achieved by the Aztecs, the Maya, and their predecessors?

If the focus of research is narrowed to the murals of Teotihuacan and the Classic Maya, both sets of images fail to fit norms that characterized warfare in early states. Although Teotihuacan may have become increasingly committed to expansive military campaigns to preserve its commercial empire, the reality of much of its existence remains an enigma. The art is depersonalized and timeless, the images corporate. Even figures of warriors present types or classes rather than portraits.

Although tombs have been discovered and massed human sacrifices excavated, the pharaohs of Teotihuacan remain elusive. With few exceptions, even the architecture appears standardized and repetitive. Was this a deliberate "imperial" strategy to avoid the pitfalls of aristocratic warfare and the cult of kings, a strategy reinforced by their own excursions into the Early Classic Maya kingdoms (Stuart 2000)? Pasztory (1997, 13) has proposed that "Teotihuacan seems to have emerged in contrast to dynastic and aristocratic cultures, such as the Olmec and the Maya."

In the case of the Lowland Maya, there now seems little doubt that the Classic elite focused on warfare and sacrifice. However, at least until the final centuries of the Classic era, the frequency and objectives of warfare seem strangely deviant from what is known of other early states. At least in Classic Maya art, the blood of kings (Schele and Miller 1986) and Venus wars seem to dominate the bellicose agenda, not the taking of territory and resources.

Yet, once again, Teotihuacan plays a dissonant role in this scenario. The Maya elite consciously manipulated Teotihuacan warfare imagery in their presentations of kings as conquerors. The war serpent headdress and Tlaloc as violent storm god are ubiquitous images on stelae, pots, and painted walls. These representations reflect a belief in the military power of the fabled metropolis to the west; they also help to unmask the parading costume-ladened figures in Teotihuacan art and to reveal the combatants that lurk underneath. Mary Miller and Simon Martin (2004, 169) suggest that the Maya experienced cognitive dissonance between their worldview and the reality of power politics and economic conflict. To transcend these contradictions, they depicted themselves as "foreign" as they stepped outside of the norms of their traditional society decked out in their interpretations of Teotihuacan military icons, the artists even switching to the two-dimensional geometric style of Teotihuacan for their war serpent headdresses and portrayals of Tlaloc.

Somewhat gleefully, LeBlanc (LeBlanc and Register 2003, 192) claims that the Maya can now be removed from the ranks of peaceful states, but perhaps the pendulum of interpretation has swung too far. As Octavio Paz (1987) ponders, in responding to Schele and Miller's magnificent exhibition, "Once we accept the vision of the Maya world proposed by the new historians [Schele and M. Miller], we must revise it. Their purely dynastic and warlike model has obvious limitations. . . . Certainly the image that Schele and Miller present is a true one, but it requires more complex realities. The subtitle of their book, after all, is *Dynasty and Ritual in Maya Art*. The dynastic element entered into the ritual; in turn the ritual derived from a cosmogony, and was its symbolic representation."

The propositions that expressions of violence in art reflect sets of aesthetic traditions and stylistic choices and that the interpretive orientations of the observers lead them to evaluate expressions of violence in their own terms seem to be supported by the evidence summarized in this chapter. Interpretations by archaeologists and art historians reflect both the theoretical fashions of the disciplines and the larger historical context. Debates move interpretations forward, and pendulum swings are the soul of debates. However, care must be taken that the purpose of these debates is not lost in their rhetoric.

The central challenge to the scholar is not simply to identify images of warfare and sacrifice in ancient Mesoamerica but to discover the cultural values that lay behind these representations of violence.

USAGE NOTE

Many Mesoamerican scholars refrain from using the accent on the final syllable of Nahuatl words, considering this practice to be an imposition of Spanish colonial orthography on the Nahuatl pronunciations. Therefore, the accent mark has been left off of "Teotihuacan" throughout this chapter.

5 CIRCUM-CARIBBEAN CHIEFLY WARFARE

Elsa M. Redmond

In a seminal volume on the impact that expanding European states in the fifteenth century had upon the warfare waged by the societies they encountered, including the many indigenous polities in the circum-Caribbean area, editors Brian Ferguson and Neil Whitehead (1992) conclude that there were few ethnographically or historically known cases of precontact or pristine warfare (Ferguson 1995, 14). They rightly emphasize the need for a historical perspective on indigenous warfare, and they single out the archaeological record and the judicious use of early historical reports from certain cases as the only means to examine and reconstruct precontact warfare (Ferguson and Whitehead 1992,

27). I think a case in point is the warfare waged by the Taino chiefdoms on the island of Hispaniola and neighboring islands to the north and west in the Caribbean (fig. 5.1), reported by Columbus on his first voyage to the Americas. In the very earliest accounts by Columbus and his followers about the Lucayan Taino groups of the Bahamas islands and the Taino polities on Cuba and Hispaniola, there are indications of indigenous warfare being pursued at the time of Columbus's landfall. There are also references to the warfare practices of Arawakan groups in the pre-Columbian past. These findings can be used to extend, hypothetically, the time frame for certain warfare practices to the distant Arawakan past on the South American mainland. Our expectations for the archaeological evidence of warfare among pre-Columbian chiefly societies in northern South America can be assessed with archaeological data from Barinas, Venezuela, to examine how close the fit is between the earliest historical reports of precontact chiefly warfare and the observations drawn from the archaeological record of prehistoric chiefdoms.

FIRST SIGNS OF INDIGENOUS WARFARE

Let me begin by presenting a chronological time line of excerpts drawn from the journal Columbus kept during his first voyage to America in 1492; Columbus would be "the only one ... to describe the Tainan islands in their original state, while powerful caziques still were maintaining their courts" (Lovén 1935, 658). The first excerpt is from the entry of October 11, 1492, which includes the events that took place on the following day, when Columbus went ashore on the island of Guanahaní (San Salvador)—Peter Hulme (1994, 157) has accorded this account the distinction of being "the first words in the ethnographic discourse" of the Americas. Columbus described the gathering of young naked males, their body and face paint, and their spears with fire-hardened, sharp points, some tipped with a fish tooth or fish bone, which they took up to defend themselves when other groups came to harm them (Dunn and Kelley 1989, 65–67; Las Casas 1951, 202, 204). Columbus added, "I saw some who had marks of wounds on their bodies and I made signs to them asking what they were; and they showed me how

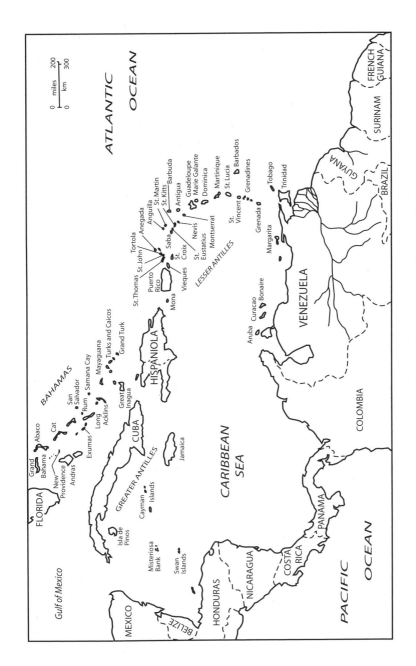

5.1 The circum-Caribbean area. (Redrawn from Keegan, Maclachlan, and Byrne 1998, fig. 9.1)

people from other islands nearby came there and tried to take them, and how they defended themselves" (Dunn and Kelley 1989, 67).

Proceeding to the northeastern coast of Cuba, where the coastal villages were small and deserted, Columbus learned from Lucayan informants onboard of warring kings and of alliances formed by "all of these islanders" to wage war against a common enemy (Dunn and Kelley 1989, 125–29). The Lucayans divulged more when they noticed that Columbus was heading southeast toward Hispaniola; they warned him that it was very large and that its inhabitants were well armed and included people "whom they called cannibals, of whom they showed great fear" (Dunn and Kelley 1989, 167). On November 27, 1492, the caravels came upon the largest settlement that Columbus had seen to that point on the coast of Cuba; there he saw "a great number of men come to the seashore shouting, all naked, with their javelins in their hands. . . . The Indians made gestures threatening to resist them and not to let them land" (Dunn and Kelley 1989, 179–81). At the final landfall in Cuba at Puerto Santo on December 3, 1492, many Indians gathered and approached the launches. One of the Indians came "up to the stern of the launch and made a big speech that [Columbus] did not understand, except that the other Indians from time to time raised their hands to the sky and gave a great shout"; the gist of the harangue was revealed by the altered, trembling, waxen demeanor of one of Columbus's Lucayan guides, who with gestures warned Columbus to shove off "because the Indians wanted to kill them" (Dunn and Kelley 1989, 195). The significance of this short-lived threat, according to Hulme, is "in its being the first reported verbal resistance to Europeans in America" (Hulme 1994, 196). As the launches made their way out of the river, Columbus described large numbers of Indians on shore, all painted red, some wearing feather headdresses, and all carrying bundles of spears (Dunn and Kelley 1989, 197).

Approaching the port of San Nicolás on the northwestern coast of Hispaniola on December 6, 1492, Columbus reported seeing "many fires that night, and, by day, much smoke like signals that seemed to be warnings of some people with whom [the inhabitants] were at war" (Dunn and Kelley 1989, 203). Along with repeated sightings of smoke signals from lookouts, which Columbus had not observed on neighboring islands, were abandoned villages. The following entry on 7 December alluded to further defensive measures practiced by the inhabitants of Hispaniola, whose main settlements Columbus thought were probably located inland on high ground that afforded long-range views and from which they "made smoke signals like people at war" (Dunn and Kelley 1989, 213, see also 229).

The final excerpt is from the entry on January 13, 1493, at the tail end of Columbus's largely successful first voyage of discovery, after friendly encounters marked by feasting and exchange with one of Hispaniola's paramount chiefs (Guacanagarí), who promised access to sources of gold inland, led Columbus to establish the fort of La Navidad (fig. 5.2) and leave thirty-nine of his men there (Dunn and Kelley 1989, 286–300; Las Casas 1951, 285; Redmond and Spencer 1994a). At the last landfall on eastern Hispaniola before returning to Spain, Columbus ordered seven of his men to go ashore and barter for more bows, arrows, and wooden broadswords (*macanas*) from the assembled party of fifty-five Indians wearing black face paint and feather headdresses. After two bows had been acquired, the Indians did not wish to hand over any more weapons; taking up their arms, they boldly confronted the sailors, with ropes in their hands to bind their intended captives (Dunn and Kelley 1989, 332–33). Although the Spanish sailors armed with swords and crossbows promptly repelled the attackers, Bartolomé de Las Casas noted that this hostile action in the Golfo de las Flechas (fig. 5.2) marked the first fight between the Indians and the Spaniards in the Indies (Dunn and Kelley 1989, 332; Las Casas 1951, 305). The many smoke signals observed afterward were another indication that the period of pristine, precontact indigenous warfare on Hispaniola had ended.

REFERENCES TO CHIEFLY WARFARE IN THE DISTANT ARAWAKAN PAST

On his second voyage, Admiral Columbus returned to Hispaniola and reached the fort of La Navidad (fig. 5.2) on November 28, 1493. There was no sign of life in the burned ruins of the outpost, only the burials of some of the thirty-nine sailors who had been stationed there (Las

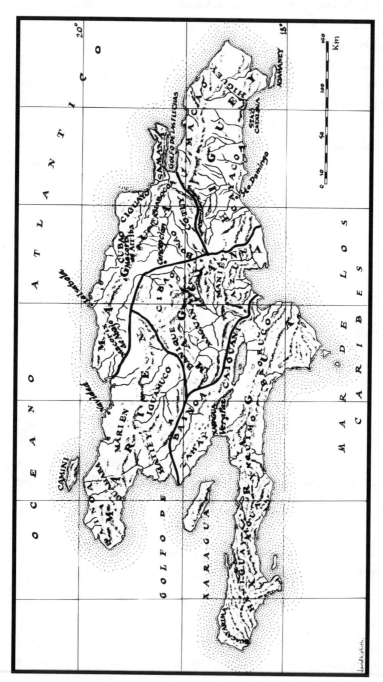

5.2 Hispaniola, showing the territories ruled by the Taino chiefdoms in 1492 and the locations of the early Spanish settlements of La Navidad and La Isabela. (Redrawn from Vega 1980, map 2, in Redmond and Spencer 1994a, fig. 10.2)

Casas 1951, 357). Moving east in December to establish a new Spanish settlement at La Isabela (fig. 5.2) early in 1494 (Las Casas 1951, 363–65), Columbus would initiate the subjugation of the native Taino chiefdoms inland, where the sources of gold lay, a campaign that began on March 12, 1494, when Columbus led his troops inland across the Vega Real and established the fort of Santo Tomás in Cibao (fig. 5.2). The following year, when Columbus ordered that the fort of Magdalena be erected in Macorix de Abajo on the Vega Real (fig. 5.2), four of the island's five paramount chiefs responded to the Spaniards' incursions into their territories by mobilizing large allied fighting forces numbering in the thousands (Las Casas 1951, 378, 400, 403, 429).

One of the Spaniards at the besieged fort of Magdalena late in March 1495 was Ramón Pané, a Catalonian Hieronymite friar who had come to Hispaniola on Columbus's second voyage and had been proselytizing members of the local chief's family. Columbus ordered Pané to the fort of La Concepción (fig. 5.2), erected farther to the southeast on the Vega Real, a half league from the paramount center of chief Guarionex, with whom Pané lived for almost two years, until the growing resistance by Guarionex and his allies to the Spaniards' encroachments led Pané to retreat to another chief's territory (Pané [1498] 2001, xiii–xvi, 40–45; Las Casas 1951, 400, 429–30). By the time Columbus embarked for Spain on March 10, 1496, paramount chief Caonabó (recognized as the island's mightiest paramount), who had been responsible for the destruction of La Navidad and in whose mountainous territory of Maguana lay the gold sources of Cibao (fig. 5.2), had been captured and was bound for Spain (Las Casas 1951, 357–58, 406–8). Chief Guarionex mounted one last stand with an allied force of 15,000 warriors at Concepción de la Vega in 1497, only to meet Caonabó's fate in 1502 (Las Casas 1951, 446, 465).

It is in this context that Ramón Pané wrote his account of Taino myths and rituals, based on his dealings with the chiefs he lived among, whose language he learned, whose ceremonies he witnessed, and whose beliefs and myths he transcribed as they were told to him. Antillean scholars agree that the value of this primary, eyewitness account of Taino beliefs and practices recorded between 1494 and 1498 rests in its authenticity, making Pané's *relación* a source, second only to Columbus's journal and letters, about the Taino chiefdoms in their original state (Pané [1498] 2001:xi; Lovén 1935, 658). Also recognized is the fact that Pané's informants were paramount chiefs such as Guarionex, who had privileged access to the body of ritual knowledge about their ancestors and mythical figures. Not only did the chiefly elites preside over Taino rituals (Pané [1498] 2001, 33; López-Baralt 1985, 37, 39–40; Lovén 1935, 560), but they also commanded war parties. In view of the conditions of heightened warfare during which Pané wrote his account and the fact that his informants were Taino chiefs, let me point out the references to warfare in Pané's relación.

The first mention of warfare comes in the description of the divinatory *cohoba* ritual. Pané specified that the cohoba was celebrated many times each year by male members of the chiefly elite. One occasion was when Taino chiefs were preparing for war, and they assembled in a special sanctuary and sat before wooden or stone sculptures of *cemís* (Arrom 1975, 104; Zayas y Alfonso 1931, 192), to seek the augury of the ancestral supernatural spirit, or *cemí*, about the war's outcome. The presiding chief inhaled the narcotic cohoba powder through the nose and invoked the cemí while sounding an instrument, then awaited the vision and revelation. Finally the chief would raise his head and relate the vision and prophecy he had received: that they would achieve victory, or that the enemy would take flight, or that many lives would be lost, or that many wars would be fought, or hunger suffered (Pané [1498] 2001, 33). Pané's intimate description of the cohoba enhances the reports we have of the pre-war rituals celebrated at chiefly war councils throughout the circum-Caribbean in the sixteenth century (Anglería 1964, 351; Las Casas 1967, 174–76; Redmond 1994, 27, 32, 40).

In the following chapter of his relación, Pané related how the staple root crop, manioc, became domesticated. In a war, the cemí Baibrama was burned by the enemy. Later, when the cemí was treated by being bathed with manioc juice, it grew new arms, its eyes reappeared, and its body grew. From then on, manioc became big and fat (Pané [1498] 2001, 34; see also Las Casas 1967, 176). José Arrom has pointed out that this myth about the domestication of manioc alludes to the clearing and burning of a garden, the germination of the cuttings, and the process of detoxifying the root crop with the same metaphorical language practiced by mainland South American Arawakan speakers in their formal discourse (Arrom 1975, 112–13). Yet Pané's indication that the cemí Baibrama was burned in war–not by slash-and-burn horticultural techniques–is supported by the final reference to warfare in his account. Pané ([1498] 2001, 35) recounted that once, when they were at war among themselves, the enemies of Guamorete (whose name in Arawak means "our creator") burned the house in which his cemí was stored (Arrom 1975, 124). These references to chiefly war councils and the divinatory rituals performed by the attending chiefs to invoke ancestral spirits, as well as to endemic warfare and the tactic of setting fire to chiefly sanctuaries containing the enemy's precious cemís shed light on the warfare waged by the Taino chiefdoms in precontact times.

Antillean scholars have long recognized the resemblances between the Taino myths transcribed by Pané and the myths of Arawakan groups in northern South America (Arrom 1975, 17; Goeje 1943, 23, 101, 107; López-Baralt 1985, 42–44; Lovén 1935, 560, 661; Roth 1915, 146–47). Since manioc was probably domesticated in the northern South American lowlands by the end of the third millennium BC (Pearsall 1992, 194; Piperno and Pearsall 1998, 286), the many archaic elements of Pané's account, which he appropriately entitled "On the Antiquities of the Indians," along with the abovementioned references to indigenous warfare, allow me to propose that such warfare must have been waged also by Arawakan societies in lowland South America in the distant pre-Columbian past.

CHIEFLY WARFARE IN THE PRE-COLUMBIAN PAST

The writings of Columbus, Pané, and those who followed them offer an especially thorough appraisal of the conquest warfare being waged by the Taino chiefdoms on Hispaniola at the time of European contact. Data gleaned from the available fifteenth- and early-sixteenth-century literature reveal the underlying motives, the preparations for war (including the defensive measures taken), the dissemination of information among allies, the chiefly war councils, the tactics pursued by allied fighting forces armed with missiles and macanas, the seizing and binding of captives, and related postwar practices. The raids and large-scale allied attacks mounted by Taino paramounts with armies composed of 5,000 to 15,000 warriors are consistent with the forms of expansionist warfare waged by chiefdoms throughout the circum-Caribbean area (Anglería 1964, 148, 155; Carneiro 1990; Redmond 1994; Whitehead 1990).

One way to assess the possibility that such warfare was waged by militaristic chiefdoms long before 1492, as alluded to in Pané's relación, is by presenting some of the results of the archaeological investigations that Charles Spencer and I carried out in the western Venezuelan *llanos*, or plains, of the Orinoco River basin (fig. 5.3) to investigate the emergence of complex societies and their relationships with neighboring groups. Our study region in the upper Canaguá River of Barinas extended across the high llanos, where in 1530 Nicolaus Federmann encountered mighty Caquetío chiefdoms, and up into the Andean piedmont, occupied by the Jirajara. The Caquetío and the Jirajara were members of the widespread Arawakan-language family (Oramas 1916).

Systematic regional survey revealed that the mound site of El Gaván (B12) out on the llanos occupied the top tier of a regional settlement hierarchy, as a regional center linked by causeways to secondary centers and villages (fig. 5.4). The regional center of El Gaván featured two large earthen mounds at either end of a 500-meter-long plaza, an encircling earthen causeway, and causeways radiating from it. Our map also shows the many lower mounds flanking the plaza and the locations of our test excavations and the horizontal excavations on two of these low mounds (Areas A and D), which exposed the remains of rectangular wattle-and-daub houses (fig. 5.4). First occupied by AD 300, El Gaván had by AD 600 increased its extent to cover the thirty-three hectares enclosed by the oval causeway. Linked by causeway were the secondary center (B97), whose mounded architecture replicated the linear plaza and mounds at El Gaván on a smaller scale, four village sites similar to the one numbered B26, and an expanse of drained fields at B27. Our test excavations at the drained fields yielded high frequencies of maize pollen, as did the pollen samples from our excavations at the adjacent village site (B26), but also present at B26 were root crops, plant dyes, and the same narcotic plant (*Piptadenia peregrina*) used by the Taino for divination, or cohoba (Lovén 1935, 387–88; Pittier 1970, 187; Spencer, Redmond, and Rinaldi 1994, 131–33). Since we estimate

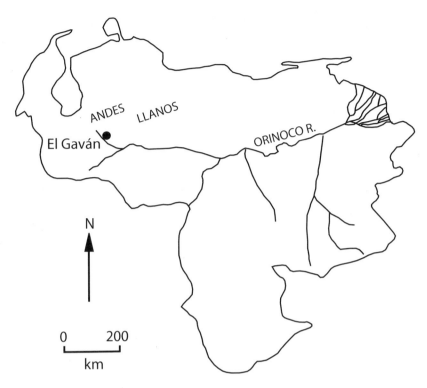

5.3 Venezuela, showing the location of the prehistoric chiefly center of El Gaván on the Canaguá River in the western plains (llanos) of the Orinoco River basin. (Redrawn from Spencer 1998a, fig. 4.1)

that the drained fields would have generated agricultural surpluses far beyond the subsistence needs of the nearby village at B26, they were most likely transported by way of the causeway to El Gaván, to be stored in granaries of the sort described for the Caquetío as large bins of maize raised on posts (Redmond and Spencer 1994b, 427). The degree of centralized regional organization and diversity of public architecture support the proposition that El Gaván was the center of a chiefdom (Spencer 1990).

Along with evidence of El Gaván's far-flung exchange, we have reason to think that the chiefdom centered at El Gaván was involved in mounting war parties and taking captives. The causeways, six to eight meters wide, would have made possible the rapid recruitment and deployment of fighting forces (Spencer and Redmond 1998, 107). Three

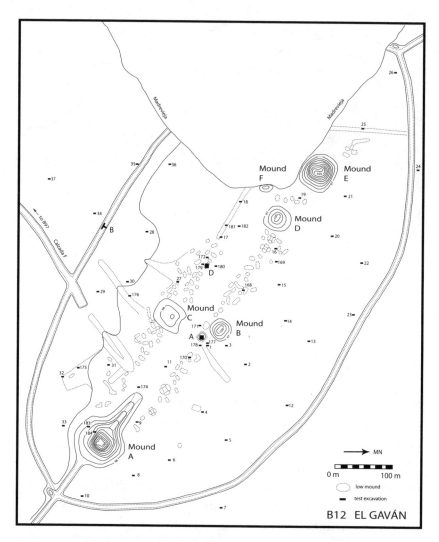

5.4 The prehistoric chiefly center of El Gaván, showing the major mounds, causeways, the encircling earthwork, smaller house mounds, numbered test pits, and the areas of horizontal excavation.

test excavations at El Gaván (T. 17, T. 18, T. 183) placed in nonresidential earthworks, including the base of the large southern mound, encountered disarticulated and incomplete human skeletons. Our use-wear analysis of the chert axes recovered in these contexts revealed the distinctive bone polish associated with such butchering (Keeley 1980, 43).

In addition to mounting raids and seizing and sacrificing captives, the Gaván chiefdom was also repelling attacks through a series of defensive measures, including the packing in of villages in the immediate vicinity of the regional center, the stockpiling of agricultural surpluses, and the building of a palisade. The oval causeway that encircles the regional center rises more than one meter above the present-day ground surface and measures six to eight meters wide on top and twenty to twenty-five meters wide at the base. It seems to have functioned in part as a defensive earthwork topped by a palisade of logs, akin to the palisade of tree trunks, timber, and earth that fortified the main village of a seventeenth-century Achagua chiefdom (Rivero 1956, 46), of which we exposed a line of carbonized post molds along its centerline in a trench we purposefully excavated atop the causeway (Area B; see fig. 5.4).

Around AD 900, however, the chiefly center of El Gaván was evidently attacked and set on fire, as attested by the burned-down palisade and the widespread occurrence of burned daub, most of it from the topmost levels of our excavations at B12, in far higher frequencies than at any secondary center or village we excavated (Spencer and Redmond 1998, 106). We suspect that a rival chiefly polity centered at El Cedral in the adjacent river valley was responsible for the attack, destruction, and abandonment of El Gaván, which was accompanied by the abandonment of all the secondary centers and villages that made up the Gaván chiefdom on the high llanos along the Canaguá River (Redmond, Gassón, and Spencer 1999).

ADDITIONAL EVIDENCE OF PRECONTACT CHIEFLY WARFARE

These archaeological findings from western Venezuela reflect the military organization, defensive measures, and outcomes of the expansionistic chiefly warfare alluded to in the earliest historical accounts about the Taino, and extend its practice back many centuries. Similar archaeological evidence has turned up on the northwestern coast of Hispaniola at the 9.5-hectare Taino mound site of En Bas Saline, which on the basis of its location and its prominent position in the regional settlement hierarchy is considered by Antillean historians and archaeologists to have been the seat of paramount chief Guacanagarí, Columbus's ally (Deagan 1989, 53–54). The site has an oval configuration with an alignment of three oval mounds across the center of a 300-meter-wide plaza and is enclosed on three sides by a 20-meter-wide earthwork that rises 0.5–0.8 meters in height (Deagan 2004, 606, fig. 3). Kathleen Deagan's excavations have revealed that the earthwork "was apparently constructed purposefully in a single episode prior to contact," and the paucity of cultural debris in its construction fill suggests that the raised earthen ridge "served as a boundary for the village" (Deagan 2004, 607). Excavations in the central mound have exposed a large wattle-and-daub residence, more than 15 meters in diameter, constructed between AD 1200 and 1250 of thick posts and referred to as a chiefly residence. In the plaza north of this centrally located chiefly residence were single-event pits containing the material remains of communal feasts (*areytos*) that are known to have been presided over by Taino chiefs on many occasions, including their war councils (Anglería 1964, 351; Deagan 2004, 608, 619). The evident defensive measures taken in a single construction effort and the public feasts and cohoba rituals did not prevent the chiefly residence from being destroyed by fire in the second half of the thirteenth century (Deagan 2004, 607, table 1), probably by an enemy war party. Such archaeological evidence of the chiefly warfare pursued on Hispaniola and in western Venezuela in precontact times is mounting and agrees surprisingly well with the earliest historical reports. Demonstrating the antiquity of chiefly warfare in the circum-Caribbean area is only the first step, however, in the process of examining objectively the role assumed by warfare in pre-Columbian times.

ACKNOWLEDGMENTS

Our investigations in Barinas, Venezuela, were supported with grants from the National Science Foundation (BNS-85-06192), the Wenner-Gren Foundation (4798), the Connecticut Research Foundation, and a University of Connecticut Faculty Summer Research Fellowship. In Venezuela, we were visiting collaborators in the Departamento de Antropología at the Instituto Venezolano de Investigaciones Científicas. Christina Elson in the Anthropology Division at the American Museum of Natural History helped prepare the figures.

6 CONFLICT AND CONQUEST IN PRE-HISPANIC ANDEAN SOUTH AMERICA

ARCHAEOLOGICAL EVIDENCE FROM NORTHERN COASTAL PERU

John W. Verano

Multiple sources of evidence indicate that conflicts on both local and regional scales played integral roles in the rise and fall of complex societies in pre-Hispanic Andean South America. These sources include ethnohistoric accounts of warfare from late prehistory (Rostworowski de Diez Canseco 1999; Rowe 1946), archaeological evidence of fortified sites and intrusive administrative centers (Arkush and Stanish 2005;

Billman 1996; Dillehay 2001; Isbell and McEwan 1991; Proulx 1985; Wilson 1987), and osteological evidence and iconographic depictions of warfare and the sacrifice of prisoners (Proulx 2001; Verano 1995, 2001b). While evidence of armed conflict is often difficult to identify in the archaeological record (Arkush and Stanish 2005; Redmond 1994; Topic and Topic 1987), some convincing cases have been documented by recent field research in Peru.

Osteological collections can provide direct physical evidence of conflict in the form of healed and unhealed skeletal trauma, which can support hypotheses suggested by archaeological data. However, recent studies of Andean skeletal collections have documented substantial regional and temporal variation in the evidence for violent injury (Standen and Arriaza 2000; Verano 1997, 2003), indicating that the frequency and intensity of armed conflict varied significantly across space and time.

HISTORIC AND ETHNOHISTORIC DATA

When Francisco Pizarro and his small contingent of Spanish soldiers reached Cajamarca in 1532, they came upon a massive military force encamped on the valley floor and surrounding hills (Pizarro 1986). These troops, who reportedly numbered in the tens of thousands, were accompanying the Inca emperor Atahualpa on his triumphant march back to Cuzco following the defeat of his half-brother Huascar in a bloody civil war. Eyewitness descriptions by the Spanish invaders of their encounter with the Inca army at Cajamarca, and during the subsequent campaign to complete the conquest of the empire, provide direct evidence of the military might of Andean South America's last indigenous empire (Hemming 1970). In the years following the Spanish invasion, chroniclers, priests, and native writers such as Guaman Poma and Garcilaso de la Vega would record Inca accounts of their dominion over numerous peoples of the Andean highlands and coast, and of the armed conflicts involved with groups such as the Chanca, Chachapoya, and Chimú, who actively resisted Inca expansion, but were conquered nonetheless and incorporated into the empire (Rostworowski de Diez Canseco 1999).

THE ARCHAEOLOGICAL RECORD

Further back in time, beyond the range of direct ethnohistoric accounts of the Inca and the peoples they conquered, the evidence for warfare and conquest becomes more cloudy, as it relies primarily on the interpretation of archaeological evidence. John and Teresa Topic provide an excellent review of the challenges involved in identifying evidence for Andean warfare (Topic and Topic 1987), in which they note that warfare does not always leave easily recognizable physical evidence. A good example of an ethnohistorically known military campaign that has left no archaeological trace is the Inca conquest of Cajamarca and the powerful Chimú state of northern coastal Peru. Although native accounts describe determined armed resistance by the Chimú and their allies (Rostworowski de Diez Canseco 1999; Rowe 1948), no archaeological evidence has been found to document the battles that culminated in their defeat. While the presence of fortified sites suggests a need for defense, Topic and Topic (1987) emphasize that high walls and hilltop locations for architecture do not necessarily indicate strictly defensive functions. However, a recent review of the archaeological evidence for Andean warfare by Elizabeth Arkush and Charles Stanish (2005) presents a convincing argument that evidence of warfare is in fact widespread but has been overlooked or downplayed by some Andean scholars.

OSTEOLOGICAL EVIDENCE OF WARFARE

Osteological evidence, such as healed or unhealed injuries to bone suggestive of violent encounters, constitutes another important source of information—particularly when found in a well-controlled archaeological context. Early studies of Andean skeletal material by anthropologists such as Aleš Hrdlička and Julio C. Tello noted high frequencies of skull fractures produced by sling stones and clubs (fig. 6.1) in collections they made from the central and southern highlands of Peru (Hrdlička 1914; Tello 1913). Unfortunately, these collections, which consisted of material gathered from the surface of disturbed cemeteries and burial caves, lack detailed information on provenience and dating and thus are of limited research potential. In recent decades, however, several mass burials with good archaeological context have been discovered at archaeological sites on the northern coast of Peru. These discoveries are important in that they provide detailed evidence for the killing of prisoners in pre-Hispanic Peru. I excavated two of these deposits (at the sites of Pacatnamú and the Pyramid of the Moon) of the northern coast and have studied the skeletal material from a third (Punta Lobos) (fig. 6.2).

THE PACATNAMÚ MASS BURIAL

The first is a mass burial of sacrificed captives from the site of Pacatnamú in the Jequetepeque River valley (fig. 6.3), found in 1984 in the bottom of a 3-meter-deep defensive trench (Verano 1986). The fourteen victims—all adolescent and adult males—were killed by a variety of methods, including stabbing, blows to the head, decapitation, and cutting open of the chest. Their bodies were not buried but were left to decompose in the bottom of the trench. Excavation revealed the skeletons of two black vultures and masses of fly pupa cases, indicating that the bodies had been accessible to scavengers (Faulkner 1986; Rea 1986). Traces of rope around ankles and wrists, as well as wound patterns, confirmed that they were captives and not individuals killed in combat. Moreover, the presence of numerous healed fractures on their skeletons suggested previous combat experience (Verano 1986). Stable isotope analysis of bone collagen revealed that more than half of the victims had a dietary signature distinct from that of the local Pacatnamú population, suggesting that they were not locals (Verano and DeNiro 1993). Radiocarbon dating and architectural context place the Pacatnamú mass burial in the Late Intermediate period, circa AD 1100–1200. Although the identities of the victims and the circumstances surrounding their deaths are unknown, ethnohistoric and archaeological data indicate that the Jequetepeque Valley was conquered by the Chimú in the twelfth century (Topic 1990); the mass burial victims may be captives taken during battles between Pacatnamú and invaders from the Chimú homeland.

PYRAMID OF THE MOON

The second example of prisoner sacrifice comes from two nearby plazas at the Pyramid of the Moon in the Moche River valley, discovered

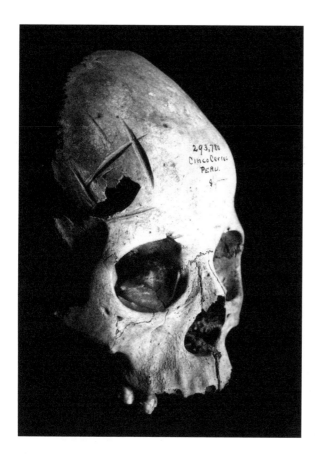

6.1 A depressed skull fracture with an incomplete trepanation. Cinco Cerros, central highlands of Peru; collected by Aleš Hrdlička. (National Museum of Natural History, Smithsonian Institution, catalog no. 293,780; photo by the author)

in 1995 and 1996 (Bourget 1997, 1998; Orbegoso 1998; Uceda and Proyecto Arqueologico Huacas del Sol y de la Luna 1998; Verano 1998). The two plazas date to different construction phases of the pyramid and represent temporally distinct episodes, but both contain the remains of captives executed by the Moche between the third and seventh centuries AD. The victims total over one hundred individuals; as at Pacatnamú, they are all adolescent and adult males. Most were dispatched by having their throat slit (fig. 6.4), as indicated by cut marks on the bodies and transverse processes of their cervical vertebrae (Verano 1998, 2001b). Some individuals had broken ribs, shoulder blades, and "parry" fractures (forearm fracture resulting from an attempt to parry a blow) that were in the early stages of healing at the time of death, suggesting that these were wounds incurred in battle or shortly following capture. Their presence

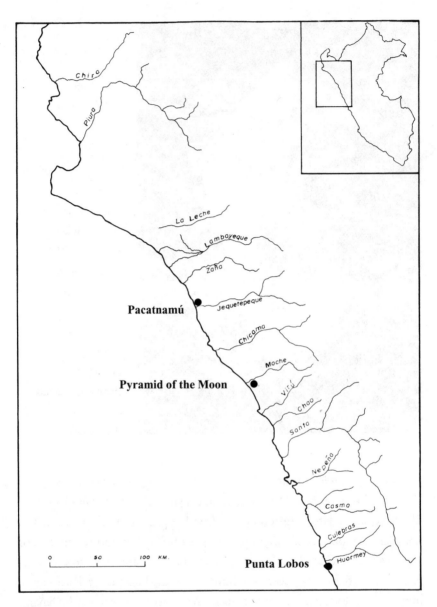

6.2 The study area.

6.3   The Pacatnamú mass burial during excavation.

indicates that victims were not killed immediately following capture but after a period of at least several weeks (Verano 1998, 2001b). Similar to what was found at Pacatnamú, the Pyramid of the Moon victims showed numerous examples of healed injuries suggesting prior combat experience.

Of some assistance in interpreting the context for Moche prisoner sacrifice is the rich representational art style of the Moche, who depicted in detail scenes of combat and the capture and sacrifice of captives (Alva and Donnan 1993; Donnan 1978; Kutscher 1955; Shimada 1994). Not until 1995 could these depictions be compared with actual osteological evidence, but we can now confirm that Moche combat and sacrifice scenes depict events that actually occurred. Debate continues, however, as to whether Moche combat was largely ritual or secular, and whether Moche artists depicted combat in a realistic fashion or in a simplified and stylized manner (Alva and Donnan 1993; Donnan 1997; Topic and Topic 1997; Verano 2001b). Unfortunately, the subsequent Late Intermediate period north coast cultures (Lambayeque, Chimú) did not share the Moche interest in depicting combat scenes, although artistic representations of captives and trophy heads are known (Lapiner 1976; Jackson 2004; Uceda 1999; Verano 1986).

ARCHAEOLOGICAL CONTEXT

A common feature shared by the Pacatnamú mass burial and the Moche sacrificial deposits at the Pyramid of the Moon is the treatment of the victims' bodies. At Pacatnamú and in Plaza 3a of the Pyramid of the Moon, bodies were not buried but left on the surface to decompose. In Plaza 3c, they were either left exposed or incorporated into the architectural fill of the plaza as it was being constructed. In Plaza 3c, many of the bodies were defleshed (as indicated by cut marks throughout the skeleton), and only partial remains were found in many cases. Clearly, these remains were not returned to family or kin groups for proper burial. Denial of burial and desecration of the body through exposure to scavengers was recorded as a punishment for serious crimes in the Inca Empire (Verano 1986), and depictions of bound captives being devoured by vultures are known in Moche and Chimú art (Donnan 1978; Lapiner 1976). Concern for the proper treatment of the dead has deep roots in the Andean area (Dillehay 1995). It is likely, therefore, that the exposure of victims' bodies at Pacatnamú and the Pyramid of the Moon had real significance both for the sacrificers and for their victims.

PUNTA LOBOS

The third and most recently discovered sample is a mass burial found at Punta Lobos in the Huarmey River valley (Walde 1998). It dates to the Late Intermediate period and may be associated with the southward military expansion of the Chimú state during the late thirteenth or early fourteenth century (Mackey and Klymyshyn 1990; Walde 1998). Two radiocarbon determinations from ropes used to bind the victims produced calibrated dates of between AD 1250 and 1300 (Verano and Walde 2004), which corresponds temporally with the early Chimú southern expansion into the Casma valley (Mackey and Klymyshyn 1990).

The Punta Lobos mass burial is unusual for its size—nearly two hundred victims—and for its location and context. The site is located on a coastal promontory facing the Pacific Ocean and has no associated architecture or other evidence of human activity in the immediate vicinity. The only possible associated feature is an offering of simple ceramic and gourd vessels, a fish net, and other textiles buried on an adjacent hillside, possibly by relatives of the victims (Walde 1998). The victims are predominantly adult males and teenagers, but boys as young as seven to nine years old (identified as male by their loincloths and short hair) are present as well. The remains are very well preserved: most individuals have mummified feet and legs; a few have mummified hands, arms, and heads as well. Rope and cloth bindings of the ankles and wrists, as well as cloth blindfolds, were found still in place on most individuals. Laboratory analysis revealed cut marks on neck vertebrae, first ribs, and clavicles consistent with slitting of the throat (Verano and Walde 2004). The bodies at Punta Lobos appear to have been left where they died, face down in the sand. All were found quite close to the surface, suggesting that only a minimal attempt was made to cover them.

The Punta Lobos massacre is unlike the Pacatnamú and Pyramid of the Moon sacrifices in that the event took place in a remote area unassociated with architecture of any kind. There is no clear evidence of any ritual behavior associated with this mass execution—victims seem to have been tied up and blindfolded, led to the site, and summarily executed. The age distribution of the Punta Lobos victims is also distinctive. Whereas the Pacatnamú and Moche victims were all adolescents or young adults (men of fighting age), the Punta Lobos sample includes men over the age of fifty as well as boys clearly too young to be combatants. Overall, my impression of Punta Lobos is one of a reprisal killing, perhaps following a rebellion or resistance to external conquest. Mass executions of rebellious groups occurred during the expansion of the Inca Empire (Rostworowski de Diez Canseco 1999); Punta Lobos may represent an example of similar behavior by the Chimú. However, Héctor Walde does not rule out the possibility that the killing also served a ritual purpose as an offering to the Chimú sea god Ní, in celebration of the conquest of the Huarmey Valley.

6.4 Cut marks on upper thoracic vertebrae, Punta Lobos.

INTERPRETATION OF MASS BURIALS

Human skeletal remains, and the archaeological contexts in which they are found, constitute a unique source of information for reconstructing evidence of conflict in ancient Andean societies. The examples described here clearly document the killing of captives, although reconstructing the events that led to such killings is more complex. There is continued debate among Moche specialists, for example, about whether Moche warfare was purely ritual, largely secular, or some combination of the two. It is also reasonable to ask whether mass killings such as that of Punta Lobos should be considered ritual human sacrifice or simply the summary execution of captives. The common way in which bodies were treated in these three cases (exposure to scavengers rather than considerate burial) suggests that captives sacrificed at Pacatnamú and at the Pyramid of the Moon were not members of the elite involved in some form of ritual combat, as has been suggested for the Moche by some authors (Donnan 1997). The fact that captives were executed and denied proper burial likewise does not support the hypothesis that Moche combat was similar to ritual battles (*tinku* or *juego de pucará*) still enacted in some areas of highland Ecuador, Peru, and Bolivia today (Topic and Topic 1997). In ritual battles such as tinku (see chap. 7, this vol.), physical injury is common and occasionally deaths occur, but participants are not captured, killed, and left exposed for scavengers to feed on. Likewise, the treatment of the Pacatnamú, Moche, and Punta Lobos victims is very different from that seen in ritual offerings such as the high-altitude child sacrifices associated with the Inca sacrificial cycles of Capa Cocha, in which children are buried with fine textiles and objects of gold, silver, and *Spondylus* shell (Ceruti 2003). As I have argued elsewhere, these carefully prepared human sacrifices are quite different from mass burials of executed captives and served very different purposes (Verano 1995).

Debates over the interpretation of mass burials such as those described in this chapter will continue as scholars attempt to better contextualize the evidence of human sacrifice in the Andean archaeological record. Careful examination of the archaeological context of these deposits, and details such as the manner in which victims were killed and the treatment of their remains, will aid in interpretation. Terms commonly used in both scholarly and popular writing to describe these discoveries, such as ritual "sacrifice" and "offerings," should be used with caution, since they imply motivations that may not be supportable by archaeological evidence alone.

In a recent cross-cultural review of ethnographic data on warfare, Keith Otterbein notes that the killing of captives is a common practice in many warring societies (Otterbein 2000b). The mass burials at Pacatnamú, Moche, and Punta Lobos provide archaeological evidence of such practices among ancient societies of northern coastal Peru.

ACKNOWLEDGMENTS

Field and laboratory research was supported by funding from the National Geographic Society (Research Grants 6784-0, 7024-01), the Roger Thayer Stone Center for Latin American Studies, Tulane University, and Engel Brothers Media.

7 THE INTI RAYMI FESTIVAL AMONG THE COTACACHI AND OTAVALO OF HIGHLAND ECUADOR
BLOOD FOR THE EARTH

Richard J. Chacon, Yamilette Chacon, and Angel Guandinango

The San Juan, San Pedro and San Pablo, and Santa Lucia festivals conducted by the Cotacachi and Otavalo of highland Ecuador are linked to the Inca Inti Raymi solstice celebration and the Pachamama cult. These fiestas still occur in a modern form in the communities of Otavalo, Peguche, Iluman, San Juan Pugio, Cotacachi, and San Pedro de Cotacachi. The Inti Raymi fiesta was and still is to a great extent an agricultural fertility rite associated with blood sacrifice (Diaz Cajas

1995; Guaña 1992; Guandinango 1995; Guaman Poma 1943), despite efforts employed by local secular and religious authorities alike to put an end to the shedding of human blood associated with these festivities. Participation in the ritual battles concomitant with this fiesta complex serves as a mechanism for affirming ethnic identity as well as a means of asserting political rights.

STUDY POPULATIONS

The Cotacachi and Otavalo are both Quechua-speaking groups that are culturally very similar. They reside as neighbors in the Imbabura Province of northern Ecuador. Currently, most Cotacachi and Otavalans either corporately or individually own land; although many are successful entrepreneurs, many remain relatively poor subsistence agriculturalists.

The data presented in this chapter were collected in the following locations (fig. 7.1):

> Otavalo: a city of 26,000 inhabitants found at 2,805 meters in elevation located approximately 110 kilometers north of Quito and roughly 150 kilometers south of the Colombian border;
>
> Peguche: a village approximately 2 kilometers northeast of Otavalo;
>
> Cotacachi: a small town approximately 8 kilometers north of Otavalo;
>
> Iluman: a small village approximately 6 kilometers north of Otavalo;
>
> San Juan Pugio: a freshwater spring approximately 6 kilometers northeast of Otavalo; and
>
> San Pedro de Cotacachi: a small village approximately 3 kilometers northwest of Cotacachi.

Ritual activity has been documented as observed in various locations instead of only one community because exposure to differential levels of Westernization has resulted in the maintenance of certain traditions in some localities and their loss in others. Therefore, to obtain a fuller understanding of the celebrations, the authors have found it necessary to compile data gathered from various sources.

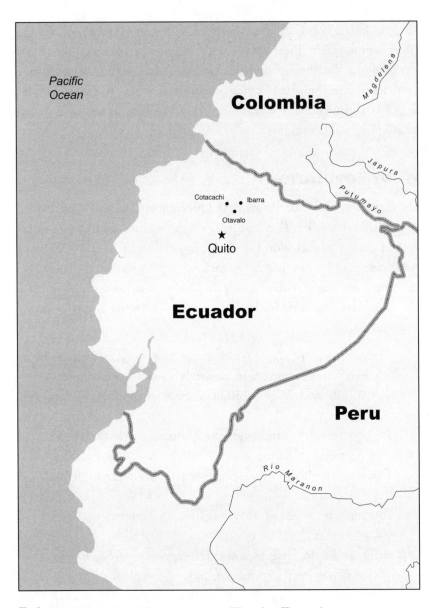

7.1 The Cotacachi and Otavalo regions of Ecuador. (Drawn by Christopher Storie)

Prehistory of the Region

Prior to the arrival of the Incas, northern Ecuador was occupied by various fiercely independent and militarily powerful chiefdom-level societies such as the Caranqui, Cayambe, Otavalo, and Cañari (Caillavet 2000; Espinoza Soriano 1971; Moreno and Oberem 1981). In the 1460s, the Inca emperor Tupac Yupanqui began a military incursion into the region that resulted in the unification of various Ecuadorian chiefdoms into a military coalition formed to resist the Inca invasion. Yupanqui's son, Huayna Capac, continued the fight against the united chiefdoms and after a protracted campaign defeated the local Ecuadorian coalitional forces at the battle of Yaguarcocha that occurred in the early 1520s (Brundage 1963; Cieza de Leon 1998).

The Incas employed several strategies for maintaining control over still-hostile conquered regions; these included indirect rule, intermarriage with local elites, forced relocation (*mitimaes*), imposition of the Quechua language, the establishment of a network of roads and forts, the bifurcation of settlements, and the imposition of the "sun cult" (Brundage 1963).

Incas and Ritual Battles

At Cuzco, the Inca emperor Pachacuti (ca. 1391–1473) established the practice of dividing communities into two sectors, and from then on, the practice was extended into conquered regions (Betanzos 1996; Brundage 1963). Settlements were divided into two districts, called *hanan* and *hurin* (upper and lower sections, respectively). This artificially imposed dichotomy served to stifle the ability of subjugated peoples to form a unified front against their Inca colonizers.

Seventeenth-century Spanish chronicler Bernabe Cobo (1979, 196) described this dichotomy:

> Another reason that moved them to make this division was to give their subjects occasion for competition and rivalry in the jobs that they were ordered to perform; since those of each faction considered themselves to be as good as their opponents, they made every effort to surpass them and they were embarrassed if

they lagged behind; and since they were eager to gain honors in things of less importance, when these people were needed for some important undertaking from which they would come out with either glory or disgrace, owing to the fact that the people of each group were identified, they would do great and distinguishing things.

According to Cobo, the Incas employed this strategy to ascertain "who were the most diligent in serving them on the occasions that came up in peace and war because the members of each tribal group were always present together and the people of one group did not mix with the people of the other one; and in the fiestas and public festivities, each group took great pains to distinguish themselves and perform better than their rivals in the inventions and festive dress that they came up with" (1979, 196).[1]

Furthermore, throughout the empire, local Inca governors were faced with the dilemma of keeping the peace among rival factions while at the same time the militaristic state needed skilled warriors. The Incas took advantage of preexisting animosities by channeling this legacy of local warfare into controlled and ritualized, regular events that pitted one group against the other (Gorbak, Lischetti, and Munoz 1962). These ritual battles encouraged by the Incas permitted subjugated locals to keep their military skills honed while the manipulation of populations prevented the formation of a unified rebellion (Morris 1998; Ogburn 2004).

Cobo reported the association between ritual fighting and Inca days of ritual importance:

Of the festivals and sacrifices that were performed during the second month, which was called Camay. . . . One day when the new moon could be seen this month, those who had been knighted came to the square with new clothing, black tunics, tawny mantles, and bunches of white feathers, and with their slings in their hands, they divided into bands, one composed of those from Hanancuzco and the other of those from Hurincuzco. They threw a certain fruit at each other. This is a fruit like the tunas that we call pitahayas.

Sometimes they would come to blows to test their strength. This would last until the Inca stood up and made them stop. This was done so that it would be known who among them were the bravest and strongest.2 (Cobo [1653] 1990, 135)

Spanish records indicate the persistence of ritual battles well into colonial times. In the sixteenth century, a Spaniard documented indigenous fiestas held in Cuzco in which combatants would employ hard fruit and slingshots as weapons in competitive encounters (Gutierrez 1905). The Spanish chroniclers recorded that these bloody ritual battles involved the hurling of projectiles: "Cotacotabamba, was a flat place between Choco and Chachona where a festival was held on certain days of the year in which they stoned one another" (Cobo [1653] 1990, 81). Court documents dating to 1772 report that a mestizo girl was killed when accidentally struck by a rock during ritual fighting between Cuzco's Hanansaya and Urinsaya factions (Hopkins 1982).[3]

SUN CULT AND INTI RAYMI

The Incas were worshippers of the sun, which they considered to be the god Inti, and the sun cult was imposed in all conquered regions. It is important to note that the Incas permitted the continuation of the worship of local deities as long as these were acknowledged as being inferior to Inti (Brundage 1963). Early Spanish chroniclers were amazed at the Incas' devotion. Cristóbal Molina (1873, 91) wrote, "As soon as the sun would rise, they would begin singing with great pomp and harmony[;] they did not rest until the sun had set and as it became hidden, they all performed an act of reverence, raising their hands and they worshipped it with profound humility."

The Peruvian-born chronicler Garcilasco de la Vega reported that the grand Inti Raymi festival was celebrated during the June solstice (after the corn harvest) and was meant to give thanks to Inti for the year's produce. High-ranking individuals who wore clothes adorned with gold and silver along with elegant headdresses and who represented all parts of the empire would come to Cuzco to honor the Sun and the Inca, who was believed to be the divine "Son of the Sun" (Garcilasco de la Vega 1966). Spanish chroniclers stated that for the Incas, the Inti Raymi festival was the most important of all festivals celebrated to honor the sun god (Cobo [1653] 1990), and such events included the ritual intoxification of participants (Ramos Gavilán [1621] 1976).

Spanish chroniclers document that sun worship involved the practice of blood sacrifice along with much drinking and dancing. The Incas made offerings of llamas, guinea pigs, rabbits, and all sorts of game birds to their sun god Inti (Cobo [1653] 1990; Garcilasco de la Vega 1966; Salcamayhua 1873). The Peruvian-born chronicler Felipe Guaman Poma de Ayala reported that the Incas "killed livestock for ceremonies and opening up their hearts as a rule among shamans. They first drink the blood and eat the rest of the animal afterwards" (Guaman Poma 1943, 65). During the solstice celebrations, Inca priests distributed receptacles filled with the blood from sacrificed llamas and would then drink it as part of a sacred rite (Tierney 1989).

Spanish chroniclers also reported that for the Incas, the most important form of sacrifice was human blood (Cobo [1653] 1990). Human offerings were called for whenever a new ruler died or assumed the throne. Additionally, humans were killed to end a drought, to stop an earthquake, or in response to an eclipse. Human sacrifices were also conducted during the two most solemn events in the Inca ceremonial calendar: the June and December solstices (Betanzos 1996; Cobo 1979, [1653] 1990; Hadingham 1987; Guaman Poma 1943).

The Italian explorer Girolamo Benzoni traveled extensively throughout Peru and Ecuador in the early sixteenth century and corroborated Spanish accounts of human sacrifice when he reported that the Incas

> had the sun as their supreme god and when they wish to make petitions, lords and priests alike climb a stone mound constructed for such a purpose and maintaining their heads lowered, strike one hand against the other, then rub them together and raise both hands to the sun as if they wished to touch it; and at the same time recite certain prayers asking for what they need ... they make sacrifices of adults and children but do not eat their flesh; likewise they sacrifice sheep (llamas), birds and other animals rubbing the

blood on the face of the idol and on the doors of the Temple. (Benzoni 2000, 115–16)

Guaman Poma also reported that human sacrifices were conducted during the month of June during the Inti Raymi celebrations, when "They made sacrifices to the Sun of many innocent children" (Guaman Poma 1943, 38).

Archaeological findings have largely substantiated ethnohistorical reports of sacrificial killings among the Incas. An 1892 excavation on the Isla de La Plata in Ecuador uncovered a lavish burial of two children in a configuration consistent with the specific burial instructions mandated by Inca emperors for dealing with the remains of sacrificial victims, as recorded by Europeans in the sixteenth century (McEwen and Silva 1992).

In 1995, the remains of a mummified Inca girl buried with sumptuous goods were uncovered on Mount Ampato in Peru, with all evidence from the find clearly indicating that she was part of a sacrificial ritual (Moffet 1999). In addition to the killing of children, enemy warriors were also said to have been sacrificed after being made to sing, dance, and recite an acceptance speech to those who were about to perform the execution (Taylor 1987). This report of adults being ritually offered up was substantiated by the recovery in 1964 of the mummified body of a young man who had been intentionally killed by the Incas on Mount Toro in Argentina (Tierney 1989). To date, the remains of approximately twenty-five individuals who were most likely sacrificial victims have been recovered at precontact high-altitude locations throughout Andean South America (María Constanza Ceruti, pers. comm. 2005; see also Ceruti 2003).

PACHAMAMA

The earth goddess played a very important role in the Inca pantheon: "They all worshipped the Earth also, they call her *Pachamama*, which means Earth Mother. And it was their custom to put a long stone in the middle of their fields or chacras as an altar in honor of this goddess. They would pray to her before this altar-stone, call upon her, and ask her to protect their chacras and make them fertile" (Cobo [1653] 1990, 34). The blood sacrifice of animals and humans was also offered to the Earth Mother. Llamas were offered as a propitiatory sacrifice to her during festivals, and every new moon four or five unblemished virgins, male or female, were sacrificed at a rock cleft called the "golden womb of Pachamama," located on Isla del Sol in Lake Titicaca (Brundage 1963; Cobo 1979).

INTI RAYMI OF THE POST–SPANISH CONQUEST

The Inca Inti Raymi celebrations were conducted during the summer solstice at the end of the agricultural cycle in what were the European calendar months of late June and early July. The Spanish *conquistadores* took this indigenous Inti Raymi festival and imposed the Catholic feast days of San Juan, San Pedro and San Pablo, and Santa Lucia on the festivities that coincided with the Inca solstice celebrations. Hence, the traditions associated with Inti worship and Pachamama devotion became Christianized, with the resulting syncretic rituals continuing to be practiced to this very day (Conejo 1995; Diaz Cajas 1995; Guaña 1992; Guandinango 1995; Obando 1988).

The Spanish friars evangelized the native peoples by assigning a patron saint to every settlement, with each community having its major saint's day celebration (Parsons 1945). Each saint was assigned a local native *prioste* (captain or manager) who was in charge of organizing the patron's fiesta. In addition to these individuals were the local native *alcaldes de la capilla* or *alcaldes de la fe* (mayors of the chapel or mayors of the faith), whose responsibilities included aiding the prioste in church-related activities and resolving disputes within their respective communities. The Spaniards issued *varas* (wooden staffs) to these alcaldes as symbols of their religious and secular authority (Steward and Faron 1959).

The prioste-alcalde system, comprised of indigenous assistants, was set up in Quito in 1573, and by 1580, as a Spanish report on highland Ecuador stated, "All the towns have churches and alcaldes and . . . they (the Indians) live in an orderly manner and are intelligent people" (Vasquez 1940, 98). This prioste-alcalde arrangement has been referred to as a "cargo system" by anthropologists who have documented its presence among native peoples of highland Mesoamerica and also among the Andean regions of South America.

Large religious festivals are organized by priostes, who are responsible for ensuring that the entire community have sufficient food and drink for the duration of the festivities. To sponsor such a fiesta is to take on a *cargo* (burden). Organizing such an activity is extremely expensive, and sponsors may sometimes seek extra work in cities to help defray the costs. As an individual assumes progressively more onerous cargos, their fellow villagers will accord them more prestige. Once an individual has fulfilled all of the fiesta sponsorship obligations, he is referred to as a *pasado* (elder), whose opinion carries considerable weight in community gatherings.

THE MODERN-DAY INTI RAYMI FESTIVAL: JUNE 22 TO JULY 1

In preparation for the celebrations, men will allocate more time working on their farms, or some may temporarily leave their own villages to seek out wage labor to ensure that a plentiful supply of food will be available for the duration of the fiestas. This is of utmost importance because many individuals will cease all subsistence activities once the festivities commence. Women will start the preparation of extra food and drink for the guests who are sure to come to visit a few days before the fiestas commence. Concomitantly, musicians will spend time practicing for the upcoming events.

On the night of June 22, regardless of what day of the week this date falls on, individuals prepare for the upcoming holidays by disrobing and then taking a ritual bath (*armaichisi*) in a local lake, stream, waterfall, or spring, with men and women bathing separately. This act is believed to bring both spiritual and physical health to individuals. It is additionally purported to provide them with the stamina necessary for the prolonged dancing that they will engage in over the next several days. Significantly, Spanish chronicler Juan Betanzos (1996) noted that many Inca rites were preceded by a midnight ritual bath in a river. Modern-day Cotacachi males who plan on participating in the violent and dangerous "taking of the plaza" ritual (beginning June 24) will scrub themselves with a stinging nettle plant while bathing or will make offerings of guinea pigs and liquor at the waterfalls at Peguche in the hopes of obtaining both courage and protection from their rivals.

If an individual wishes to honor a particular Catholic saint during this ritual period, he will conduct the *huarcuic huasi* ritual in his private home to obtain the saint's intercession. In this manner, he becomes a "giver of a castle." Construction of such a *huarcu* (castle) takes up most of the day of June 23 and consists of eucalyptus wood or cane sticks tied together to form a square latticed rack. This approximately frame, approximately one meter square, is then hung from the ceiling or placed high against a wall with the saint's image on it (thus making it a type of altar). Devotees will also provide the saint's statue with a new cloth cape. Attached to the castle/altar are foodstuffs including various forms of bread, corn, bananas, pineapples, oranges, tree-tomatoes, and tangerines along with roasted guinea pigs. In addition to these exotic items, paper money (U.S. dollars) and bottles of hard liquor are often found on such structures.

At approximately 4 p.m., friends, relatives, and neighbors begin arriving to admire the castle and to pay back debts incurred in the previous year (see below for an explanation of this payment). Visitors always bring with them two candles that will be lit and then placed in front of the saint's image. It is considered appropriate that the builder of the castle serve all visitors the following foodstuffs: *chicha* (a beverage made from corn), *colada* (a soup also made from corn), potatoes, and *mote* (boiled corn), along with guinea pig and chicken.

At approximately 7 p.m., after all guests have been fed, the host will set off three firecrackers as a way of publicly announcing that he has met all of the duties of being a "giver of a castle," and after this act, he is no longer obligated to feed any latecomers. The castle will remain in place until the *huarchuic fiti* ritual takes place on June 26.

After giving a castle, an individual becomes *compadre* (godparent) with the saint and has the obligation to offer a mass for the "heavenly kinsmen" for the next three consecutive years. Failure by devotees to faithfully perform all of the obligations due their supernatural compadre will result in their requests for the saint's intercession going unanswered.

Fireworks are set off throughout the day of June 23 as a way of announcing the imminent arrival of Inti Raymi, and by early evening, groups of individuals (both male and female) begin making their rounds, dancing throughout the village of Peguche. On this night, they speak in high-pitched voices (thus imitating spirits), wear *aya huma* (spirit head) masks of various kinds, and carry musical instruments (flutes, pan pipes, conch shells, and guitars). Every home visited by these dancers is obligated to provide a space for them to perform the Sanjuanito and to serve them chicha, alcohol, and perhaps some food as a reward for their "hard work," which will continue well into the early morning hours.

The Sanjuanito dance is conducted in a circle with individuals stomping their feet loudly and alternating their movement first in a clockwise and then in a counterclockwise fashion in accordance with commands given by the group's leader. Those playing musical instruments remain rotating in the center of the circle while the others dance around them.

Because these nocturnal visitors are masked and speak in unrecognizable voices, their identities remain hidden. This allows for male dancers to openly flirt with any single women who may be present at each house they visit. They will sometimes say to the male head of a household, "Give me your daughter!" Dance troops will spend little time at locations lacking the presence of nubile women and will conversely be reticent to leave those homes where young women are present. In fact, fights have been known to occur when males from different dance troops arrive at the same house at the same time and express a sexual interest in the women present. Some men will seek to impress others (especially women) by demonstrating their strength by dancing until sunrise without rest, and Luis Alberto Conejo (1995) reports that fights can occur as a result of this competition. This observation of sexual jealousy is in stark contradiction to Elsie Clews Parsons' (1945) reporting that fighting over women does not occur in Otavalo.

Because becoming intoxicated during fiestas is an accepted behavior for adults (Parsons 1945), individuals (both male and female) have little difficulty arranging trysts with their lovers on this night, as parents or spouses are in diminished capacity owing to the effects of alcohol or are engaged in their own clandestine liaisons. As one Otavalan leader stated, "Anything can happen during the Inti Raymi festival. People can fall in love and any woman can become pregnant" (Chacon's field notes). Significantly, Burr Brundage (1963) noted that certain Inca rituals called for not only ritual intoxification but also sexual license (see also Hopkins 1982; Muelle 1950; Urton 1993; Zecenarro 1992).

Several rituals that involve the shedding of blood mark the June 24th San Juan feast day (Inti Raymi proper; see also Crespi 1981; Morote 1955; Wibbelsman 2004). The village of Iluman is known throughout the region for the large number (approximately thirty) of male and female *yachacs*, or shamans, who reside there (Obando 1988). On the morning of June 24, many of the Iluman yachacs gather together publicly at the sacred springs of San Juan Pugio, where they ritually bathe and purify themselves before conducting an animal sacrifice. Purification is accomplished by each shaman taking hard liquor into his or her mouth and then spraying it on each other.

After this ritual, they then climb to the top of a very large and prominent rock outcrop located at the springs and offer prayers to Inti, to Imbabura (a local male mountain deity responsible for bringing rain), and also to Cotacachi (a local female mountain deity associated with rain as well as soil fertility) and to Pachamama (see also Wibbelsman 2005). The worship of Imbabura by the Cotacachi very likely predates the Inca conquest.

After voicing their petitions, the yachacs take a live sheep, slash its throat open with a knife, and collect its blood in a gourd. Then they pass this container around, with each shaman consuming some of the fresh blood mixed with hard liquor. This ritual reportedly gives these individuals great strength (recall the above-mentioned Spanish account of Incan high-ranking individuals ceremonially drinking the blood of sacrificed animals on a stone mound). At the end of this event, roosters are ceremonially brought to the spring area.

The ritual of *la entrega de la rama de gallos* (the giving of the "branch" of roosters) involves the ceremonial exchange of thirteen roosters between fiesta priostes called *capitanes de gallos* (rooster captains). After the yachac ceremony, the gallo capitan from Iluman who has taken on the cargo of sponsoring this year's festivities (i.e., paying for food, "castles," music, and pyrotechnics) will set off fireworks to publicly announce that la entrega will soon take place (de la Torre 1995).

In the early afternoon, the gallo capitan will set out from his home toward the sacred springs accompanied by his supporters (those who have helped him meet his cargo obligations). They transport the live roosters from the gallo capitan's home to the springs by tying the birds upside down by their feet to two separate poles, each carrying six roosters. The wife of the gallo capitan brings the thirteenth rooster on her back. The entourage also carries various "castles" bearing items such as various forms of bread, corn, bananas, pineapples, oranges, tree-tomatoes, tangerines, and roasted guinea pigs as well as bottles of hard liquor. They arrive at the springs in procession to the accompaniment of flutes and dancing with a great multitude of people who have come to admire the castles along with the rama de gallos. The term *rama* means "branch," and because these poles with roosters attached to them are said to resemble trees, they are named as such (de la Torre 1995).

Upon their arrival, the gallo capitan is served chicha and hard liquor, then fireworks are set off and the castles along with roosters are propped up for public display at the springs. The gallo capitan then ceremonially hands over the rama de gallo to the individual who has pledged to sponsor next year's feast and has promised to likewise give a rama de gallo to his successor. With this act, the current gallo capitan has successfully fulfilled all of his cargo obligations, thereby gaining the admiration of his fellow villagers (de la Torre 1995; Diaz Cajas 1995).

After the "giving of the branch of roosters" has taken place, the current fiesta sponsor will invite next year's gallo capitan to partake in the *gallo fiti* ritual, which involves the public decapitation of a rooster's head. At approximately 4 p.m., several live roosters are publicly hung upside down from a horizontally fastened rope placed between two poles. Then with much drinking and dancing, next year's gallo capitan will attempt to tear off the rooster's head from its body using only his bare hands (gallo fiti). If he can accomplish this task in one attempt, it is believed that he will have good luck in the following year, that is, he will have no trouble in meeting his cargo obligations as gallo capitan for next year's feast. If, however, he should fail to pull off the head from the rooster's body in one attempt, then this is viewed as a portent of misfortune, that is, he will have great difficulty in meeting his gallo capitan obligations (Diaz Cajas 1995).

All of the roosters killed during the fiestas will be cooked and consumed with the understanding that all who partake of the meal are committing themselves to help the new gallo capitan meet all of his obligations for next year's fiesta (i.e., providing food, "castles," music, and pyrotechnics). Likewise, those who remove items from the castles are expected to reciprocate in the future (de la Torre 1995; Obando 1988).

THE TAKING OF THE PLAZA

On the morning of June 24, men from the various surrounding villages will begin their march into the town of Cotacachi. They wear colorful festive garb that publicly identifies their village affiliation (recall the Spanish account stating that native peoples took great pains both to distinguish themselves from and to outperform their rival factions during public festivities).

Individuals wear large black cardboard hats and leather chaps; some don aya huma masks; and all carry weapons such as whips, clubs, or stones (some individuals also apply paint to their faces to intimidate their rivals). These men come accompanied by musicians playing flutes, conchs, and pan pipes and travel in tight formation *zapateando* (stomping) in unison while chanting and/or whistling. It is important to note that Spanish chroniclers report that musicians often accompanied Inca troops into battle (Guaman Poma 1943).

The group's cohesion is enforced by at least two leaders (one at the front and the other at the rear) who maintain discipline by preventing individuals from getting too far ahead of the group or straggling behind. Anyone who does not remain in tight formation will be whipped by one of these leaders. Women accompany the men and render them support by carrying the food, liquor, and stones that will be used in the impending violent encounter (see Bolin 1998; Brachetti 2001; Gifford and Hoggarth 1976; Urton 1993).

Most groups arrive at the outskirts of Cotacachi by 10:30 a.m., and once in town, they will stop to briefly perform the Sanjuanito dance at every street corner they pass by. As they make their way through the community, large crowds of mostly indigenous spectators have already gathered at Cotacachi's main plaza to witness the festivities. Upon arriving at the center of town, each group will march around Cotacachi's town square, stopping to dance the Sanjuanito at every one of the main plaza's four corners.

According to informants, the town's principal Roman Catholic sanctuary stands on the former site of a precontact temple, and the aforementioned main plaza is located directly in front of this ancient place of worship. Important ceremonies and ritual processions may have taken place on this main plaza during the Inca occupation, and thus many of the present-day ritual activities that occur on this presumably sacred location may reasonably be assumed to have also transpired in the precontact period (but see Wibbelsman 2005).

Throughout the day, participants will visit local bars to drink, and all will stop to have lunch between noon and 2 p.m. After lunch, all of the groups from the surrounding villages are well rested, have had much to drink, and are ready for the violent *toma de la plaza* (taking of the plaza) ritual to begin in earnest. As the numerous groups return from the bars, they resume dancing, only this time they slowly coalesce into two large units as they march around the plaza.

The indigenous villages surrounding the town of Cotacachi are presently being divided into two coalitions. According to Conejo (1995) and local informants, the first faction is called *hanan* (upper) and is made up of various indigenous communities including those of San Pedro, El Cercado, Topo Grande, Topo Chico, and Arabuela. The other sector is referred to as *urin* (lower) and includes the native communities of La Calera, San Ignacio, San Martin, and El Quitugu and Morochos.[4] These two groups are very antagonistic toward each other; as mentioned above, this practice of bifurcating settlements into upper (hanan or *janan*) versus lower (urin) factions is associated with the Incas' past presence in the region (Cobo 1979).

In the afternoon, men from all the villages gradually begin fusing themselves into two large rival units (upper and lower) while marching. As the day progresses, they become increasingly hostile toward their rivals and will whistle and jeer at them as the formations pass near each other. Despite the danger, women participate in the march by walking behind their men, sometimes carrying infants on their backs while boys (some as young as six years of age) march and carry weapons with the adult males.

Despite the efforts by the local authorities to keep the two enemy groups (comprised of hundreds of males) from fighting, insults quickly escalate into an all-out battle involving rock- and stick-throwing along with whipping and clubbing, often resulting in serious injuries and continuing for up to several hours. The goal of each faction is to draw blood from one of the members of the rival group. The local police may launch tear gas canisters into the angry crowd to disperse the combatants, but this serves only to abate the fight, not to stop it. What often happens is that the rival factions will simply march away from the main plaza toward a side street to continue fighting without interference from the authorities.

On June 24, 2001, the two groups met at a location one block away from the main plaza to do battle, and this encounter resulted in the death of a twenty-nine-year-old individual from a urin village. The victim died as the result of receiving repeated blows to the head.[5] The urin allies of the victim have publicly stated that they will avenge this death by killing two janan men in the future (Lopez 2001). At the end of the Inti Raymi ritual period, whichever group (janan or urin) emerges victorious (i.e., has taken more lives) is said to have successfully "tomado la plaza." Recall that the Spanish chroniclers reported that janan-jurin factions made every effort to surpass each other during public festivities.

The combination of heavy drinking, dancing, marching, and chanting (which goes on for hours) causes some participants to enter into what appears to be a trancelike state that undoubtedly affects their judgment (see also Wibbelsman 2004). During the course of the battle, some individuals may choose to brazenly leave themselves exposed to being struck by rocks hurled by their opponents by provocatively positioning themselves directly within reach of their rivals.

Despite the public nature of these extremely violent events, to the best of the authors' knowledge, there have been no convictions in Cotacachi for any of the many killings committed over the years. This stems from the fact that in such confusion, it is very difficult for the authorities to identify a specific individual who threw the rock or who gave the blow that proved to be lethal to the victim.

By 6:00 p.m., the fighting ceases, with most groups abandoning the main plaza and heading back to their villages in the same manner in which they arrived. That is, by zapateando in tight formation, stopping only to dance the Sanjuanito at every street corner. By that time, many of the men have become very intoxicated or are injured from the fighting and require help from their friends or spouses to make it back to their respective communities. Most adult males will spend the night sleeping. However, a few individuals are known to pass the entire evening dancing in their villages until daybreak and then will return to Cotacachi the next morning to continue in the toma de la plaza ritual without getting any sleep whatsoever.

On the morning of the next day (June 25), the villagers wake up early and repeat the entire process. That is, they arrive in Cotacachi by 10:30 a.m., spend most of the morning and early afternoon marching and dancing Sanjuanitos around the main plaza, engage in violent bloody skirmishes by the late afternoon, and leave for their respective communities by 6:00 p.m. This marks the termination of the San Juan fiesta, but it does not signify an end to either the ritual period or the bloodshed. For the next two days, those injured will nurse their wounds but will return to the Cotacachi's main plaza to continue the toma de la plaza ritual on the ensuing feast days of San Pedro and San Pablo, and Santa Lucia.

Meanwhile, while most of the combatants are resting, the "giver of a castle" (first raised on June 23 in the huarcuic huasi ritual) will bring it down on June 26 in the huarcuic fiti (pulling of the castle) rite. Individuals present at this event may take any of the items that are attached to the castle with the understanding that they must repay the giver of the castle double the worth of the removed object. For example, if two oranges are taken from the huarcu, a payment of four oranges must be made to the giver of the castle at the next huarcuic huasi on June 23 of the following year. This transaction is referred to as *aumento* (increase).

While most of the adults of the village are resting to regain the strength that they will need for the upcoming celebrations, on July 27, the alcaldes de capilla or alcaldes de la fe of the community of San Pedro are busy organizing the feast day mass for the community's patron saint. Early in the morning, the alcaldes remove the image of San Pedro from the local chapel and visit every household in the village asking for donations to offer a mass in honor of the saint that will be held on the eve (June 28) of his feast day. During this event, each alcalde takes a turn carrying the image of their patron, and all walk from house to house with their varas (wooden staffs), symbolizing both their secular and religious authority (as mentioned previously, the use of these varas dates back to colonial times). The connection between the modern Christian practice of celebrating a saint's feast day with ancient agricultural fertility rites became clear to the authors when an alcalde remarked, "It has been very dry, we must have a Mass so that it will rain." Many of the native people of this region are subsistence agriculturalists who do not irrigate their fields; therefore, they are completely dependent on local rainfall for their survival.

While the alcaldes make their rounds throughout the village, most other adults are resting, but the children of San Pedro de Cotacachi will spend the entire day dancing Sanjuanitos from house to house. There will be no ritual dancing performed by adults until the eve of the feast day of San Pedro and San Pablo. The mass in honor of San Pedro is held at the local chapel in the early evening of June 28 with the hopes that this will bring the eagerly desired rain. After church services, the prioste will sponsor a dinner for all of his fellow villagers. After the meal, adults will begin dancing Sanjuanitos from house to house until sunrise.

On June 29 (the San Pedro and San Pablo fiesta), villagers from the surrounding communities arrive in Cotacachi by 10:30 a.m. and spend most of the morning and early afternoon marching and dancing Sanjuanitos around the main plaza, which contains mostly indigenous spectators. There, the janan and urin factions resume the violent skirmishes, which reach their apex in the late afternoon. By 6:00 p.m., most villagers have left the main plaza and are marching toward their respective communities.

On June 30 (San Pedro and San Pablo fiesta, continued), villagers repeat the entire process. That is, native peoples from surrounding communities arrive in Cotacachi by 10:30 a.m. (many with wounds sustained during the previous day's fighting) and spend most of the morning and early afternoon marching and dancing Sanjuanitos around the main plaza, where they resume their skirmishes. The clashes occurring between rival groups are usually more violent during the San Pedro and San Pablo fiesta than during those of San Juan. Usually, one to four deaths take place annually, with most of the killings occurring between 4:00 and 5:00 p.m. (Guandinango 1995).[6] All combatants will depart for their respective communities by 6:00 p.m. This marks the end of the San Pedro and San Pablo fiesta.

On the morning of July 1 (Santa Lucia fiesta), women from surrounding indigenous communities will come to dance Sanjuanitos and to march in Cotacachi's main plaza in the same manner that men have done on previous days, with many of them brandishing weapons similar to the ones used by males (however, no actual fighting among females was observed on this day). Some armed men join the women's groups as marchers, dancers, or musicians, but this is clearly an event for women and led by women.[7] By 6:00 p.m., most participants have abandoned the main plaza and have left for their respective communities. The completion of this event marks the end of the Inti Raymi celebrations in the region.[8]

ATTEMPTS AT ENDING THE FIGHTING

Local secular authorities have been understandably troubled by the violence associated with the Inti Raymi fiesta. Attempts to put an end to the bloodshed have consisted of arming local authorities with tear gas that is used for dispersing the large and angry crowds. Although this method has proven somewhat effective in some localities, such as Otavalo, it has not met with success in Cotacachi. As mentioned earlier with regards to this community, tear gas only abates the fighting, and skirmishes simply continue in different sections of town.

The Roman Catholic Church recently invited representatives from all janan and urin villages to attend a "peace conference" designed to establish dialogue and reconciliation between the rival factions. At first, the results of this meeting seemed promising, as parties ceremonially burned their weapons (whips and clubs) in a large public bonfire in the main plaza after attending a "peace mass." Unfortunately, later that day, fighting broke out between the factions. Thus, all hopes for a quick end to the violence were dashed.

Many indigenous leaders openly lament the fact that their communities are divided as such, and local native organizations such as the Union de Organizaciones Campesinas de Cotacachi (UNORCAC) have called for an end to the violence but have had no success.

Explanations for the Presence of Andean Ritual Fighting

The ritual violence described above has its counterparts throughout the Andes, where it is referred to as *tinku, tinkuy, juego de pucara,* or *chiarage.* Leslie Brownrigg (1972) and Roswith Hartmann (1972) believe that highland ritual battles are in effect vestigial reenactments of ancient conflicts over land (see also Zorn 2002). Structuralist explanations regarding tinku invoke a well-documented Andean dualism as well as an awareness of oppositions that are resolved through conflict (Orlove 1994). Tristan Platt (1986) sees ritual fighting as a form of ritual copulation between male and female groups. Pierre Duviols (1973) contends that the ritually sanctioned violence that occurred between the two complementary groups appealed to the long-standing antagonism by emphasizing their traditional enmity, yet at the same time, this ritual provided a foundation for their ongoing interaction and coexistence. Juan San Martin (2002, 394) holds that this particular form of ritualized violence serves "as a way of exorcising unnecessary violence between communities." Likewise, Christine Hastorf (1993) believes that ritual combat serves to assuage cumulative internal tension by serving as a safety valve.

Some report that combatants are said to target individuals to avenge past grievances (Orlove 1994; Sallnow 1987; Wibbelsman 2004; Zorn 2002). Still others see the ritual fighting associated with the fiestas as a solidarity maintenance mechanism. The violent encounter between rival groups creates social solidarity among fellow faction members by bringing people into a coalition against a common enemy: "It draws individuals together, locating them as members of a human community on a common landscape" (Sikkink 1997, 184). Inge Bolin (1998, 95) similarly recorded one Peruvian highlander who provided the following explanation regarding tinku: "Pachamama needs a few drops of blood and we all come together to provide this offering. So we meet as opponents and end in solidarity" (see also Brownrigg 1972 and Hastorf 1993).

Participation in such violent encounters is said to bestow prestige upon the combatants (Bolin 1998; Brownrigg 1972; Gorbak, Lischetti, and Munoz 1962; Hartmann 1972; Zorn 2002). Elayne Zorn (2002) also stipulates that participation in ritual fighting by young males serves as a means for them to gain the attention of young females. Conversely, able-bodied males who failed to participate in such battles could be sanctioned. San Martin (2002, 396) reports, "Young males returning to their community without signs of having participated are not welcomed. Years ago they were isolated."

Gary Urton (1993, 129) argues that tinkus are staged as tensions arise prior to the redistribution of agricultural plots of land and serve as a means of "realigning political identities, and reestablishing hierarchical relations of authority within the community in anticipation of the tensions and potential conflicts that may arise during the redistribution of communally owned potato fields." In effect, ritual battles serve to assert and maintain a group's political and geographic boundaries (Bolin 1998; see also Alencastre and Dumezil 1953; Bastien 1978; Hastorf 1993; Hopkins 1982; and Platt 1987). Similarly, Hartmann (1972) holds that tinku battles help to establish and to maintain relationships of dominance and subjugation, resulting in a political hierarchy. Hastorf (1993, 54) adds, "An important point learned from the documentary and modern evidence about tinku is that it not only seems to allow for contestation over and gain of access to resources and political power but also it is a strategy for societal maintenance between and within groups that do not have an overarching centralized political authority." Benjamin Orlove (1994), however, reports that winners obtain neither new lands nor booty, nor do they establish any form of political dominance over the losers. Yet Hastorf (1993, 54) reports that not only material but also reproductive benefits were obtained as the result of victory in ritual combat because "those who had inflicted more damage, in some cases captured more women, or even killed more, gain a good prognosis for success in the coming year and sometimes even gain new land" (see also Alencastre and Dumezil 1953; Brachetti 2001; Gilt Contreras 1955; Gorbak, Lischetti, and Munoz 1962; Platt 1986; and Sallnow 1987).

Still others hold that ritual fighting serves to send a clear signal to the mestizo population that native peoples are fierce fighters. Public displays of bellicosity are vehicles for reaffirming the highlander's reputation for violence. Native peoples are, in effect, striking fear into the psyches of mestizos (and of other indigenous groups) by publicly attacking each other during fiestas. Therefore, ritual combatants are suggesting to the nonindigenous population (and to their indigenous rivals) that they are a powerful force to be reckoned with (Orlove 1994).

In the 1940s, Parsons noted that during the Otavalo San Juan fiesta, "White people are said to be somewhat fearful of the Indians at this time because their usually submissive neighbors tend to be self-assertive and overbearing" (Parsons 1945, 108). The present-day situation is similar in that many nonindigenous inhabitants and merchants of Cotacachi temporarily leave town or simply close up shop during the festivities because of fear of bellicose native people.

FUNCTIONS OF INTI RAYMI

Several of the Cotacachi and Otavalans interviewed stated that the bloody injuries and deaths that occur during the Inti Raymi celebrations will bring about a good harvest for the upcoming year. Conversely, if no blood is spilt or if no one is killed during the festivities, informants reported that the coming year's harvest would be poor. In effect, a bloody ritual battle is considered to be proper payment to supernaturals in exchange for a fertile year (see also Barrionuevo 1971; Bolin 1998; Brachetti 2001; Brownrigg 1972; Hartmann 1972; Hastorf 1993; Orlove 1994; Sikkink 1997; and Wibbelsman 2004).[9]

Since only indigenous people participate in the hazardous ritual combat, taking part in this activity provides individuals with a vehicle for the public manifestation of their ethnic affiliation. Participation in ritual fighting distinguishes Cotacachi and Otavalo individuals from the rest of Ecuadorian nonindigenous society. Furthermore, such willingness on the part of native people to go into battle serves as a clear signal to the surrounding mestizo society that indigenous peoples are to be respected (see also Orlove 1994).

SUMMARY OF THE MODERN-DAY
INTI RAYMI CELEBRATIONS

The contemporary San Juan, San Pedro and San Pablo, and Santa Lucia fiestas that take place on the main plaza (a location directly in front of where a precontact temple once stood) are linked to Inca agricultural fertility rites that occurred during the June solstice period. The ritual intoxification, midnight bathing, circumscribed period of sexual license, sacrifice of animals (along with the ceremonial ingestion of their blood), dichotomy of "upper" and "lower" combatants all dressed in clearly identifiable garb, bloodshed, and deaths that occur during the contemporary festivities are all vestiges of the precontact rituals associated with both Inti and Pachamama worship.[10]

The shedding of animal and human blood along with the expected loss of human life that occurs during the present-day Inti Raymi festivities are considered by local highland indigenous populations to be appropriate offerings to the deities so that they may grant continued rain and fertility to the soil in the coming year. For many Andean peoples, the public performance of institutionalized conflict through ritual battles resulting in bloodshed is believed to bring about the desired shift in weather patterns (Sikkink 1997). In effect, this modern-day Inti Raymi festival complex preserves this precontact Andean association between rain, soil productivity, and the shedding of human blood.[11] Additionally, participation in the ritual fighting concomitant with Inti Raymi celebrations creates and reinforces indigenous identity and also serves as a reminder to the nonindigenous population that the rights of the Cotacachi and Otavalo people are not to be violated.

NOTES

1. There is evidence, however, that the bifurcation of settlements predated the Incas. Parsons reported that the internal walls dividing some Late Intermediate sites investigated in the Peruvian Tarama-Chichaycocha region may have served to demarcate boundaries within the community. This may have set the stage "for the performance of integrative public rituals within bifocal communities. This may have included some ritual fighting" (Parsons, Hastings, and Matos 1997, 334).

2. See also Betanzos 1996. Tunas and pitahayas are cacti of the flat-padded and columnar forms with solid, semiovoid edible fruits.

3. Rostworowski (1988) suggests that the great Inca site of Sacsayhuaman may have been the location for ritual battles.

4. Wibbelsman (2004) reports that the two factions are referred to as *hanan* (upper) and *uray* (lower). See Wibbelsman 2004 for a comprehensive list of "upper" and "lower" Cotacachi communities.

5. In addition to this incident, several individuals were seriously injured during the ritual combat witnessed by the authors in 2001.

6. Wibbelsman (2004) suggests that there has recently been an increase in violence exhibited during Inti Raymi ritual combat and that this may be associated with the psychological aftereffects that young men possibly suffer after having served in the Ecuadorian armed forces.

7. Many of the males marching in the Santa Lucia fiesta were elderly individuals who did not participate in the ritual combat held previously. See Platt 1986 and Zorn 2002 for the presence of women ritual combatants in the Bolivian Andes.

8. However, the intraethnic antagonism found among the Cotacachi is not limited to the duration of the fiestas but is a year-round phenomenon. Even after the celebrations are over, it is not safe for an adult male from one faction to visit a community of the rival faction, as he could be seriously injured or even killed.

9. The association between shed human blood and agricultural fertility is dramatically illustrated in the following practice recorded among the Cañari of the Ecuadorian highlands: "In the past, when a great fighter [ritual combatant] was killed, his killer would cut the throat of the vanquished to obtain the blood which would be sprinkled in the victor's fields" (authors' translation, Brownrigg 1972, 97). Native anthropologist Luis Enrique Cachiguango (2001, 22) explains that the victims of ritual battles are in fact privileged, since they have been chosen by Pachamama as the link between humans and supernaturals. Moreover, Wibbelsman reports that after initial condemnation, UNORCAC categorized the above-cited killing of the twenty-nine-year-old urin man during the Inti Raymi fiesta as a "sacred death" (2004, 172).

10. See Cachiguango 2000 for another rain-generating ritual occurring in the Cotama area of Otavalo that also combines Inca and Christian beliefs.

11. The authors are unaware of any existing ethnohistorical documents

that specifically mention ritual combats taking place during the Inti Raymi celebrations. However, it is well established that the Incas organized elaborate public ceremonies that often included ritual battles on certain dates throughout their ritual calendar. Additionally, ritual fighting was conducted to memorialize important historical events such as the celebration of military victories or the deaths of rulers (Betanzos 1996; Cobo 1979, [1653] 1990; Morris 1998; Zuidema 1991, 1992).

8 UPPER AMAZONIAN WARFARE

Stephen Beckerman and James Yost

The first ethnographic document produced in the New World was a report prepared for Christopher Columbus by a monk whom he had sent to live among the natives of the island of Hispaniola. Fray Ramón Pané lived with two Taino chiefs in the years 1495 and 1496, learning their "beliefs and idolatries." His brief manuscript contains three references to habitual warfare among the inhabitants of the island (Pané [1498] 2001, 33, 34, 35) as well as a discussion of the practice of killing a shaman if his patient died (Pané [1498] 2001, 29–31). Despite this evidence, and the massive amount of documentation of aboriginal warfare that emerged from first contacts in other parts of the New World, there is a currently fashionable belief that warfare, if not all homicide, was introduced to the Americas by Europeans—although admittedly this belief is more prevalent in the popular, semipopular, and armchair anthropology literature than in the writings of ethnographers with extensive field experience.

Choosing a limited geographical region and assessing the earliest known and most recent manifestations of warfare provides a way of testing whether the origins of warfare preceded the arrival of Europeans. This chapter is a compilation of evidence rebutting this trendy opinion with regard to one large region of the New World, as well as an exploration of the nature of aboriginal warfare in that region. The focus is on the peoples of the upper Amazon, and among them, the Waorani in particular. We address three issues: (1) the autochthonous existence of warfare in this zone; (2) the methods and patterns of war in the zone; and (3) the question of the "causes of war." With respect to these issues, we concentrate on the data and keep interpretation to a minimum. Our emphasis is on firsthand evidence from the early colonial period, when aboriginal patterns of warfare were observed by the men who made the first contacts with the native inhabitants, and on ethnographic reports from the present day and the recent past. These periods provide the most pertinent evidence concerning the pre-Columbian existence of warfare and the richest data about its characteristics, respectively. Archaeological evidence for warfare in precontact times and data from historic records from the seventeenth, eighteenth, nineteenth, and early twentieth centuries are given less attention here.

The upper Amazon is not a rigorously defined region but is often taken to include the western lowlands of the Amazon basin, drained by tributaries reaching from the Putumayo in the north to the upper Ucayali in the south, and from an altitude of around 1,000 meters in the west to the confluence of the Putumayo and the Amazon in the east (fig. 8.1). This large, roughly triangular expanse of land—about eight degrees from east to west, and nearly twelve from north to south, at its greatest dimensions—is distinguished from other parts of the Amazon basin by a number of features. It is, especially toward its western margin, somewhat higher than most of the rest of the basin and thus, owing to orographic rainfall, somewhat wetter. Because most of the rivers that drain it originate in the Andes, they are largely whitewater rivers, carrying suspended silt and rock flour from the geologically new rocks of those mountains. This burden, when deposited along riverbanks in times of flood, produces exceptionally rich soils by general Amazonian standards. This agriculturally desirable land has been considered worth fighting over for centuries.

In terms of human geography, the upper Amazon is notable for its linguistic diversity, particularly for the number of isolated languages that are strung along the eastern slope of the Andes. This evidence probably indicates that the region has long been a cul de sac into which displaced peoples fled from farther downriver.

Another signal feature of the human geography of the upper Amazon is its proximity to the Andean civilizations along its western margin. Archaeological and ethnohistoric research (e.g., Myers 1981, 1988; Newson 1995; Santos Granero 1992; Taylor 1999; and references therein) documents the centuries-old relations between the lowland peoples and their highland neighbors—interactions that included both warfare and commerce (interactions commonly linked all over the world), as well as actual migrations of people both up and down the Andes.

Commercial relations of the upper Amazonians were not confined to exchange with Andean peoples; Anne Christine Taylor (1999, 199) summarizes contemporary findings about

> the great trans-Amazon trade circuits brought to light by recent archaeological and ethnohistorical research. Locally these circuits articulated two kinds of networks. One involved a chain of riverside groups specializing in long-distance trade, like the Piro, Conibo, or Omagua, carrying goods to and from the Colombian piedmont and the Cuzco region, and through the upper Amazon area down to the central Amazonian Solimões (Tápajos-Madeira). This latter area was itself the terminus of extensive trade networks crisscrossing over Guyana and northern Amazonia. The second network associated the riverine groups and the societies of the interfluve and high forest by means of a diffuse range of dyadic ritual trade partnerships.

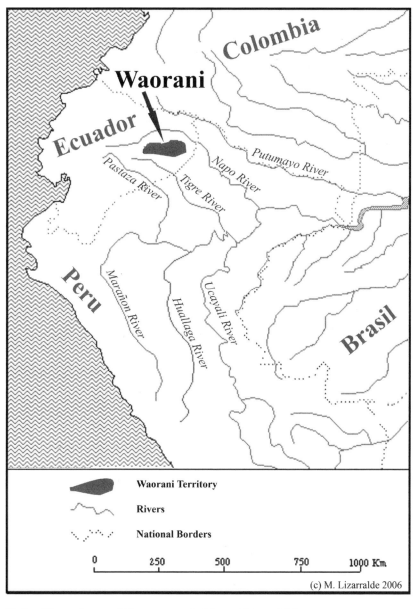

8.1 The study area. (Map prepared by Manuel Lizarralde)

PRECONTACT

Prehistoric warfare is not as well revealed in Amazonia as in other regions. Rapid decay of bone in acid tropical soils limits the likelihood that excavations in lowland South America will ever produce the abundant evidence of indigenous war that has been revealed at sites in North America (e.g., Willey 1990) and Europe (e.g., Wahl and Konig 1987). However, other forms of evidence exist.

For example, Clifford Evans and Betty Meggers (1968) describe medallions held by figures portrayed on anthropomorphic urns from archaeological excavations in the Napo basin as shields, although they are clearly too small, as represented, to have been of use in battle. Similarly, Miguel Angel Cabodevilla (1994, 58) describes other archaeological anthropomorphic urns from the same general region as showing "weapons of war as well as standards of command." In a synthetic treatment of the archaeology of the upper Amazon, Donald Lathrap (1970) presents the ethnohistory of the entire region in terms of invasions and replacements of peoples and cultural traditions, largely as waves of migration up the Amazon.

But clearly not all contact, whether peaceful or hostile, was confined to the lowlands. Copper axes manufactured in the south-central Andes have been found on the upper and middle Ucayali and dated to about 800 AD (Santos Granero 1992, 9), a time that corresponds to the expansion of the pre-Incaic Wari Empire. By the time of the Inca Empire, both war and commerce between the Andeans and their lowland neighbors had become habitual. An examination of the writings of the first Spanish chroniclers and other early accounts led Fernando Santos Granero (1992, 48; our translation) to conclude that "during their dominion the Incas carried out twenty-nine military expeditions against the inhabitants to the east of Cuzco. Of these, twelve ended in military victories, ten failed in their objectives, worn out by native resistance or by the difficult conditions of the tropical forest, and seven culminated in treaties of friendship sanctioned by the ritual exchange of prestige goods."

First Contact

If the archaeological record regarding warfare is scant and the chronicles of precontact relations sketchy, the record of war at the various moments of first contact between Europeans and the natives of the upper Amazon is almost rich. Ethnohistorian Linda Newson (1996, 20), writing of the Ecuadorian portion of the upper Amazon, summarizes a large body of archival and published material:

> Warfare was endemic and native groups possessed large repertoires of weapons. Warfare was stimulated by the need to avenge wrongs and to acquire social status, booty and sometimes slaves, although some contemporary observers attributed the constant state of warfare to the lack of effective native leadership. Among the Quijo the arms and legs of captives were consumed by leaders and, like the Jívaro, Maina and Omagua, their hands and heads were displayed as trophies. Wars were generally small scale and conducted in the form of raids but the acquisition of slaves by the Quijo and Omagua is suggestive of larger and more organized forms of warfare directed at group purposes.

The abundant documentation of war practices in early colonial records is not surprising. The one thing (other than gold) that the *conquistadores* were interested in was how hard and how well the Indians were going to fight their invaders. As professional soldiers, the Europeans evaluated their enemies with a practiced eye.

One such was a Portuguese adventurer, Diogo Nunes, who participated in the first European expedition to the Huallaga River (a southern tributary of the Amazon) in an exploration launched from the Andes under Spanish command. To the best of our knowledge, his account (Nunes [1554?] 1924–26), the ethnographic portion of which is reproduced below, has not previously been published in English. As with other newly translated documents quoted in this chapter, words supplied within parentheses are implied by and helpful in following the text, while words within brackets are explanatory comments on the text.

> In the year xxxbiij [38, that is, 1538], I went with a captain who is named Mercadillo, and we left Peru to discover and we

passed many unpopulated lands until (the place) where this captain became indisposed.

Then he sent twenty-five horsemen, among whom went I by order of this captain, and we arrived at a province after twenty-five days (where) we found good land and well populated with Indians and rich in gold according to what I saw and noted, that the Indians carried arms of gold and bracelets on their arms. These people were in garrison, because they were at war with other Indians we had already left behind us. They put themselves to defend against our entry into the land, and we defeated them by force of arms and entered the land. And these Indians would be five or six thousand and there we took many of them, among whom came other Indians of other languages and lands, as it appeared to the translators we brought with us.—This province where I arrived is called Machifaro.

These Indians whom we took there told us that they were of another lord farther on ahead from this (lord) whose vassals they were.

These two lords are at war one with the other and they capture one another's (people) and take them for slaves—Seeing the land so good, we returned to give word to our captain where we had left him and we did not find him because his (men) had taken him prisoner over a certain difference (of opinion) that he and they had had, and they took him to Peru as a prisoner, and for this reason this province was not populated (with Spanish settlers) because we all turned back to Peru.

I brought with me certain Indians from these provinces from whom I informed myself of what was there farther on, from one of these Indians whom I had in my company fourteen or fifteen years.

After we left this land there came after us fourteen thousand Indians (wanting) to know what (kind of) people we were, and on the way they came upon other Indians of another lord with whom they were at war, and they killed all of them (so) that there were not more than three hundred left alive, who went fleeing upriver in some canoes, and after a certain time they came to a town of Christians that is in Peru, which is called the Chachapoas. There would be by this route from where these Indians came (until getting) to Peru five hundred leagues. And these Indians knew the others that I brought because they were all of one land and one lord and the report of the land I have from my Indians and that which these told was one and the same. And these three hundred Indians are now in Peru.

In this province of Machifaro that I saw, one could populate five or six very rich towns because without a doubt there is in it much gold, and as it seemed to me, (it) is land abundant in provisions and healthy[?] as that of Peru. This land is between the Ryo da Prata and the Brasil, inland; through this land passes the Great River of the Amazons and in the transit of this land this river has many islands in the river and (these are) very populated with intelligent people and on the other bank of the river there are many towns of the same people, in such manner that one bank and the other are (both) well populated.

(Of) the provisions of this land, there is maize, which here is called mylho, and acaçaby [cassava], which serves as bread and of this there is a large quantity. There is in this river (so) much fish of all kinds, as in Spain, that in every town (where one) arrives one finds many houses full of dried fish that they take to sell to the forest, and they have their contractings with other Indians. The roads run very open and very followed because many people use them.

There is wild game in this land: deer, danta[?], wild pigs, ducks, and much other game. I had word that towards the Ryo da Prata in this same land there were sheep like those of Peru [llamas], which is the best sign that there could be in these parts because where there are sheep there is everything else in abundance. (Nunes [1554?] 1924–26, 367–68; our translation)

Just a few years after Mercadillo's exploration, the first European journey (1541–42) from the Andes to the Atlantic began, under the command of Francisco de Orellana. He and his fifty-seven men descended the Napo River, a northern tributary of the Amazon, without hostile encounters. Generous with gifts to the villagers who provisioned him, and claiming to be the son of the sun (i.e., to be the Inca himself), Orellana did not face armed resistance until he arrived at the confluence of the Amazon and its next major northern tributary after the Napo, the Putumayo. There he entered the province of Machiparo (the question of whether this Machiparo was the same as the Machifaro encountered by Nunes four years earlier has been endlessly argued by historians). The resulting battle was described in detail by Friar Gaspar de Carvajal, Orellana's chaplain and scribe, revealing a good deal about aboriginal warfare. We excerpt below from the Heaton edition, with bracketed material retained as in that source. Our comments are inserted in italics.

When twelve days of the month of May had gone by, we arrived in the provinces belonging to Machiparo, who is a very great overlord and one having many people under him, and is a neighbor of another overlord just as great, named Omaga, and they are friends who join together to make war on other overlords who are [located] inland, for they [i.e., the latter] come each day to drive them from their homes. This Machiparo has his headquarters quite near the river upon a small hill and holds sway over many settlements and very large ones which together contribute for fighting purposes fifty thousand men of the age of from thirty years up to seventy, because the young men do not go to war, and in all the fights that we had with them we did not see any, but it was the old men, and these [were] quite expert, and they have thin mustaches and not beards.

Before we had come within two leagues of this village, we saw the villages glimmering white, and we had not proceeded far when we saw coming up the river a great many canoes, all equipped for fighting, gaily colored, and [the men] with their shields on, which are made out of the shell-like skins of lizards and the hides of manatees and of tapirs, as tall as a man, because they cover them entirely. They were coming on with a great yell, playing on many drums and wooden trumpets, threatening us as if they were going to devour us. Immediately the Captain gave orders to the effect that the two brigantines should join together so that the one might aid the other and that all should take their weapons and look to what they had before them and take heed of the necessity on their part of defending their persons and fighting with the determination to come through to a haven of safety, and that all should commend themselves to God, for He would help us in that serious plight which we were in: and in the meantime the Indians kept coming closer, with their squadrons formed to catch us in the center, and thus they were coming on in such orderly fashion and with so much arrogance that it seemed as if they already had us in their hands. Our companions were all [filled] with so much courage that it seemed to them that four Indians to each one of them were not enough, and so the Indians drew near to the point where they began to attack us. Immediately the Captain gave the command to make ready the arquebuses and crossbows. Here there happened to us a misfortune by no means slight when one considers the situation in which we were at the time, which was that the arquebusiers found their powder damp, in consequence whereof they turned out to be of no use, and it was necessary for the crossbows to make up for the deficiency of the arquebuses; and so our crossbowmen began to inflict some damage on the enemy, as they were close up and we [were] fear-inspiring; and when it was seen [by] the Indians that so much damage was being done to them, they began to hold back, [yet] not showing any sign of cowardice, rather it seemed as if their courage were increasing, and there kept coming to them many reinforcements, and every time that some came to them they set about to attack us so boldly that it seemed as if they wanted to seize hold of the brigantines with their hands. In this manner we kept on fighting until we came to the village, where there were a great number of men stationed on the high banks to defend their homes. Here we engaged in a perilous battle, because there were many Indians on the water and on land and from all sides they gave us a hard fight; and so, of necessity, although seemingly at the risk of the lives of all of us, we attacked and captured the first spot [we could], where the Indians did not cease to leap out on land at [i.e., to attack] our companions, because they continued to defend it [i.e., the land] courageously; and had it not been for the crossbows, which effected some remarkable shots here . . . the landing would not have been won; and so, with this help already mentioned, the brigantines were beached and one half of our companions jumped into the water and fell upon the Indians in such a manner that they made them flee, and the other half stayed on the brigantines defending them from the other warriors who were out on the water, for they did not cease, even though the land was won, to fight on, and although damage was being done to them by the crossbows, they nevertheless did not give up [their attempt] to carry out their evil design. The beginning of the settlement being won, the Captain ordered the Lieutenant with twenty-five men to run through the settlement and drive the Indians out of it and look to see if there was any food [there], because he intended to rest in the said village five or six days in order to let us recover from the hardships which we had endured; and so the Lieutenant went and made a foray for a distance of half a league out through the village, and this [he did] not without difficulty, for, although the Indians were in retreat, they kept up a defensive fight like men whom it vexed to abandon their homes; and, as the Indians, when they do not meet with success in their intentions at the beginning, always run away until they feel the second impulse to return to a normal state of mind, they were, as I say, still fleeing; and, when the aforesaid Lieutenant had perceived the great extent of the settlement and of its population, he decided not to go on farther but to turn back and tell the Captain what the situation was; and thus he did turn back before the Indians could do him any damage, and, having got back to the beginning of the settlement, he found that the Captain was lodged in the houses and that the Indians were still attacking him from the river, and he [i.e., the Lieutenant] told him exactly how things were and [informed him] that there was a great quantity of food, such as turtles in pens and pools of water, and a great deal of meat and fish and biscuit, and all this in such great abundance that there was enough to feed an expeditionary force of one thousand men for one year; and the Captain, having observed what a good harbor it was, decided to gather food together in order to recuperate, as I have said, and for this purpose he sent for Cristóbal Maldonado and told him to take a dozen companions and go and seize all the food that he could; and so he went, and when he arrived there he found that the Indians were going about the village carrying off the food that they had. The said Cristóbal Maldonado toiled hard to collect the food, and, when he had gathered together more than a thousand turtles, the Indians returned, and this second time there came a great number of men, and very determined [they were] to kill them [i.e., Maldonado and his men] and push on to strike at the place where we were with the Captain; and when the said Cristóbal Maldonado saw the Indians coming back, he rallied his companions and attacked the enemy, and here they [i.e., Maldonado and his men] were held in check for a long time, because there were more than two thousand Indians and of the companions who were with Cristóbal Maldonado there were only ten, and they had much to do to defend themselves. In the end such superior skill was displayed that they [i.e., the Indians] were routed, and they [i.e., Maldonado's men] again started to collect the food, and two companions came out of this second fight wounded; and, as the country was very thickly settled and the Indians were constantly reforming and replenishing their ranks, they again came back at the said Cristóbal Maldonado, so resolutely that [it was evident that] they sought (and actually started) to seize them all with their hands, and in this assault they wounded six companions very badly, some being pierced through the arms and others through the legs, and they wounded the said Cristóbal Maldonado to the extent of piercing one of his arms and giving him a blow in the face with a stick. Here the companions found themselves in a very serious plight and need of help, for, as they were wounded and very tired . . . (*torn*), they could not go backward nor forward, and so they all considered themselves as good as dead and kept saying that they ought to return to where their Captain was, and the said Cristóbal Maldonado told them not to think of such a thing, because he for one had no intention of returning to where his Captain was, whereby the Indians would carry off the victory; and so he rallied around him those of the companions who were in a condition to fight, and put himself on the defensive, and fought so courageously that he was the means of preventing the Indians from killing all of our companions.

During this time the Indians had come around by the upper part [of the village] to strike at where our Captain was from two sides, and as we were all tired out from so much fighting and off our guard, thinking that we were protected from the rear because Cristóbal Maldonado was out there, it became evident that Our Lord had enlightened the Captain [by inspiring in him the idea] of sending out the aforementioned [Cristóbal Maldonado], for had he not sent him out, or had he [i.e., Cristóbal Maldonado] not happened to be just where he was, I hold it for certain that we should have run a great risk of [losing] our lives; and, as I am saying, our Captain and all of us were off our guard and with no armor on, so that the Indians had an opportunity to enter the village and fall upon us without being noticed [before we could get ready for them], and, when they were noticed, they were right in among us and had felled four of our companions, [leaving them] very badly wounded; and at this moment they were seen by one of our companions named Cristóbal de Aguilar (13), who took his stand facing them, fighting very courageously, giving the alarm, which our Captain heard, who went out to see what it was, with no armor on, with a sword in his hand, and he saw that the Indians had the houses where our companions were, surrounded; and, besides this, a squadron of more than five hundred Indians was in the square. The Captain began to call aloud, and so all our companions came out behind the Captain and attacked the squadron with so much intrepidity that they routed them, inflicting damage upon the Indians, but they [i.e., the Indians] did not cease from fighting and putting up a defense, so that they wounded nine companions with grievous wounds, and, at the end of two hours during which we had kept on fighting, the Indians were vanquished and routed and our own men [were] greatly fatigued. . . . *Maldonado returned, he and all his men wounded, one mortally.* . . . At this juncture they came and told the Captain how the Indians were coming back and that they were close to us in a gully, waiting till they got reorganized; and, in order to drive them out of there, the Captain ordered a cavalier named Cristóbal Enríquez (17) to go there with fifteen men, and he went, and when he got there one of the arquebusiers that he had taken with him had one of his legs pierced; in that way we lost an arquebusier, because thereafter we could not make use of him. The said Cristóbal Enríquez promptly sent back someone to inform the Captain of what was taking place and to ask him to send more men, because the Indians were in great numbers and were being reinforced every hour; and the Captain at once sent orders to the said Cristóbal Enríquez that, without showing that he was retreating, he should come along little by little to where they [i.e., the Captain and the rest] were, because now was not the time for them to risk the life of single Spaniard. . . . *Orellana addressed his men and ordered them not to provoke the Indians* . . . and he began to load food on board, and as soon as it was on board the Captain commanded that the wounded be placed on board, and those who were unable to go on their own feet he ordered to be wrapped in blankets and be carried aboard on the backs of other men, as if these latter were carrying loads of maize, so that they might not embark limping and so that the Indians on perceiving this might not regain so much courage that they would not let us embark; and after this had been done, the brigantines being ready and unmoored and the oars in hand, the Captain with the companions in good order went down [to the river], and they embarked, and he put off, and was not a stone's throw away when there came more than four hundred Indians on the water and along the land, and, as those on the land could not get at us, they served no purpose but to call and shout; and those on the water attacked again and again, like men who had been wronged, with great fury; but our companions with their crossbows [and] arquebuses defended the brigantines so well that they turned away those wicked people. This was around sundown, and in this manner, attacking us every little while, [they kept] following us all the night, for not one moment did they allow us a respite, because they had us headed off. In this way we kept on until it was day, when we saw ourselves in the midst of numerous and very large settlements, whence fresh Indians were constantly coming out, while those who were fatigued dropped out. About midday, when our companions were no longer able to row, we were all thoroughly exhausted from the cruel night and from the fighting which the Indians had forced upon us. The Captain, in order that the men might get a little rest and eat something, gave orders that we put in on an uninhabited island which was in the middle of the river, and, just as they began to cook something to eat, there came along a great number of canoes, and they attacked us three times, so that they put us in great distress. It having become evident to the Indians that from the water they could not put us to rout, they decided to attack us [both] by land and by water, because, as there were many Indians, there were enough of them for [undertaking] anything. The Captain, seeing what the Indians were making ready to do, decided not to wait for them on land, and hence embarked again and pulled out into the river, because there he thought he could better fight back, and thus we began to move on, with the Indians still not ceasing to follow us and force upon us many combats, because from these settlements there had gathered together many Indians and on the land the men who appeared were beyond count. There went about among these men and the war canoes four or five sorcerers, all daubed with whitewash and with their mouths full of ashes, which they blew into the air, having in their hands a pair of aspergills, with which as they moved along they kept throwing water about the river as a form of enchantment, and, after they had made one complete turn about our brigantines in the manner which I have said, they called out to the warriors, and at once these began to blow their wooden bugles and trumpets and beat their drums and with a very loud yell they attacked us; but, as I have already said, the arquebuses and crossbows, next to God, were our salvation; and so they led us along in this manner until they got us into a narrows in an arm of the river. Here they had us in a very distressful situation, and so much so that [if luck had not favored us] I do not know whether any one of us would have survived, because they had laid an ambuscade for us on land, and from there they would have surrounded us. Those on the water resolved to wipe us out, and they being now quite determined to do so, being now very close [to us], there stood out before them their captain-general distinguishing himself in a very manly fashion, at whom a companion of ours, named Celis, took aim and fired with an arquebus, and he hit [him] in the middle of the chest, so that he killed him; and at once his men became disheartened and they all gathered around to look at their overlord, and in the meantime we seized the opportunity to get out into the wide part of the river; but still they followed us for two days and two nights without letting us rest, for it took us that long to get out of the territory occupied by the subjects of this great overlord named Machiparo, which in the opinion of all extended for more than eighty leagues, for it was all of one tongue, these [eighty leagues] being all inhabited, for there was not from village to village [in most cases] a crossbow shot, and the one which was farthest [removed from the next] was not half a league away, and there was one settlement that stretched for five leagues without there intervening any space from house to house, which was a marvelous thing to behold: as we were only passing by and fleeing, we had no opportunity to learn what there was in the country [farther] inland. (Carvajal [1542] 1934, 190–98)

Carvajal's moment-by-moment account of this battle reveals that warfare was a well-practiced activity in Machiparo's domain (shields and trumpets and formations have no use in tropical forest hunting) and that it involved leaders or officers of some kind who were able to coordinate forces on land and on water. However, this chronicle also shows that, while raids were common, pitched battles were not. Machiparo's forces kept regrouping, but losses kept driving them off again; they were never able to mount the sort of determined, relentless assault that would have overwhelmed the outnumbered Spaniards (even discounting the obvious exaggeration of Indian numbers) despite the superior weapons and armor of the former.

Not all conflicts in the upper Amazon were as well organized and resolute as Machiparo's battle with Orellana. Around 1550, Hernando Benavente explored the valley of the Río Upano, encountering Jivaroan-speaking peoples living in dispersed longhouses. They burned their longhouses and fled at his approach. Eventually, Benavente

sent certain soldiers who saw a road on which they encountered some Indians, naked, and each one with a spear and a buckler, of whom they could only take one man and one woman, whom they brought to me, and (they being) brought I spoke through a translator to the Indian man that he might tell me about this land and where was the chief, (and he) responded why did I want to know and that his chief was very great and that if he took me and the others that he would kill us and drink from our heads and sow the road with our bones. (Benavente [1550] 1994, 60–61; our translation)

Less than a decade after that undiplomatic encounter, 1557–59, Juan de Salinas Loyola made a two-year expedition down the Santiago River (one of the westernmost tributaries of the Amazon) to the Amazon (which, above its confluence with the Napo, is today called the Marañon), down the Amazon, past its confluence with the Huallaga, as far its meeting with the Ucayali, and then up the Ucayali for three hundred leagues, so he claimed, meeting many indigenous groups along the way. In general, he found the locals to be less formidable than Orellana and Benavente had. On the Santiago, Salinas Loyola ([1571] 1965, 199; our translation) reported that "the natives likewise are of *behetría* [an archaic Spanish word describing a settlement or local population that had the traditional right to choose its own lord, rather than belonging to a hereditary overlord; the conquistadors used it to describe native communities not subject to a paramount chief], each village not recognizing more than its chiefs or captains, and although they are not bellicose people, among themselves they have their continuous wars, killing and robbing each other." On the upper Marañon, he reported similarly (Salinas Loyola [1571] 1965, 200; our translation): "The natives of the land and this aforesaid province are very tame and not at all warriors or bellicose, although among themselves they continuously have their differences because they do not obey or (even) have a general lord whom they respect, (nothing) more than (that) each village and (local) population (respects) its chiefs and captains in the way of those behind on the aforesaid Santiago (River)." Somewhat farther down the Marañon, the expedition found different natives when they arrived (Salinas Loyola [1571] 1965, 201; our translation) "at a province called Maynas, (populated by) people (who were) very lucid and of good disposition in comparison with ordinary Indians. It was a different language than (that of) those behind, people very warlike and bellicose and for that they were feared by their neighbors; they wore cloths of cotton, very colorful, and used a great deal of feather work of all colors, which they placed with fine workmanship on their buckers and spears and other instruments of war."

In generalizing about the people of the Marañón between the Santiago and the Ucayali, Salinas Loyola ([1571] 1965, 201; our translation) reported, "All these aforesaid people and provinces are of more orderliness than those behind them, and bellicose. The weapons are spears and shields and staffs–throwing sticks [atlatls] and some that they call *macanas* that are of the size of a two-handed sword, of palm wood. They are great water people; they have many and very good canoes, in which they navigate." However, despite all this evidence of indigenous warfare, Salinas Loyola rowed three hundred leagues upriver on the Ucayali, encountering several native groups, and met no serious resistance, although he noted (Salinas Loyola [1571] 1965, 202; our translation) in reference to the territory of the Pariaches, "On entering this province and land they [the natives] disposed themselves in the manner of resistance, which later changed to peace, and they kept it and sustained it as long as the aforesaid language and province lasted."

The picture that emerges from this brief review of early documents is in no way surprising. There were cultural differences with respect to warfare, just as with respect to subsistence, settlement pattern, social organization, role within the trade network, and language. In some large regions, the people were largely peaceful, particularly in the face of Spanish firearms and crossbows. In others they were more warlike, with the tempo of fighting ranging from more or less continuous to intermittent. Motives for war were similarly varied, ranging from personal vengeance to territorial dispute and slaving. Where the upper Amazonians were at war, their military activities reflected their social organization, in some places organized under a paramount chief and in some places manifesting only local mobilization. These differences in the motives and organization of Amazonian war have been emphasized by Elsa Redmond (1994).

LATER HISTORY—SEVENTEENTH THROUGH TWENTIETH CENTURIES

There can be no doubt that the arrival of the Spanish invaders had enormous effects on aboriginal patterns of war, the most obvious change being the addition of a new and formidable foe, so widely hated that previous native animosities were sometimes submerged in the face of allied resistance to a common enemy. Fernando Santos Granero (1992, 213–36), the main source for this section, discusses four general rebellions against the Spanish conquistadors—by Jivaroan speakers, by the Cocama and various allies, and by Panoan speakers, as well as by a multiethnic alliance.

There was an early and quickly extinguished uprising of Jivaroan speakers in 1569, followed by the successful Jívaro general revolt of 1599—which according to Santos Granero (1992, 217–20) actually began in 1579 and lasted twenty years before the Spaniards were definitely driven out of most of Jivaroan territory—an expulsion that held until the early twentieth century. This revolt was apparently marked by a degree of coordination among independent settlements and different tribes (speaking related languages, however) that continues to attract the curiosity of anthropologists. Traditional enemies coordinated attacks, fought together, and even recruited some Andean Indians and mestizos to expel the Spanish colonizers.

Farther downriver, in 1635 the Maina Indians attacked the small city of Borja on the Marañon just below its confluence with the Santiago, killing a large number of landowners. Spanish punitive expeditions responded with enormous brutality, and Jesuit missionaries came in the next year to attempt to pacify the Indians. There were several ethnic groups downstream of Borja, where the Jesuits had their missions south of the Marañon, mostly in the lower basins of the Huallaga and Ucayali. Among them were the Jebero (not to be confused with the Jívaro, who lived much farther upstream), the Cocamilla, the Cocama, and the Shipibo. The Cocamilla apparently had friendly relations with both the Jebero and the Cocama, but the latter two peoples were enemies. The Cocama were also traditional enemies of the Shipibo. Nevertheless, these mutually hostile peoples managed to fight together sufficiently well to bring Spanish advances in this area to a standstill for the decade 1659–69, after which date they were definitively defeated by a combined Spanish-Indian force.

The most famous Indian uprising in the upper Amazon was the revolt of Juan Santos Atahuallapa, 1742–52. The Campa, the Amuesha, the Conibo, the Shipibo, and the Piro all took part. This rebellion was successful in driving the Spanish colonizers from the middle and upper Ucayali valley and adjoining regions and keeping them out for over half a century (Taylor 1999, 221). Rather than a loose confederation of like-minded independent groups, this uprising was led by a single charismatic leader who appears actually to have given orders. Juan Santos Atahuallapa, an Andean with extensive knowledge of the Spaniards, remains an iconic figure in indigenous lowland Peru. Under his messianic and revitalistic leadership, the five tribes mentioned above, joined by some blacks and mestizos, formed a fighting force that was able to meet the Spanish forces on their own terms. He "routed two generals sent from Lima, captured all the forts overlooking the montaña, caused the death of over 600 Spaniards and 50 missionaries, and ruined several important towns" (Taylor 1999, 221). Then in 1752 he retreated to an isolated region of rain forest and never attacked the Spanish colonizers again.

A series of events more similar to the Jivaro and Cocama rebellions took place in the lower Ucayali and Huallaga basins a few years after Juan Santos Atahuallapa's withdrawal, this time among speakers of Panoan languages, who drove Franciscan missionaries from their homeland between 1766 and 1790. Again, formerly hostile peoples (Setebo, Shipibo, and Conibo) united to fight the Spanish invaders.

Despite the temporary halt in intertribal hostilities that each of these four alliances entailed, none produced a lasting peace. Traditional enmities reemerged as soon as the Spanish forces withdrew. But the Spanish colonizers never withdrew permanently. And before they left and after they returned, their presence added three additional motives for interethnic conflict.

One came from the virtually universal use of Indian allies in Spanish military expeditions to round up Indians for service on *encomiendas* or for outright slavery (a distinction probably lost on the captives) or to punish fleeing or rebelling Indians. Men from one tribe joined these expeditions because they were conscripted, because they had been raised at missions and "tamed" (as the writers of the time said), or because they saw such service as a way to settle old scores with an enemy tribe, under the protection of Spanish firearms. Thus old enmities were reinvigorated by new outrages.

Another new motive for interethnic warfare was arguably the most important influence that the inhabitants of the Old World brought to those of the New—infectious disease. The native disease mortality that accompanied contact with the European and African migrants has been sufficiently documented that there is no longer any doubt of its enormous magnitude. What is not perhaps sufficiently appreciated is the extent to which disease mortality led to war mortality.

The link was the common belief that most if not all deaths were the result of human malice. A snake bite, a fall, a death from a contagious disease were interpreted as evidence of witchcraft. When Old World epidemics reached the upper Amazon (Salinas Loyola's men may have been among the first agents of contagion; Newson 1996, 16), these disasters were almost certainly understood as the work of traditional enemies. The few survivors of such scourges as smallpox or plague understood their duty to avenge their dead family members.

A third motive for tribal-tribal warfare was the displacement of populations, as group after group of native peoples fled the European invaders and, in so doing, invaded the territory of other peoples. The "fourteen thousand Indians" who "came after us" according to the Nunes report on the Mercadillo expedition were Tupí-Guaraní migrants coming upriver from Brazil. They were searching for a "land without evil," a precontact Guaraní practice (Wright with Carneiro de Cunha 1999, 316) but one that had been augmented by the desire to escape Portuguese slavers. According to Nunes, by the time the fourteen thousand reached the Andes, their number had been reduced, by combat with other tribes, to three hundred.

Despite all this evidence for the general exacerbation of war and warfare mortality as a result of European influence, the issue should not be closed on that note alone. There were also times and places where the Spanish influence diminished war. The conquistadors made considerable efforts to suppress intra- and intertribal warfare when they first entered the upper Amazon, because warfare interfered with putting the

Indians to work. Salinas Loyola, for instance, wrote with pride about "pacifying" native peoples and stamping out local wars, so that the Indians could be distributed to work on Spanish encomiendas. Only when the pacified natives fled their masters did the more lasting practice of setting tribe against tribe become the dominant note.

The related disasters of Old World diseases, warfare, and brutal forced labor combined in some places to diminish, disperse, and defeat the native populations to such a point that some remnant peoples no longer had accessible enemies to fight and lacked the sense that they had available to them any response to the appearance of outsiders other than flight. Accounts of this situation, not rarely encountered by the pioneer ethnographers of the early twentieth century, may be the evidence that led inexperienced interpreters to posit an inherent pacifism among Native Americans and a pre-Columbian golden age without war.

The last two widespread disasters to overtake virtually all of the native peoples of the upper Amazon, without respect to location or ethnic identity, took place around the turn of the nineteenth century. The rubber boom, which began around 1880 in this region, was one of the great atrocities of New World history (Hardenburg 1912). In the production of latex, Peruvian, Colombian, and Brazilian entrepreneurs enslaved and worked to death thousands of Indian men, casually murdering their wives and children as well. It was a generations-long massacre with the impact of a series of major epidemics.

On top of this genocide, there appeared a real epidemic. The influenza pandemic of 1918 reached the Amazon, with horrific results. Although this worldwide scourge is sometimes claimed to have killed up to 2 percent of the entire population of the world, its effect among Amazonian natives, who had no epidemiological experience of the pathogen, was proportionally far worse. There are no reliable figures, but the mortality was sufficient to erase the possibility that the Amazonian peoples will ever recover demographically (Hemming 1987).

ETHNOGRAPHIC CASE: THE WAORANI

It is in the context of the massive depopulation brought about by these two disasters as the twentieth century began that the violence of the

Waorani, the tribe sometimes believed to have been the most warlike people on earth, must be understood. The ethnographic data presented below speak only to patterns of behavior manifested after this devastation; there is no reliable information as to the culture of the Waorani before the twentieth century. In discussing Wao warfare, we deal with the same topics emphasized in the historical sketch above: the autochthonous nature of Wao warfare, the methods they employed in war, and their motivations for going to war.

The Waorani (Robarchek and Robarchek 1998; Yost 1981, 1990) are a small (precontact population about 500, currently about 2,000) interfluvial tribe living south of the Río Napo in Ecuador. Before peaceful contact in 1958, they were the only human inhabitants of an area about the size of Massachusetts. Their subsistence practices were much like those of the interfluvial Jívaro, with sweet manioc (consumed as a mildly alcoholic beer) as the dietary staple and game supplying the animal protein fraction of the diet. The repeated claim by Laura Rival (1999, 2002) that they were hunters and gatherers is false.

At the time of peaceful Western contact, the Waorani lived in four geographically separated, mutually hostile groups. These groups inhabited dispersed neighborhood clusters (Yost 1981) of closely related and friendly Waorani living in communal houses within one or two days' walk of one another. Each communal household usually maintained two or three different houses and associated gardens scattered up to a day's walk from each other and moved among them every few months. Hostile groups, in contrast, maintained their neighborhood clusters at least several days' walk from each other.

Marriage was prescriptively with a bilateral cross cousin and was arranged by the parents of the young couple, often without their knowledge. Marriages were most common within the neighborhood cluster. Completed fertility was low for a natural-fertility population. In a sample of 17 postreproductive women, James Larrick and colleagues (1979) found a mean of only 5.7 live births per woman.

Because the Waorani lived interspersed among at least five other indigenous groups between the Napo River on the north and the Villano River on the south, it is impossible to determine with any confidence whether early contacts in that area were with Waorani or with other tribes. Similarities between the Waorani and their neighbors in aspects of culture that could be observed by a foreign explorer, combined with the lack of linguistic data, confound reconstruction of historical contact. Long-standing hostility between the Waorani and all other groups motivated the former to keep to the hills and hinterlands, far from the riverine cultures. This settlement pattern makes it likely that the early European contacts were with the riverine groups, not the Waorani. In 1664, Padre Lucas de la Cueva appears to have been the first European to travel the length of the Curaray River, which bisects traditional Wao territory. He noted that of the six "nations" he contacted, two were hostile and the rest were peaceful. However, it is not possible to connect any of these groups with the contemporary Waorani. Even much later explorers, such as F. W. Up de Graff (1921), who visited the area in 1897, left accounts that yield no reliable conclusions as to whom they were encountering. Rolf Blomberg's (1957) well-known foray into the area in 1947 is of little help, since the few phrases he quotes are not from the Wao language.

At the point at which a definite identification can be made of the Waorani, they were noted to be aggressive and hostile, not only internally but also against all other groups, both indigenous and European (Tessman 1930, 73). They fiercely repelled all incursions into their territory and, based on their own accounts, were likely the ones responsible for numerous raids documented against European settlers near Wao territory and against explorers and travelers at least as far back as the end of the nineteenth century. Wao oral history is rife with accounts of raids against *cowode*, "non-Waorani." Their hostility was serious enough that in an attempt to stem the killings, the Ecuadorian military issued an edict in the 1950s prohibiting crossing to the south bank of the Napo River. Lowland Quichua Indians who attempted to settle there or ventured into the area to hunt were often met with Wao spears, and an army outpost established on the lower Cononaco River was abandoned in the late 1960s because of attacks from the Waorani.

The hostility was exacerbated throughout time by retaliatory raids on the Waorani from surrounding peoples. In addition, at the turn of the nineteenth century, rubber gatherers plying Wao rivers and territory deepened Wao fears, suspicion, and anger by capturing Waorani for slaves or killing them. Because the Waorani did not distinguish among various groups of cowode, regarding them all as cannibals and subhuman, they vented their anger on all cowode. If a Wao family was incited to kill for whatever reason and if cowode were living or traveling nearby, these cowode became the first target of the hostility, whether they were connected to the matter or not.

The Waorani were ever alert for signs of cowode. Even after two decades of peaceful contact with the cowode, the Waorani were anxious about them. For example, hunters often carried a pair of swimming trunks tucked into their g-strings, and if they encountered evidence of anyone else in the area they immediately donned the trunks, thereby signaling that they were not a hostile group and should not be shot on sight. In addition, until the 1980s, Wao mothers went to great length to explain to children the evils of cowode and the need to avoid them and conceal evidence of travels where cowode might venture.

WAORANI SELF-REINFORCING WARFARE

While the Waorani were hostile to the cowode, they were even more bellicose among themselves. Legend says that the first killings took place right after the creation of man when one group trespassed on the hunting territory of another. The home group killed the trespassers, beginning a vendetta that continued until late in the twentieth century. In the five generations preceding 1975, nearly half of all deaths were homicides from that internal vendetta. Our records show that from the 1910s to the 1970s, the Waorani undertook at least sixty raids on other Waorani (certainly an undercount). Of these sixty raids, twelve resulted in the killing of a single individual, usually from ambush, and the rest produced multiple homicides.

Consequently, spearing raids and revenge dominated Wao thinking and emotions until the most recent generation (those who have grown up since around 1980). In fact, as will be seen in the development of this discussion, a great deal of Wao culture has been shaped by internal warfare. During Yost's fieldwork in the early 1970s, scarcely a day passed that conversations did not turn to spearing raids. Anything could act as a mnemonic. In the evenings, as people lay in their hammocks, elders recounted past raids; on the trail, the way the sun filtered through the leaves stirred a memory of how someone raided a family; birds flushing in the underbrush ignited a tale of how Lives Badly (this name, like all other Waorani names in this chapter, is fictitious) almost killed the hunter Yost was with; passing a rotted tree stump served to remind Poison Pot how his parents were killed. Inevitably, the tales were lengthy and gruesome in detail. The causal antecedents to the raid, the time of day, what the weather was like, and who was doing what when the raiders appeared were all repeated. Then came the chaos of the raid—who came to kill, who got away, who got speared and in exactly what part of the body, how he or she suffered, and the reactions of the killers. Every detail was seared into memories repeated countless times down the generations. Those stories reminded later generations of whom they needed to kill in revenge, and also functioned as critical models for survival strategies.

Childrearing also centered on both defensive and offensive strategies concerning the vendetta. Defensively, children were instructed never to give their names to a stranger or to tell a stranger who their parents were, since lack of traceable kinship was a sure guarantee of getting speared. They were instructed in how to recognize an imminent raid, how to escape one, and what to do following it. They were never to tell where their parents were or when or how their parents might return. In hamlets that felt vulnerable, mothers with two or three young children moved together as a cluster, much like a hen and her chicks, ensuring that they could escape as a group if danger appeared.

Offensively, adults repeatedly reinforced upon children who their enemies were and whose deaths needed to be avenged. Particularly in the longhouse at night, children listened as their parents and grandparents related the horrors of being raided by enemies who needed to be eliminated before they returned to kill again. More overtly, men just returning from a raid beat the arms and legs of children, even infants in the carrying sling, with thorn-vines or the flat of wooden machetes to pass onto them the ability to carry spears long distances, to run fast, and to kill efficiently. Grandmothers would call out the names of enemies to young boys as they practiced chunking spears into banana roots or other surrogate enemies.

But most effectively, hardly any children ever made it through childhood without personally experiencing the horrors of raids on their houses. The indelible memories of parents, siblings, or other family members being killed in front of children were easily molded into a drive to avenge.

WAORANI METHODS AND PATTERNS OF WAR

The following first-person accounts of war were collected by Yost in the 1970s and translated by him.

Motmot (female)

I was about four years old, down playing in the stream at the time. All of us kids were swimming and splashing around in the narrow stream. No rocks, just a sandy bottom and not deep. Suddenly we heard lots of screaming, and my sister Armored-Catfish, who was the oldest of the bunch, runs up the hill toward the house and sees men outside with spears and Aunt Longvine running down the hill with a spear in her side. Armored-Catfish scrambles back to us, [yelling out,] "They've already speared!" We scattered in all directions. Armored-Catfish and I took off downriver, Armored-Catfish holding my hand. Cries-for-Food [four years old] and Always-Enters [two years old] turned and ran back up to the house. The men speared and killed them. We found the trail and fled up toward Uncle Woodpecker's house. We met him on his way to visit us. He and the other men continued on toward our house to bury the dead, and we fled to his house with the women.

Woodpecker (male)

Skinny-Fish came running up: "Wooley-Monkey has just speared Stinging-Ant and your father, Another-Tree! The spears just nicked me. I'm going to go spear them in return!" I said, "No! Don't go now. Let it rest and if we wait a long time they'll think we're all dead and will drop their guard. Then we can tuk! spear them." So we fled across land to the headwaters of the Dayono River, being very careful all the time we lived there to keep our tracks hidden. After almost a year, I said, "Now is the time. All my life I have said we should go spear them because of what they have done in the past. Then they killed again, so now is the time."

Running, running, running we went down intending to spear. Bamboo, Pygmy-Squirrel, myself, Lives-in-Son, Thorn-Cluster, Skinny-Fish. On the way we took a wrong trail and accidentally came across Kicker and Hidden-Woman's bodies rotting with flies swarming over them. Wooley-Monkey had just speared again. Seeing his brother's body being eaten by maggots, Bamboo became insanely furious. After two more days just at dusk we reached Wooley-Monkey's house setting on top of the hill, with the trees cleared all the way down. We waited in hiding for dark and for Wooley-Monkey's return. As we approached the house, we heard chanting. "Who do you think it is?" Then we heard someone call out Palm-Spear's name. "Palm-Spear! He's one of those who killed Stinging-Ant!" Pygmy-Squirrel and Skinny-Fish could see in through the leaves at the edge of the door and thought they could spear right through the leaves. Thorn-Cluster and I went to the door at the other end of the house.

Thorn-Cluster takes his foot and slams it against the door, flattening staves and all. Wooley-Monkey yells out, "Badogaa!" As he yells, Pygmy-Squirrel and Skinny-Fish at the other end of the house spear both him and Stingray in the back through the thatch. Thorn-Cluster and I burst in. I spear Green-Parrot, and dying, he falls into the fire, scattering it. The house becomes pitch black. Spearing anything that moves and does not sound like us, I kill three women. Someone fans up a fire, and I see Wooley-Monkey staggering through the house with three spears in him. He staggers to the door where Bamboo is standing. Bamboo puts another spear, then another and another into him. He then stands over Wooley-Monkey, chanting, taunting. Whirling, Bamboo then grabs a spear from a body and mortally wounds two infants the same ages as Cries-for-Food and Always-Enters, whom Wooley-Monkey had killed with Stinging-Ant.

Wounded, Stingray escaped out of the house because the young men who were stationed there were too inexperienced to get him.

He stood out in the garden clapping his hands yelling, "You're all going to die! You're all going to die!"

I realized Wooley-Monkey's young daughter was sitting there in a hammock, terrified, frozen in place, unscathed. "Hey, Pygmy-Squirrel," I said, "here's a girl sitting here. Take her for your wife." He is still married to her today.

We fled up the trail about two hundred yards, then went back and set the house on fire with all of the bodies inside. We ran upriver and across to the Dayono. All night and all the next day we ran, concealing our tracks until we got home. Then we took our families and fled far, far downriver, floating on a fallen log to throw off any pursuers. Later we crossed overland and finally settled at Damointado.

That's how we lived in the old days. Back and forth we killed. Back and forth, back and forth. Together we died.

The Waorani had no chiefs, village council, or specialized leadership, and their warfare reflected this egalitarian social organization. Any man could initiate a raid; when he decided to undertake one, it was up to him to recruit and motivate followers. In most cases, a man in his twenties would initiate and lead a raid, but if a younger man wanted to instigate one, he normally sought first to enroll the service of an older, more experienced man to lead the raid. In the case cited above, Woodpecker was the only man above twenty years of age; the rest were scarcely more than teenagers. Often young teens, and sometimes even ten-year-olds, accompanied raiders and were allowed to dispatch the wounded or very young as the raid reached its conclusion. The preparation period might be spontaneous and rapid if the initiation was a reaction to a raid that just took place, or it might take several days if the stimulus for the raid was a long-standing grudge that had to be satisfied and necessitated motivating men who were not or only tangentially involved in the original dispute. As the leader tried to incite men to follow him, he reminded them of any past injury or raid that had not been avenged. The memory did not need to relate to the proposed victim. As he recounted past injuries, he began to make a number of spears, decorating each with his own distinctive combination of feathers, vine, cotton string, *achiote* painting, notching, and edge shapes. Even the length and weight of the spears was his, resulting in a unique weapon that anyone would recognize as his. The goal was to ensure that survivors of the raid would know exactly who killed whom and be overcome with terror of the owner. Although in raids the only weapon carried was the spear, in an ambush or spontaneous killing a hardened palm machete or axe might be used.

Once the spears were prepared, the men chanted during the night before departing to induce a dream that involved the intended victim, since dreams were portents of the future and of success. Before departing, they sent their families off into hiding; then the party set out, each man with a wrapped bundle of spears on one shoulder and a single spear ready for use on the other. The average number of men in a raiding party was about eight, but parties ranged in size from a single man to over thirty. They might have to travel four or five days over high ridges and across rivers and swamps, often pushing into the night and covering up to sixty miles in a day. (Repeated and cross-checked, independently gathered information tying raider movements to known landmarks verifies this remarkable figure. The raiders' determination was fierce, and Wao endurance and stamina truly astounding.)

Overwhelmingly, the stealth surprise raid, reinforced by whatever deceit was available, was the primary tactic of Wao warfare. The object was to avoid a position whereby the victims might be able to defend themselves or fight back. "Battles" were unheard of. Likewise, if a house was attacked, the occupants never chose to engage the attackers; instead, they fled in whatever manner they could, and it was up to every individual—adult or child, male or female—to fend for himself or herself. Escape was their tactic and the dense forest their ally.

Raiders preferred to attack during the darkest hours of the night, waiting for signs that all activity inside the thatch house was quiet, with no one alert to their approach. The raiders wanted all the psychological advantage possible. A night thunderstorm was even better, since lightning could be someone's soul ascending into the heavens and an uneasiness accompanied nearby lightning strikes. In addition to the lightning, the raiders smeared the spears and their bodies with achiote (*Bixa orellana*) because it gave off an odor that they hoped would strike fear into their victims. If possible, they would send someone known to the household into it to spend the night and relay signals to them when the time was opportune for them to attack. On signal, they burst into the doorways at each end of the A-frame thatched house. Each raider carried as many as a dozen spears on one shoulder, leaving one hand free to thrust spears into anyone who moved. In the darkness and chaos of people screaming, coals from fires getting kicked around, children shrieking, and victims rushing to break through the thatch sides or ends, the raiders always took the chance of impaling one of their own party. If possible, young boys inexperienced in raiding stood outside the house waiting for those who tried to escape through the thatch walls. When the pandemonium had subsided, the raiders grabbed what booty they wanted and set fire to the house with the bodies inside. Before they left, they often destroyed all gardens and anything else that might help those who were not home during the raid. In most cases, they made no effort to pursue those who escaped, preferring to flee home as quickly as possible in case some other households had been alerted and might ambush them.

On occasion, raiders agreed before a raid to spare either someone closely related to them or a girl or woman who could be taken as a wife. For this purpose it was preferable that the raid take place in the daytime, giving much greater opportunity to identify someone and let him—or more often her—live. At such times, women might accompany the men to make it look like a peaceful visit, or just before they burst into a house they might even call out to their relatives within the house, instructing them to grab and hold those they intended to kill. If only children were home, the raiders forced the children to tell where the parents were and when and how they would return. After then killing the children, the raiders could set up an ambush.

Various informants stated that if a raided group had no kin, they would all be killed if possible so there would be no one to retaliate. Some Waorani insisted that if the raided group did have relatives else-where, the raiders tried to spare somebody to discourage the remaining relatives from retaliating—preferably young children, since they were no threat for years to come. (Our data indicate that revenge was always eventually forthcoming, no matter what.) The point may have been to impress upon the absent relatives, by means of a horrified eyewitness account, the ferocity of the attackers and thus dissuade them from a counterattack in the near future.

Upon returning to their own homes, the members of a raiding party usually burned their houses and fled to small, remote, hidden gardens (*wayomo*), where they remained until they were certain that no one was searching for them in revenge. If they suspected that they were being followed, they hung their hammocks in the dense forest up to a kilometer from the hidden garden, building only temporary shelters and not clearing any trees. For the first month after a raid, they followed a number of taboos to purify themselves. After a few months, they sought out relatives to live with for up to a year. They might then return to their old house site, or if they felt that it was vulnerable, they might never return and would instead build at the wayomo or near kin.

Although the vast majority of spearings were conducted in raids on households, occasionally men would single out one individual they wanted to kill and devise methods of isolating and ambushing him. For example, one or two men might invite another to go hunting with them to a location where they knew a nest of birds was ready for blowgunning. They would conspire with another man to hide in ambush so that as the victim raised his blowgun and focused his attention on the birds, the spearer could drive a spear into his back. Or they might reconnoiter a household, determine where a man's trails to his gardens or hunting grounds were, and devise a trap along his trail. In one instance, a man's hunting trail passed through a bamboo patch. The spearer sliced and telescoped one of the bamboo stems into a pattern that appeared it would release when pushed, but instead continued to tighten. He felled that stem across the hunting trail, so that when the hunter came by and encountered it, he started to push it away but found that it would not move. He started to examine it closely, giving the spearer the opportunity to burst from ambush and spear him in the back.

All of these tactics demanded that hamlets and individuals maintain vigilance and develop methods of defense. Houses were constructed with that in mind—situated on hilltops with the trees cleared to the bottom of the hill, giving maximum visibility; doorways constructed intentionally small, requiring one to bend over deeply to enter; thatch kept as tight as possible to prevent entrance without creating a lot of noise, which would alert the occupants. Some houses had vertical palm staves concealed within the walls, and senior males positioned their hammocks at the ends of the houses on each side of the doors. Trails were kept as small and light as possible to avoid leading enemies into the territory. The trails leading up to a house were often footholds chopped into the steep hillsides. Some of those footholds might have three-inch bamboo or *chonta* palm spikes placed in them, covered with leaves. The residents knew where not to step, but a raider pursuing someone escaping down the hill would likely run a spike through his foot.

Since fleeing into the forest alone after a raid was extremely demanding and could even result in death, the Waorani had developed a number of means of increasing their chances of survival when fleeing. First, by planting several gardens, at least a day's travel from one another, families could flee to other gardens and survive. The location of those wayomo gardens was kept secret from all but the closest relatives, and the gardens were planted well away from anyone else's hunting grounds and in a direction opposite of enemy groups. Maintaining a semisedentary lifestyle by rotating between those sites kept obvious signs of use at a minimum, making discovery much more difficult, at the same time that it dispersed pressure on the resources. The neighborhood cluster of friendly houses scattered within a few hours' walk meant that when one house was raided, those who escaped could flee to the others to warn them and escape with them. Also, by keeping possessions to a minimum, the Waorani could flee on a moment's notice, carrying things such as weapons, hammocks, and fire kits with them. Their hammocks, for example, were not tied to posts but were held in place by bones or sticks that could be slipped out of place and rolled up in a matter of seconds.

WAORANI MOTIVES AND CAUSES OF WAR

The causes of Wao warfare can be viewed from at least two levels: the proximate level of immediate, mostly conscious, motivations; and a higher level of functions that must be inferred. When talking with the Waorani, one finds that they refer almost exclusively to the first, conscious emotional level (Boster, Yost, and Peeke 2004). In fact, it would be difficult to overplay the role of emotion in Wao warfare. In answer to the question "why did he/they carry spears to kill x?" the Waorani invariably respond, "because he was angry." Only with lengthy follow-up were we able to elicit what it was that made him or them "angry."

Summarized elsewhere (Boster, Yost, and Peeke 2004) are the recorded immediate causes of raiding, but we present an abbreviated list here, with three provisos helpful in sorting through it. First, among the Waorani, killing was principally a reflection of a burning emotion; it acted to make graphically explicit the extreme to which the negative emotion had reached. Consequently, the killing did not have to have a logical relation (from our Western point of view) between the "cause" and the victim. Second, the time that transpired between the provocation (that is, the "cause") and the killing was indeterminable. He who contemplated killing may have fulminated for months to years, or he may have exploded into the immediate expression of emotion. Third, a Wao man gained status through the display of rage that led to the killing. (We do not believe that a man killed only with the goal of proving himself to the people, but it did serve as an impulse when joined with other provocations that facilitated the killing.)

The listing below serves to give an idea of the variety of ethnographically reported "causes" for a killing. The grouping is one of analytic convenience and does not attempt to reflect any reality felt by the Waorani.

Vengeance/Frustration/Resentment

> For a death for whatever cause: accident, sickness, violence
> For a sickness even though it did not lead to a death
> For a previous killing (vendetta)
> For someone becoming lost in the forest
> For an accident resulting in an injury
> For a killing done by the cowode
> For having hoarded something, food in particular
> For not permitting one to marry
> For the fury that results from an argument
> For a series of events of bad luck, for example, continued lack of
>   success in hunting
> For the birth of a deformed child

Acquisition

Of wives (or husbands) from another group

Of food or material goods, either of native manufacture or from the cowode

Of status and approval in the eyes of the cowode

Prevention

Of the entry of cowode, who presumably would kill and eat them or would carry away children or adults to slavery, or steal their women

Of the taking away of their territory, foreseeing threats real and imaginary

Of an anticipated raid by other Waorani

Of the effects of the actions of a shaman, whether of actions proved or only suspected

Two themes underlie many of these motivations. The first is fear—that others would take preemptive action and raid one before one had a chance to prevent it. The second theme is the occurrence of uncontrollable events such as a death from illness or an accidental injury. The Waorani were extremely confident people who felt very much in control of their lives, but uncontrollable events, such as death, provoked them to intense emotion. They lost control of themselves when they confronted the uncontrollable. On numerous occasions, we observed people erupt into fury at the news that a relative died (for example, of snakebite) in a distant village. In fact, just dreaming that a relative died could disturb someone enough to motivate him to undertake a raid. In most instances, the immediate motivation for embarking on a raid was violent reaction to a stressful situation, such as injury or death; but inevitably, a long-standing unsettled score underlay the action. For example, one man knew that his parents had been killed by Mingi when he was a child. That knowledge festered within his soul. Then, when the timing was right, a seemingly unrelated, minor event—missing a shot with a blowgun—was sufficient to cause him to erupt into exacting revenge. The connection between cause and victim was not necessarily obvious on the surface, but in-depth probing could usually reveal it. Yost's field notes recorded the necessity of constant awareness of these volatile emotions when he wrote of an event in November 1989 in a remote household that had almost no exposure to the outside world:

> while I was filming a garden-clearing scene today River-Otter began felling the last remaining tree in the center of the garden plot. The 120 foot tree forked near the top into two huge branches. As the tree began to groan and lean River-Otter looked up to see his 3 year old granddaughter walk toward him into the clearing directly in line with the groaning tree. He yelled, threw down his axe and leaped from fallen log to fallen log in the garden, yanking her into his arms and stepping aside just in time to have the fork crash astraddle him and his granddaughter. The hair stood up on the back of my neck as I froze helpless on the near side. In an instant I felt horror at the girl's danger. I felt amazement at River-Otter's catlike instinctive response. But the moment it was over I knew without a doubt that I too had just escaped death. If either of them had been seriously injured or killed I would not be leaving alive.

The remaining few days he spent in that hamlet, Yost lived at a level of heightened alertness, watching for signs that the near miss itself could trigger someone into violent action.

The role anger played in war is illustrated in the numerous occasions when raiders returned to the raid site to desecrate the graves of those they killed. Yost's informants underlined this point.

Motmot (female)

Some spearers come back the next day to see whether the bodies have been buried yet. Others wait until the flesh has rotted and bones are all that is left. They dig up the bodies, scatter the bones, [and] take the ritual drinking pot that was left on the grave and hang it up on a spear. "Will he ever drink from that again! His soul will starve now!" If the bodies are still rotting, they throw three spears into them instead of messing with them.

Tiny-Jaguar (female)

When relatives come to see the graves of their dead relatives, they find the bones scattered and bury them again in the same place. This time they don't bother to put the ritual drink on the grave. They get furious, though, and go spear in return. When they spear in revenge, they dig up those people's graves in the same way for revenge.

In addition to reflecting institutionalized responses to immediate emotions, raiding had more long-term consequences, some of them perhaps recognized by the Waorani, others probably not. Chronic raiding functioned at an ecological level to disperse the population and reduce pressure on resources. Some Waorani made this function explicit as they described exactly how closely another group would be allowed to hunt or plant if that other group did not want to risk being attacked. But even in this context, the element of emotion—anger and fear—surfaced.

Fat-Fish (female)

If a nonrelative came and planted nearby, like as close as Wood-pecker's house on the OdaeÁedo River from here, we were angry. "They've come to do us badly," we said. If we went hunting and saw them hunting, we were really scared. If they came and met us and said, "We've just come to live, not to spear," we agreed. But thn later we made spears and went to spear them. If they were relatives, we weren't angry and let it go.

"Others" [nonrelatives] came and built houses over on the Kedemeneno River near Chambira-Palm's grave site. People here saw them while on a sleeping [extended overnight] hunt, became furious, came home, and made spears immediately.

This population dispersal not only reduced the competition for resources and allowed their regeneration but also reduced the impact of disease. The Waorani have been less subject to Old World infectious diseases than their more densely settled former neighbors because their hamlets were small and dispersed. Of course, this epidemiological result was not intentional on the part of the Waorani.

Raiding also had genetic consequences. First, individuals who were mentally or physically marginal were quickly eliminated in the warfare and did not propagate their alleles. Second, because women from outside the usually tiny pool of locally available mates might be captured for wives during raids on more distant locations (including lowland Quichua houses), the gene pool gained variability.

Finally, raiding served to maintain an exclusive territory by keeping other tribal and nontribal peoples off their land. In 1958, such was the reputation of the five hundred–odd Waorani that they were the only human inhabitants of an area the size of Massachusetts.

CONCLUSION

As the historical and ethnographic data presented above demonstrate, the native inhabitants of the upper Amazon needed no help from Europeans to initiate or perpetuate their own wars. The presence of their own native neighbors provided potential enemies. The universal human emotions of fear, grief, rage, and self-protection and the desire to acquire and defend sexual partners, territory, food, and status provided the immediate motives. The presence of the same motives and their consequent behaviors in neighboring groups provided proximate provocations. The basic conditions of evolutionary biology provided the ultimate causes. Most of the motives were, once set in motion, self-perpetuating. The explosion of Old World peoples and diseases into this region altered the context, scale, and consequences of warfare immensely but did not introduce war to the upper Amazon and was not necessary for its persistence.

9 COMPLEXITY AND CAUSALITY IN TUPINAMBÁ WARFARE

William Balée

The term "Tupinambá" denotes a geographic continuum of peoples from the sixteenth century who were united by essentially a common tongue and culture across much of the Atlantic Coastal Forest of Brazil while simultaneously politically divided by acerbic, militant, and lethal intergroup relations (Fernandes 1963, 15–16; Métraux 1948, 95; see fig. 9.1). Tupinambá society proved to be a principal model for European thinkers' views of the Savage, encapsulated largely within the notion of a mirror of their past selves, albeit one displaced in space and, from their peculiarly Western perspective, time (McGrane 1989). The Indians represented a living, transoceanic version of European savagery, the "wild man" (Colin 1999).

The French essayist Michel de Montaigne, a forerunner of cultural relativity, in 1580 published "On Cannibals" regarding the Tupinambá (Montaigne 1933). This essay was based on his firsthand knowledge of Tupinambá Indians who had been brought to Rouen, France, by French Huguenots who had been expelled by the Portuguese from what would one day become Rio de Janeiro, and Montaigne's information derived probably also from the splendid account of Jean de Léry (Lestringant 1999, 37), who had been one of those Huguenots in Brazil during 1556–58 (Léry 1990). Montaigne gave the documented anthropophagy of the Tupinambá the benefit of the doubt when he intuitively compared it to the bloodthirstiness and cruelty of European wars and massacres of his own day, such as the St. Bartholomew's Day Massacre of August 1572, which involved post hoc cannibalism wherein "mobs or individuals, in paroxysms of hatred, threw themselves on the bodies of slain Huguenots and tore into them to devour their hearts or livers" (Whatley 1990:xxviii). Montaigne's account was translated into English in 1603 by John Florio and likely read by William Shakespeare, whose not-so-stereotypical savage (or "salvage" as he is listed in the Dramatis Personae) Caliban (an anagram of "cannibal") in *The Tempest* probably derived from it (Smith 1974, 1607). The scintillating amateur ethnography by Hans Staden (a Hessian harquebusier captured by Tupinambá Indians along the São Paulo coast and held for several months), as related by himself to a ghostwriter and eventually translated from German into Dutch, English, Flemish, French, Latin, Portuguese, and Spanish, launched several hundred years of European home entertainment, in the form of captivity literature. By these and other accounts, the Tupinambá acquired notoriety in the Western world for their alleged cannibalism, warfare, and anarchy.

The Portuguese Jesuits who would translate and describe (as best they could, given the linguistic naïveté of the time) the grammar of the Tupinambá language, called the Língua Brasílica, which in turn would form the bedrock of Língua Geral, the language of Catholic missions in Brazil and the Amazon, claimed that because the indigenous language lacked the letters *L*, *R*, and *F*, by the doctrine of signatures, it was understandable why these Indians also lacked, therefore, "lei" (law), "rei" (king, or kingship, or loosely, the state), and "fé" ("faith" or reli-

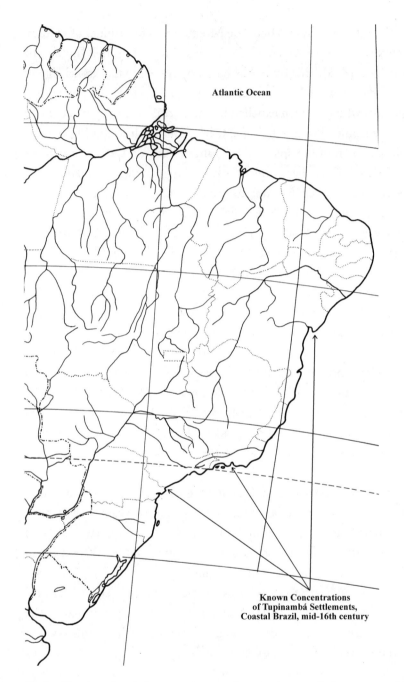

Atlantic Ocean

**Known Concentrations
of Tupinambá Settlements,
Coastal Brazil, mid-16th century**

9.1 Northern South America, showing the ethnohistorically known area of the Tupinambá in the early sixteenth century.

gion) (see Clastres 1995; Lestringant 1999). The savagery that native Tupians instantiated to the European mind was evident in their nudity and, above all, in their cannibalism (Colin 1999, 16–17; Métraux [1950] 1979, 137), itself intimately a facet of warfare because theirs was "exo-cannibalism" (i.e., eating of members of different groups, not one's own [known as endocannibalism], hence associated with violent appropriation of other bodies, other flesh, from their point of view).

It is on the question of "sem rei" (without a king), however, widely remarked upon by their Portuguese-speaking interlocutors—a state of anarchy, or the state of being a nonstate, to sixteenth-century European thinking—that a reassessment of theories on Tupinambá warfare and its motives seems apropos. The key question that arises in examining indigenous political complexity in coastal Brazil is determining whether the Tupinambá, in isolated demographic units or on a large scale along the thousands of kilometers of coastline that they inhabited and held, were organized into something more than autonomous villages, at least during some times, in certain places.

DIVERGENT VIEWPOINTS ON COMPLEXITY

In terms of political complexity and intergroup warfare, two scholarly interpretations have been derived from essentially the same data. Data that exist on the Tupinambá are almost exclusively of a documentary, ethnohistorical character,[1] provided by the *cronistas* (European writers of colonialist accounts of contact in sixteenth-century Brazil, such as Catholic and Protestant missionaries, explorers, and soldiers). Archaeology of the region where the Tupinambá villages were located—eastern and southern Brazil—has mostly focused on the *sambaquis* (oyster shell mounds) that predate agriculture.

One view based on the chroniclers' accounts holds that the Tupinambá basically lacked complexity in this manifold-settlement sense (Fausto 1992, 1997; Fernandes 1963; Sturtevant 1998); the other envisions various Tupinambá societies to have been complex in the sense of exhibiting a social-organizational construct known as the "chiefdom" (Balée 1984; Carneiro 1998; Dean 1995; Noelli 1998). Once one reviews the analytical literature on Tupinambá warfare, likewise two principal schools of thinking may be discerned. One school holds that the Tupinambá of the Brazilian coast exhibited complex warfare patterns above and beyond the level of single, autonomous village raids and feuds (Balée 1984; Carneiro 1998; Dean 1995; Noelli 1998) and that they were (at least some of the time, in given places) involved in conquest of land (fertile, coastal land), not merely subjugation and execution of war prisoners for the purpose of ritual cannibalism and revenge. The other school rejects that proposition and eschews a notion of Tupinambá society as complex or conquest-oriented in any territorial sense, even though the main architect of that school, the late sociologist Florestan Fernandes, recognized that Tupinambá societies had expanded and migrated over a vast land area—most of the Brazilian Atlantic coastline—in a relatively brief though indeterminate period before the arrival of the Europeans (Fernandes 1963).

Indeed, the fact that the Tupinambá language was spoken along coastal Brazil from Maranhão in the north to São Paulo in the south, a distance of more than three thousand kilometers, with only a few exceptions (and these confined to relatively truncated segments of coastline), while Tupinambá societies, by contrast, were in and of themselves numerous, disjunct, and sometimes mutually hostile, represents a challenging research problem. If Tupi-Guarani pottery (a style of ceramics only, not known to be affiliated a priori with a language in prehistory, though it was clearly associated with the ethnohistorically known Tupinambá) appears at circa AD 500, as is widely thought among archaeologists (Brochado 1989), and if (a big if) such pottery was associated with the arrival of Tupí-Guaraní-speaking people, and finally, if these Tupians were not overtly territorial (as a state or an empire), how did the language stay the same for so long across such a vast area?[2]

Such constancy might be expected where one would find some form of centripetal power in the Atlantic Coastal Forest, perhaps as in a chiefdom, or several chiefdoms, depending on the definition of this term. Or was the Tupinambá migration across this immense territory recent, perhaps even within a memory of only two or a few human lifespans?—a plausibility in Bahia, according to the firsthand account of planter Gabriel Soares de Sousa ([1587] 1948, 240; Balée 1984, 248–49; Métraux 1948, 97–98), who noted that the oral accounts of elderly indigenous people there referred to successive waves of invasions in recent memory, by dissimilar groups, until the Tupinambá came to dominate the shorelines. If the migration was that recent, linguistic studies for the age of the language family would have to be significantly revised. In any event, since Fernandes wrote his opinion on the matter, several other scholars have argued against political complexity for the Tupinambá, seeing political autonomy and power essentially distinguishable only within the context of the village (e.g., Sturtevant 1998, after Viveiros de Castro 1992). The data to be presented, however, would seem to justify an evaluation of the Tupinambá as having been at least minimally complex, in political terms.

When one considers causality in Tupinambá warfare, the central issue seems to be whether people fought for trophies, revenge, and other ritualized, emically comprehensible motives that ultimately would have had psychological underpinnings or whether, in contrast, they fought (unconsciously, as though a group motive) to acquire more land, resources, and labor to fuel their expanding population and economy (Dean 1984, 1995), with such expansion, of course, ending abruptly in the sixteenth century, with the arrival of the Europeans, epidemics, and slavery (Dean 1984; Marchant 1942). This latter view would hold up well with "hawks," as Keith Otterbein (1997, 268–69) refers to them; the other view seems to make warfare in simple (nonstate) societies seem more innocent, a view of the "doves," in Otterbein's phraseology.[3] It is hawkish, though I argue essentially correct, in this sense, to reason from the data that Tupinambá warfare had significant effects on land, resources, and people and was not easygoing or uncommon, lacking in severe casualties and other harsh consequences for both winners and losers, and hence to be dismissed as only spurious warfare or mere feuding.

Although no evidence indicates that the Tupinambá and their enemies inland traded in food or shared food (Fausto 1997, 213–14; cf. Balée 1984, 258), a speculation I had earlier offered, the same belligerent parties did engage in formal if temporary cessations of hostility toward one another (Lévi-Strauss 1942, 143; Métraux 1928, 277). The warring parties at such times exchanged luxury goods (especially greenstone labrets and toucan feathers; Métraux 1928, 277). Ironically, these truces constitute evidence for the existence of *real* warfare (Kelly

2000, 105–19). At a later time, in the early colonial period, the coastal Tupí traded iron axes and knives with the interior peoples (Métraux 1928, 277), not unlike the Tupí trade with the Yanomamö of northern Amazonia more recently (Ferguson 1995).

The truces, as evidence for organized warfare, are not incompatible with contemporary observations that the Tupinambá had military engagements involving large numbers (hundreds if not thousands) of opposing forces culled from a multitude of locales. Ethnographer and ethnohistorian Carlos Fausto (2000) would avoid describing Tupinambá society as having been "simple" (perhaps what Kelly [2000] would call "unsegmented"), using the same logic by which he would not argue that modern Tupian societies of the Amazon forests are "simple." This argument is in line with the recently espoused view that aboriginal Arawakan speakers were hierarchical, perhaps even politically centralized, whereas Tupinambá and other Tupí-Guaraní-speaking polities, by contrast, were and still are lacking in such attributes (Hill and Santos-Granero 2001). Some essentialism, perhaps as linguistic reductionism, adheres to this viewpoint, and it does not fare well in light of historical and comparative analysis; for whatever the ambiguities attendant upon Tupinambá complexity, their linguistically and geographically close neighbors, the sixteenth-century Guaraní, by wide agreement, evinced numerous settled maize-growing villages affiliated with large territories subordinated to individual chiefs (Monteiro 1992, 481). Javier Ruedas (2004) has noted inconsistencies and other problems with widespread assumptions in anthropology of pan-Amazonian egalitarianism, in the ethnographic present; in addition, he has noted an essentialist tendency in the usage of concepts such as "hierarchy" to refer to earlier societies of the tropical forest. At least it is clear that political complexity and simplicity are highly nuanced concepts when referring to Amazonia: one is not simply present or absent in ethnographic and ethnohistorical reality. We need operational definitions of these notions. In other words, even if Léry seems to have the upper hand, partly by virtue of being a better writer and having had longer field experience with the Tupinambá, the jury is still out on the extremely different views of what would have been the same or very similar Tupinambá political reality by André Thevet and Jean de Léry (Lestringant 1999). The right answer is somewhere between these two poles.

For Carlos Fausto, the problem with the notion of political simplicity of the Tupinambá is that it usually is rendered in a negative definition, inappropriate to discussing people having intentionality and living in a society with features of its own (1992, 381). He wrote, "We don't intend to affirm that the Tupinambá were very 'simple' like small contemporary Amazonian groups, but, in contrast, that they were not so 'elementary' as these"[4] (1992, 381; translation mine), by which he seems to mean that some kind of complexity (ritual or otherwise, perhaps) can be discerned in what anthropologists have traditionally called "simple, egalitarian" societies. Clearly positive characteristics may indeed be used in delimiting the range and meaning of "simple" societies.[5] Although such a viewpoint, in the context of Amazonian historical ecology, has been similarly expressed by Laura Rival (2002), at least some of the Tupinambá did demonstrably have political organization above the village level, which traditionally among cultural anthropologists indicates complexity.[6]

In perceiving such complexity, one can understand why Tupinambá warfare was often referred to by the sixteenth-century chroniclers and their twentieth-century commentators as "continual" and "constant" (e.g., Métraux 1948, 119) even though truces occurred. Characterizing Tupinambá warfare as simultaneously episodic and frequent is likely more accurate. Frequent warfare, however defined, was not a given of society, but a developmental situation in which the Tupinambá, unlike subsequent Tupian societies of the Amazon region, found themselves.[7] As Robert Carneiro (1998, 27) noted, a pioneer of Tupinambá ethnohistory sympathetic to Léry's viewpoint, the Swiss-born ethnologist Alfred Métraux, did refer to such an example of supravillage organization in Bahia in observing that "some chiefs extended their power over a whole district and commanded a great many villages" (Métraux 1948, 113).

In contrast, Fausto's explanation of Tupinambá warfare is focused on what seem to me to be psychological motivators of behavior that he uses to account for a complex group phenomenon (Fausto 1992) that is perhaps not attainable only at the level of individual village organization based exclusively on kinship (cf. Sturtevant 1998). I do not see this as alien to the position espoused here, but it is insufficient as a single cause of collective behavior, especially that instantiated by warfare; my reasoning on this is related to the very definition of warfare (see below). Fausto's interpretation grasps part of what is in fact a situation of multiple causality (one I too failed to recognize earlier; see Balée 1984). A notion of multiple causality of Tupinambá warfare corresponds to the varied social, political, historical, and environmental contexts in which that warfare played itself out before Paradise, if it ever existed, ceased to be at some point during the contact situation of the sixteenth-century Brazilian littoral.

DEFINING TUPINAMBÁ WARFARE AND POLITICS

Raymond Kelly's recent definitional model of warfare (2000, table 1, p. 7) can be employed to help frame this debate and the rethinking of issues regarding the Tupinambá. Although the model's seven criteria have been seen by some (e.g., Thorpe 2003, 146) as overly restrictive, these permit one to make an intuitively useful distinction between war and other forms of lethal violence, such as feuding and capital punishment. This model allows for more than a negligible sample of peaceful societies also, which in turn enables more sophisticated cross-cultural comparison with control groups (of peaceful societies) that are not simply rare (cf. Otterbein 1997, 260). Kelly's model becomes an especially robust definitional construct when used together with David Fabbro's (1978) eight "criteria of peace" (Kelly 2000, 12).

Indeed, in Amazonia today, one can point to a number of hunting-and-gathering societies within the same linguistic family as the Tupinambá (i.e., Tupí-Guaraní), that share some of the same concepts and lore yet have had only minimal warfare both historically and in the ethnographic present. Their warfare occurred normally only for defensive purposes (as with the Guajá and the Sirionó—among whom I have done fieldwork; the Sirionó are widely considered to be one of the few societies without war [Fabbro 1978, cited in Kelly 2000, 12–13], and the Guajá engaged in it only for defense).

One means of testing propositions concerning the causality of Tupinambá warfare, a phenomenon that essentially ended with the contact-induced extinction of the society and the assimilation of its survivors along the Atlantic coast into a nascent Brazilian identity, toward the end of the sixteenth century, is to look within a language family. To be sure, the Parakanã (Fausto 1997, 2000), who are also Tupí-Guaraní speaking, engaged until recently in frequent warfare, as did the Ka'apor (Balée 1988) and many other Tupí-Guaraní societies known in the ethnohistoric and ethnographic record. As far as I know, these groups did not have episodic truces with their enemies. In other words, once peace was contracted between two groups, as ineluctably occurred between indigenous societies and the national society, intergroup conflicts of the deeply hostile kind that existed previously did not tend to recur. Even if cannibalism (and trophy taking) is an intrinsic, definitional feature of Tupian societies generally, as Eduardo Viveiros de Castro (1992) has suggested, such a feature would not have originated in an abstract context, that is, without historical and environmental underpinnings.

My point is that the Tupinambá had episodic but frequent warfare related to aspects of their developmental history, their political organization, their migratory expansion, and the biological richness of their habitat. Other internal factors, such as the marital requirement of a man to kill an enemy, preferably just before a cannibalistic feast (Fausto 1992), were no doubt operative, but in and of themselves, they do not well explain the origins of Tupinambá warfare and its continuation in late prehistory and into the early colonial period.

The argument best suited to the data suggests that the Tupinambá constituted minimally complex societies in the process of expansion at the time of the European conquest. The Tupinambá were expanding at the expense of other societies in a physical space essentially limited by the extent of the Atlantic Coastal Forest (which does not mean, contra linguistic reductionism, that Tupian societies cannot exist outside such milieus—the Chiriguano [or Bolivian Guaraní] have since the sixteenth century lived in the Andes and adjoining piedmont, and the Avá-Canoeiro have since probably the eighteenth century been a people of the *cerrado* country of central Brazil). The Tupinambá fought both people who shared their language and culture and those who did not; they fought enemies from the interior savannas as well as enemies along the coasts they either occupied or would come to inhabit.

Tupinambá warfare seems to have possessed much in common with that of complex societies (especially chiefdoms of various types) elsewhere. Psychological motivators of behavior are not likely to be able to explain this warfare by use of comparative ethnology, because the same factors are not present in other societal situations. However, the political and environmental features associated with the context of Tupinambá society are not unique and can be found in other parts of the world where prehistoric warfare was deemed to have been frequent or intense, with or without truces. Statistical evidence leads one to expect frequent warfare between dissimilar groups in a favorable habitat in terms of its biotic diversity, a relatively high population density, a relatively complex political order, and well-established rules of engagement of forces as well as means for contracting truces (Kelly 2000; Otterbein 1970).

Let us examine directly Kelly's criteria (2000, table 1, p. 7 et passim) for the existence of war and decide on the evidence whether the Tupinambá meet any of them.

1. "Collective armed conflict." The Franciscan friar and royal cosmographer of King Charles IX of France, André Thevet (1944, 225), in 1557 wrote that warfare involved "villages against villages,"[8] while Lopes de Sousa referred to naval engagements involving tens of canoes with numerous determined fighters inside each one (cited in Hemming 1978, 35). Hostile engagements between enemies involved groups (i.e., collectivities), and these groups bore arms, principally the bow and arrow and the club (Balée 1984, 253).

2. "Collectively sanctioned by participants' community." The rewards for going to war were potentially great for a young man; inflicting vengeance on one's enemies by capturing one or a few of them, executing them, and consuming their flesh in grand feasts involving all of society was the only ritually approved way he could acquire a wife from his community (Fausto 1992, 391; Moore 1978, 182–83). Elsewhere I have criticized reliance on this view of causality in Tupinambá warfare (Balée 1984, 246–47) on the basis of its being circular—as a cause, revenge only begets revenge. Jonathan Haas (2003, 7) more recently has noted, "Although a revenge motive may continue a pattern of war beyond its initial causal conditions, war is ultimately a costly alternative that is not self-sustaining." Haas (2003) indicates that the causal conditions for warfare on a regular basis are rooted in the Neolithic, the origins of agricultural society.

On the Tupinambá, Fausto (1992, 391) stated, "The principal objective of the warring expeditions, whether small or large in scale, was to take captives to be executed and eaten in the public square" and "Revenge, thus, was embodied in society: it was necessary that everyone have his vengeance" (translations mine).[9] The argument in fact dates back to the 1570s, in the writing of Léry (1990, 112). One could argue that revenge was part of the psychological manifestation of motives that would lead individuals to risk their lives in combat, and combat was risky, since not all victims of warfare were taken on the battlefield alive—some were shot or clubbed and died at the scene (Léry 1990, 118). Those who were taken alive, especially males, were sacrificed later. Fausto (1992, 392), citing Viveiros de Castro, sees this revenge pattern not so much as tit for tat, but as the socially approved means of reproducing and expanding society itself. It is not, however, in and of itself contradictory of the primordial combination of political complexity and conquest-oriented warfare.

3. "Morally justified in participants' viewpoint." This is the case, for in slaying a prisoner, the killer claimed to be gaining vengeance for his previously slain kinsmen, considering kinship to be at the basis of any system of morality. It was, as Fernandes pointed out (1963, 311), a question of "honor." Léry (1990, 113) likewise noted that the Tupinambá near Rio de Janeiro considered war against their enemies to be a matter of "honor."

4. "Participants esteemed by others of their collectivity." The ritual slayer of a prisoner, himself a warrior who captured the prisoner, was awarded a series of honors for his deed, such as taking new names that would in turn be sung and repeated, and his wife or wives as well could take as many new names as captives her husband had killed (Fausto 1992, 392; cf. Métraux [1950] 1979, 142).

5. "Entails organized, planned, and premeditated attack(s)." Hans Staden (1929, 152, quoted in Balée 1984, 253) wrote that "when they desire to make war in an enemy's country the chiefs gather together and take counsel how best to achieve their purpose."

6. "Serves identifiable instrumental objectives (e.g., defense, revenge, excision, appropriation)." All these factors were involved in Tupinambá warfare, as discussed in the other six items here.

7. "Social substitution governs the targeting of individuals for lethal violence." This criterion is what distinguishes warfare from capital punishment—a particular, known individual is not targeted, but rather, any member of the enemy group can represent an appropriate target for killing or capture. The anonymity (or social substitution) of Tupinambá warfare is evident in a passage written by Léry (1990, 118), who witnessed a battle near Rio involving thousands of warriors from opposing forces:

> As soon as they were within two or three hundred feet of each other, they saluted each other with great volleys of arrows, and you would have seen an infinity of them soar through the air as thick as flies. If some were hit, as several were, they tore the arrows out of their bodies with a marvelous courage. . . . When they finally met in hand-to-hand combat, it was with their wooden swords and clubs, charging each other with great two-handed blows; whoever hit the head of his enemy not only knocked him to the ground but struck him dead, as our butchers fell oxen.

The concept of social substitution not only was applied to Tupinambá military engagements but also was embedded in the kinship system, for they had the levirate (Métraux 1948, 112), and the children of a local woman whose father had been a war captive could also be executed and eaten, indicating a concept of patrilineal transmission of status (as either edible or inedible). Another indicator of social substitution is Tupinambá classificatory (bifurcate-merging) kinship terminology (Fernandes 1963, 205–13; see discussion in Kelly 2000, 47).[10]

COMPLEXITY AND WARFARE

In terms of these seven attributes of war, Tupinambá battles qualify as warfare. Using this definitional construct of warfare, warfare would be expected even if the Tupinambá were not politically complex (if they were an unsegmented society, in Kelly's terms) and if intergroup conflicts were spontaneous (as opposed to planned), because the area they lived in was rich in resources, both aquatic and terrestrial (similar to the Andaman Islander case study that Kelly reviews) and their population density was much higher than 0.2 persons per square kilometer (Kelly 2000, 136); indeed, Tupinambá population density in the coastal zone of São Paulo and Rio de Janeiro has been reliably estimated at 9 persons per square kilometer (Dean 1995; cf. Dean 1984). The point I am making is that the internal characteristics of Tupinambá society relating to motive factors for war, such as a seemingly unquenchable thirst for revenge, ritual cannibalism, trophy taking (as with necklaces made from dead enemies' teeth—Métraux 1948, 107), the wish by both men and women to acquire new names (Fausto 1992; Métraux 1948, 116), and the hope of a man to acquire a local wife, may be less related to the origins of Tupinambá warfare than to aspects of their habitat and demography.

To be sure, not all cases of Tupinambá wars involved the conquest of land. Léry, ever the dedicated Calvinist and ultimately antiroyalist (Lestringant 1999), wrote, "These barbarians do not wage war to win countries and lands from each other, for each has more than he needs" (1990, 112). But it is significant that some cases did involve such conquest, and most wars involved the capture of prisoners as well as the killing of enemies.

The Tupinambá could be expected to have had intensified warfare after it began in this milieu, and such intensification is evidenced by their displacement of enemies from particular locales; this was well documented regarding the forced removal of the Tapuya people by the Tupina people and the subsequent removal of the Tupina people by the Tupinambá people along the Bahian coast shortly before the Portuguese arrived (Métraux 1948, 98; Soares de Sousa [1587] 1948, 240). Another aspect of the intensification of fighting among the prehistoric Tupian peoples of the coast would have been resource concentration, or circumscription (Balée 1984, 244–45; Carneiro 1998, 32). Some of the concentrated resources were soils appropriate for agriculture; fish; aquatic mammals (manatees); shrimp, lobster, and, in mangrove forests, crabs; and shellfish (Balée 1984, 244). Circumscription is seen in a fairly narrow band of Atlantic Coastal Forest defined by two starkly different adjoining areas, both nonforest, being the ocean on the eastern side and mountains, savanna, or steppe country on the western side (Balée 1984).

Political complexity is usually dependent on numbers of people that, as aggregated multitudes, exceed individual village populations. What can be said of Tupinambá villages and their typical size? The arithmetic mean from a sample of six estimates of longhouse size, at different times and places in the sixteenth century, is 104 persons (Balée 1984, 255). The median is 75, and the standard deviation is an uncomfortably large 77. Even if the typical longhouse (*maloca*) contained only about 30 persons, however, a distinctly plausible though conservative number (for a more liberal estimate, see Dean 1984), given the limitations of the ethnohistoric sample, that number is already comparable to modern village sizes of groups with dispersed settlement patterns in the Amazon region, and these usually had been ravaged by epidemic disease shortly before censuses were taken. The point is, with more than one longhouse per village and each longhouse being the size of a contemporary Amazon village, village size was larger in the coastal forest than in modern Amazonia. What we see today is thus not what existed in prehistory (Heckenberger et al. 2003; Roosevelt 1989).

How many longhouses were there per village (a question I [Balée 1984] asked independently of Warren Dean [1984])? Again, the data are scant and variable, but suggestive. The arithmetic mean from a sample of five sixteenth-century estimates (Balée 1984, 255) is 2.11. The median is 7.25, and the mode is 4. Even if typical villages only had four longhouses per village, continuing with this conservative statistical reasoning, the typical village population would be 4 × 30 = 120. Such a number is probably far below what the villages in the most heavily populated Tupinambá areas—such as coastal Rio de Janeiro, the São Paulo coast, and Bahia—were like (Dean 1984, 1995).

Military expeditions also present certain statistical problems, with widely varying eyewitness numerical estimates (Dean 1984) and small sample sizes of these. At least it is clear, however, that these numbers were in the hundreds, since the lowest known estimate is 300 (Carder 1906, 140). Eyewitness Jean de Léry saw a battle on the beach in which one side (the side he happened to be on) had in arms "about four thousand" fighters (Léry 1990, 118); that number is very close to the arithmetic mean from six estimates that I had calculated at 4,422 men (Balée 1984, 254). If Léry is to be believed, this Tupinambá society near Rio de

Janeiro in the sixteenth century was a chiefdom using Sturtevant's criteria (1998, 141) or a maximal chiefdom using Carneiro's criteria (1981). Eyewitness Staden saw military expeditions in the hundreds of men under arms (1929, 104). This leads me to conclude that if typical village numbers were somewhat more than one hundred but expedition sizes exceeded that number, we are dealing with prehistoric collectivities of forces from at least two villages.

That armed constellation of persons from diverse locales in singly united formations, risking their lives together as it were, apart from bonds of kinship and residence, suggests, accordingly, the existence of political leadership above the village level. Perhaps such leadership amounted to power over only a chieftaincy (Redmond 1998, 3) or a minimal chiefdom (Carneiro 1981; see discussion on this concept by Otterbein [1997, 268]). But probably in certain cases, especially near the São Paulo and Rio de Janeiro coastlines, political power exerted by Tupinambá chiefs in warfare over large numbers of warriors was much more centralized than that. Those polities are what I mean when I stated earlier that Tupinambá societies were *at least* minimally complex. That political complexity, the richness of resources in the habitat, and the circumscription of the habitat are more connected to the origins of Tupinambá warfare than are psychological motivators, such as a burning inner craving to avenge the killers and eaters of one's kinfolk. Such motivators would have been associated principally with the perpetuation of warfare and its emic acceptance by the community, not the episodic yet frequent and intense nature of warfare as it unfolded over time along the Brazilian coastline.

NOTES

1. Sturtevant (1998, 140) has pointed out that the ethnohistorical data on the Tupinambá are probably superior to those of any other sixteenth-century New World society except the indigenous states of Mesoamerica and the Andes.

2. I am indebted to Eduardo Viveiros de Castro (pers. comm., 2002) for discussion on this point. Also see Sturtevant 1998, 142. The actual estimates for the time of arrival of people speaking the Tupinambá language (or something very close to it) vary widely, as is to be expected where considerable inferring

is drawn from depauperate data. Scholars over the centuries have been fundamentally in disagreement as to where the ancestral Tupinambá first arrived, and how and in order of which cardinal directions their migratory journeys took in colonizing the Atlantic Coastal Forest (as reviewed in Susnik 1975, 7–10). Somewhat discordant estimates of Tupinambá arrival dates on the coast, however "recent," moreover, doubtlessly reflect a certain amount of conjecture. In modern times, the late historian Warren Dean suggested a time frame of AD 1 to AD 700 for a Tupinambá arrival along the Atlantic coast (1984, 5); ethnohistorian John Hemming proposed a date of about AD 1000 for the same event (1978, 51). Fine-grained linguistic research may help elucidate the time frame at some future point.

3. Otterbein's division of scholars on indigenous warfare into hawks and doves does not refer to their moral or political views on the validity of warfare (Otterbein 2000a). It also does not reflect on their conceptualization of human nature. Few cultural anthropologists would disagree with Otterbein's comment, "Man is neither, by nature, peaceful nor warlike" (1997, 272). Otterbein's usage of these terms differs also from Santos-Granero's use of the terms *hawk* and *dove* in another South Americanist context (Santos-Granero 2000).

4. "Não pretendemos afirmar que os Tupinambá eram tão 'simples' quanto os pequenos grupos amazônicos atuais, mas, ao contrário, que eles eram tão 'não elementares' quanto estes últimos."

5. In referring to the "tribe" of Australian Aborigines, Kenelm Burridge (1973, 128) wrote, "We think of a tribe as a group of people who speak the same language or dialect; who regard a particular portion of land as their own even though rights of exploitation, economic or religious, may be subdivided among individuals or sections of the group; who think of themselves as forming a unity as against others; who give themselves a name to express this unity; amongst whom intermarriage is possible; who are as though kin, or who can address each other in terms of the kin idiom."

6. Michael Heckenberger and colleagues (2003; one of the coauthors of the article is Carlos Fausto) discuss complex prehistoric polities of the upper Xingu River basin, to the west of the Atlantic Coastal Forest in north-central Brazil, dated from ca. AD 1250 to AD 1650. If such complexity could exist contemporaneously in a relatively rich resource area, such as the well-attested case of the upper Xingu, and if complexity also existed in the Amazon and Orinoco River basins (Roosevelt 1989), as it arguably did in the Llanos de

Mojos (Erickson 2000), one might have difficulty in specifying factors that would have precluded similar complexity in the Atlantic Coastal Forest, the occupation of which predated agriculture.

7. Those subsequent Tupian societies were all unsegmented, a category of society to which the only ethnographically known warless societies pertain, which for Kelly (2000, 44) are defined as societies that "manifest only those social groups that are cultural universals, present in every society, and nothing more. . . . There is no level of organization beyond the local community (although there is a sense of shared language and culture that extends outward to adjacent communities, and diffusely beyond these as far as is known and is applicable)." Tupinambá society was not unsegmented by this definition.

8. To be sure, Thevet expounded on the Tupinambá as though they lived in a monarchy, in contrast to Léry, who tended to emphasize what he considered to be their egalitarianism (Lestringant 1999). But in the implication that Tupinambá warfare tended to involve fighting men from multitudes of villages against like, complex formations, the two Frenchmen, one Catholic and the other Calvinist, seemed to be in implicit agreement.

9. "O principal objetivo das expedições guerreiras, seja de pequeno ou grande porte, era fazer cativos para serem executados e comidos em praça pública." "A vingança, assim, era socializada: era necessária que todos se vingassem" (Fausto 1992, 391). This echoes the view of Florestan Fernandes (1963, 311), who, in quoting Yves d'Evreux, a French missionary also, wrote, "The *vendetta* was seen as a necessary solution, given that the Tupinambá believed 'their honor depended on vengeance.'" ("A *vendetta* era encarada como uma solução necessária, pensando os Tupinambá que 'sua honra depende de vingança,'" italics in original, translation mine).

10. In this specific sort of substitution, however, complexity is not necessarily entailed. Dravidian forms of nomenclature, which equate cross- and lineal relatives, in fact tend to be associated with simpler (or nonsegmented) societies (Viveiros de Castro 1998), though not always; this contrasts with Iroquois terminology, found with more complex societies (Viveiros de Castro 1998) and exhibiting highly descriptive forms of kinship terminology or those that lack bifurcate-merging. These include Sudanese, which was the system used by many European languages of the past and by contemporary Sudanic languages (Murphy 1989, 133), commonly associated with societies that are not merely "simple."

10 HUNTER-GATHERERS' ABORIGINAL WARFARE IN WESTERN CHACO

Marcela Mendoza

Hunting and gathering societies of the South American Western Chaco presented a threat to Europeans who began settling the fringes of this area in the mid sixteenth century. Colonial chroniclers described Western Chaco indigenous groups as nomadic and brutal nations, without permanent homes or property but with so many warriors that, had the Spaniards not arrived, these warlike peoples would have conquered and decimated the more sedentary indigenous agriculturalists who lived in nearby valleys. For example, in 1584, Captain Hernán Mejía Miraval reported to the Spanish governor of the Tucumán Province that he had captured and killed many Western Chaco Indians, recovering scalps and trophy heads that they had taken from their enemies (Cabrera 1910, 17). European expansion has been credited with suppressing the violent resistance of the indigenous groups and pacifying the region. Lawrence Keeley calls this explanation for imposed pacification "one of the apologies for imperialism during its heyday" (1996, 150). Much has been written about the conquest of Gran Chaco by the Argentine, Bolivian, and Paraguayan armies; however, the study of the intergroup aboriginal warfare that continued in Western Chaco until the beginning of the twentieth century has received little attention from ethnographers.

Following the anthropological literature, I consider the raids and feuds of the hunter-gatherers of the region as unique forms of collective violence explained in terms of complex models that include environmental, behavioral, and sociocultural variables (Rubinstein 1994). Intergroup warfare in the region largely preceded the arrival of the Europeans and continued until the early twentieth century. The aboriginal warfare among hunter-gatherer societies of Western Chaco from 1875 to 1925 manifested as aggressive resistance to the encroachment upon their land by European settlers and colonists. Thoroughly defeated by the Argentine, Bolivian, and Paraguayan military, the indigenous Chacoans' resistance ended in the second decade of the twentieth century. Furthermore, the Chaco War (1932–36) between Bolivia and Paraguay eliminated the indigenous peoples' prospects of continuing a lifestyle of seasonal trekking in their home ranges. This chapter examines the territorial expansion of the hunter-gatherer bands, the shift in range areas, and the socially unstable relations between neighboring groups with reference to demographic packing—a measure of population density per square kilometer that evaluates the productivity of different habitats in relation to the size of the group (Binford 2001). My interest in this subject developed while conducting fieldwork among the Western Toba in the late 1980s and early 1990s.[1]

Indigenous Peoples of Western Chaco

The Gran Chaco is the second-largest natural biome of South America. In the heart of the continent, it extends over one million square kilometers in area. The semiarid Western Chaco includes eastern Bolivia, northern Argentina, and western Paraguay (fig. 10.1). Chacoan ethnic and linguistic groups have been known as "tribes" since colonial times. These independent ethnic groups speak mutually understandable variants of the same language and recognize the existence of social ties and cultural similarities among themselves; their modus operandi was characterized by continuous coalition building and offensive raids during which scalps, captives, and booty were taken. In the last quarter of the nineteenth century, the inhabitants of Western Chaco north of the Pilcomayo River comprised the Ayoreo and Chamacoco (Zamuco linguistic family); the Toba and Pilagá (Guaycurú linguistic family); the Izoceño, Chiriguano, Guarayo, and Chané (Tupí-Guaraní linguistic family); the Kaskihá, Sanapaná, and Enxet (Maskoi linguistic family); and the Chorote, Wichí, Nivaclé, and Maká (Matako-Maká linguistic family).

Chacoan hunter-gatherers made their living through a combination of hunting rhea, guanaco, peccary, tapir, deer, and other small animals, collecting xerophytic seeds and honey, and fishing. They occasionally planted maize, pumpkins, melons, beans, and tobacco to supplement other foraging activities. However, planting did not tie them to the land in permanent settlements (Steward and Faron 1959, 415).

The Chaco region is both an ancient and a dynamic population nucleus. The region contains one of the few heterogeneous clusters of Paleo-American hunter-gatherers that can be associated with prehistoric routes of migration (Salzano and Callegari-Jacques 1988). Current inhabitants are descendants of prehistoric hunter-gatherers who entered the basin over eight thousand years ago from different directions and adapted their foraging economies to a new natural biome. Latin American anthropologists call these societies "typical chaquenses" (typical Chacoan inhabitants). Mitochondrial DNA analysis indicates that Chacoan groups have the highest genetic variation and the lowest intergroup variability when compared to other population groups, such as tropical forest, Andean populations and the indigenous peoples of Tierra del Fuego–Patagonia—who appear to retain the phenotypic and genetic traits of the first settlers of the Americas (Demarchi et al. 2001; González, Dahinten, and Hernández 2001). Chaco genetic diversity is explained as a product of gene flow, most probably favored by the bilateral kinship system and uxorilocal residence pattern prevalent among the hunting-and-gathering bands (Braunstein and Miller 1999). Small exogamous social units would send their young males out to marry

10.1 The Gran Chaco region, with the approximate location of the major indigenous ethnic-linguistic groups.

and exchange information with other units; females were incorporated through both marriage and warfare. Fission and fusion mechanisms of social aggregation would have facilitated the dissemination of genes and culture within linguistic-ethnic groups and also among different ethnic groups in the past, as much as it effectively occurred in historical times.

SOCIAL EXCHANGES

Chacoan linguistic-ethnic groups have made alliances, fought, and traded with each other frequently, as reported in ethnographic and historical sources. Intermarriages and fictive kinship arrangements formed the basis for trade and alliance among hunting-and-gathering bands and between hunter-gatherers and horticulturalists. For example, the Chiriguano and Chané would trade garden products with Chorote and Wichí; the Toba would trade dry fish for maize with neighboring Wichí (Tebboth 1989). In 1908–9, the Chorote and Nivaclé would trade skin cloaks and wool for shell beads and European goods with the Enxet (Nordenskiöld [1930] 1979, 136). Trade and social exchange created the conditions for disagreements and violence (Sterpin 1993). In analyzing the causes of ethnographic warfare, Lawrence Keeley says, "To varying degrees, then, many societies tend to fight the people they marry and to marry those they fight, to raid the people with whom they trade and to trade with their enemies. Contrary to the usual assumptions, exchange between societies is a context favorable to conflict and is closely associated with it" (1996, 126).

Chacoans either raided one another's camp to avenge a previous attack or forged alliances to trade goods and participate in seasonal gatherings that included ritual dances and drinking feasts. During the dry season (called the "hungry season") at the end of winter and beginning of spring, folks from different bands gathered together to play a ball game resembling hockey, to dance, and to drink fermented beverages made of honey. During those gatherings, they organized war parties against neighboring groups. In the 1990s, I recorded oral stories from Toba elders about hockey games and fiestas celebrated among Toba bands and neighboring Tiagaiquipi and Cagaic'pi bands at sites called Paso de los Tobas and Toba Quemado.

SOCIALLY UNSTABLE TERRITORIES

The presence of large herbivores adapted to open country suggests that the Gran Chaco was open grassland long before human occupation. A surplus of dry vegetation covered the grassland during the dry season, when the animals migrated to riverine areas in search of water. Chacoan indigenous peoples would burn dry bush for hunting, warfare, and communication purposes, clearing large patches of land every year. The indigenous peoples' management of fire favored the dispersion of grass and herbaceous species not adapted to grazing. Fire intensity and frequency declined in Western Chaco after colonization by campesinos (small-scale cattle ranchers who display a cultural and genetic mix between Europeans and aborigines).

Western Chaco hunter-gatherers had flexible, egalitarian, and individualistic social structures similar to the social structures of the indigenous peoples of northern North America (Riches 1995). The social units I call bands are coresidential groups of related families who would trek together (and share food) in the same ranges. They considered each other as relatives and were identified with proper names. Band members explain the notion of "range" as the habitual exploitation of the same area. Members of other bands in the same linguistic-ethnic group were advised of the extension of the ranges habitually trekked by each social unit, yet they would hunt and gather in those ranges if they needed to. The ranges trekked by each linguistic-ethnic group were separated by buffer zones that included common-pool resources. These particular resources are characterized as being so widely available to all that any attempt to exclude other potential consumers from obtaining benefits from their use would prove too costly (Eerkens 1999).

These regionally oriented, mobile, hunter-gatherer-fisher Chacoan societies eventually negotiated among themselves socially unstable territories that would have taken into account the presence of newly arrived populations (Dortch 2002; Pereira, Bergman, and Roughgarden 2003). Geographically stable territorial systems are most likely to form when resources are relatively abundant and occur predictably (Baker 2003); when resources occur predictably but are relatively scarce, the result may be a home range system where some kind of ownership exists but is never exclusive because the costs of defending exclusive ownership rights are higher than the benefits of negotiating reciprocal access to natural resources (Cashdan 1983). As resources get even scarcer, cohabitation of two groups in the same habitat becomes less likely, and the group with the greatest fighting ability may obtain the whole patch.

The warlike Toba of Western Chaco exercised their fighting ability to occupy the best patches in the home ranges of other ethnic groups.

Social units that shared the same territory would not normally fight among themselves, but ethnographic accounts indicate that unannounced foraging in the home range of a band, damage to fish weirs, and unauthorized appropriation of food kept in storage have been immediate causes for retaliation and vendetta raids between neighboring ethnic groups, well into the twentieth century.

In the late 1800s, the land north and south of the upper Pilcomayo River, between latitudes 23°15' and 23°35' South, was inhabited almost exclusively by indigenous groups. North of the river (then Bolivian Chaco), the Toba occupied the ranges previously trekked by Nivaclé-Tiagaiquipi and Wichí-Cagaic'pi bands. Historical and oral records indicate that these three neighboring groups have adopted contentious attitudes and fought each other. At times, the Toba raided Tiagaiquipi and Cagaic'pi campsites, taking captives, scalps, and booty. At least two Toba camps along an old dry river course are named after fights with the Tiagaiquipi. In turn, the Tiagaiquipi and Cagaic'pi raided Toba camps and destroyed their fish traps during the height of the fishing season (Mendoza 2002).

South of the Pilcomayo, Wichí-Viac'pi and Wichí-Damacapi bands occupied the land. In 1995, I interviewed Wichí-Damacapi adults who recalled that Toba warriors had driven their ancestors away from the land south of the Pilcomayo River, a territory that the Wichí still consider their own. Some Toba bands regarded the Damacapi as friends; other Toba bands would fight them whenever unprotected Damacapi families were found in the country. In general, the Toba say that the Damacapi are adversaries with less stamina than the Cagaic'pi, Viac'pi, and Tiagaiquipi people. In fact, the Damacapi resented the Toba for a long time.[2]

By 1900, the Toba had driven away the Wichí and Nivaclé from creeks and lagoons rich in natural resources, both north and south of the Pilcomayo. Toba oral tradition carries on memories of many algarrobales (groves of algarrobo trees) and highly productive pescaderos (fishing spots) surrendered by previous occupants.

Aboriginal Raids and Feuds

In Western Chaco, warfare was a collective enterprise against other social units defined as "enemies" and viewed at the moment as a threat. Different authors have mentioned retaliation for previous raids as a common cause of aboriginal warfare. "Behind the blood-feuds," wrote Rafael Karsten ([1932] 1979, 103), "there are often earlier quarrels, especially about boundaries." Foraging, fishing, and pasturing flocks in the ranges habitually trekked by another ethnic group without asking permission were considered trespass and could cause a blood feud. For example, Giovani Pelleschi ([1881] 1886), who visited Western Chaco in 1875, said,

> Each nation of Indians has its own territory and will go to war over the smallest patch of land as we would. These wars are very frequent for the many reasons set down elsewhere and because of the marauding spirit which dominates the Indians—thus it is that whenever they learn that a tribe has become rich, for one reason or another, in animals or belongings, they try to despoil it by surprise. These actions are always followed by deaths, wounds and imprisonment, which are cause enough for new wars, made without warning, to which end each has informers and spies in the other camp.[3]

War raids were organized to surprise-attack the enemies in their villages; the warriors were expected to take booty and captives and return with scalps. The leaders of the bands were warriors who had killed an enemy during a war raid and could display head trophies and scalps. The warriors acquired prestige and supernatural power from their victims' scalps. The Toba said that the women would encourage their husbands to participate in raids, in part because the women overestimated the amount of food available in their neighbors' villages during the season of scarcity. The women reasoned that their neighbors were enjoying abundance while their own children were hungry.

War parties worked on carefully planned schemes. When the Toba planned an attack on another group, old men and warriors in allied social units gathered together at the campsite of one of the convening bands. Shamans made invocations to the spirits, and the men drank a fermented beverage and performed dances in anticipation of the coming victory. Sexual abstinence and body painting prepared them for the war expedition. Members of a war party would pierce their skins with peccary bones to gain strength and fierceness. They would pierce themselves with charata bird bones to rise up early during the journey and with owl bones to be able to see and fight in the dark.

The Toba used to attack at nighttime—preferably a moonlit night, not during the "dying" moon—but the Wichí always attacked at daybreak. In 1929, ethnographer Alfred Métraux documented an encounter between Toba and Wichí near Pozo del Tigre in the Argentine Chaco: "In consequence of that conflict, the Wichí made prisoner a Toba woman, but later on they surrendered her to her people for a payment" (1939, 117).

Before the raid, some men were sent out as spies with the purpose of getting as much intelligence as they could on the daily routine of the enemies' village. As Karsten observed, "In their actions they exercise the greatest prudence, rarely fighting in a body, and trying to overthrow the enemy with as little loss of life to themselves as possible" ([1932] 1979, 106). The targeted village was surrounded in silence, and the warriors communicated among themselves with cries that imitated nocturnal animals. At a signal, they made a sudden attack, entering the huts and killing the inhabitants. If they succeeded in taking the victims by surprise, the warriors would kill those who were not able to escape. Younger women and children from other ethnic groups were incorporated into the bands of their captors and socialized as band members.

All the hunter-gatherer societies of the Pilcomayo River were scalp hunters. The head of the slain enemy was cut off, and the scalp was stripped from the skull and kept as a war trophy. "Shortly before I arrived at the Pilcomayo in 1911," Karsten wrote, "the Nivaclé had succeeded in killing nineteen Bolivian soldiers who were marching down to one of the military settlements on the river. The heads of the young men had been cut off and taken home by the Indians. Later on it was reported that their scalps or skulls, fixed on long poles, decorated the entrance of the main Indian village, being used at the great feasts as drinking-cups which were believed to inspire the drinkers with courage" ([1932] 1979, 107).

The stamina associated with the act of killing, sometimes described as "courage," actually refers to a mystical prowess that only a few men had. The act of killing was extremely dangerous, since the assassin would become polluted by the blood of his victim and could be threatened by the victim's avenging spirit. The warrior who had killed an enemy in battle, as much as the hunter who had succeeded in killing a carnivore such as a jaguar, underwent the appropriate ritual of purification involving both prayer and seclusion (Susnik 1990). Hunters would pray over the animal just killed and bring it to camp, and then they would rest and avoid strenuous activity for a period of one or two days. Warriors participated in public rituals to celebrate victory and made themselves and their weapons clean through fasting and isolation. The Toba believe that fortunate hunters as much as successful warriors—those who were not injured in raids and brought back booty and scalps—owed their success to the supernatural aid they received from their spirit guides.

ENCROACHMENT ON THE LAND

In the early sixteenth century, before the arrival of European colonists and settlers, the Western Toba bands lived in the Andean foothills near the upper Pilcomayo River (Karsten [1932] 1979). The various Toba bands spoke the same language, shared a hunter-gatherer-fisher subsistence strategy, and celebrated periodic gatherings that strengthened alliances among social units. As a result of their successful adaptation, the bands grew in size and split into smaller groups. Some recently separated Toba groups of the Bolivian Chaco began expanding to the southeast, fighting their way down the river through lands occupied by the Chorote, Wichí, and Nivaclé. This Toba territorial expansion could have been triggered by the migration of Amazonian Tupí-Guaraní-speaking peoples into the Andean foothills (reportedly in the mid fifteenth century). The newly arrived Chiriguano horticulturalists limited the expansion of the Toba to the north and actually occupied part of their former territories. Thus, the influx from indigenous migrations as well as the incursion by campesinos resulted in great pressure being placed upon the natural food resources of the Western Chaco area.

Western Chaco indigenous peoples had been organized in small bands of hunters and gatherers focused on the exploitation of wild animals and terrestrial plants, occupying subsistence ranges over which the groups moved. For a long time, population density apparently remained low in relation to the availability of plant and animal resources in the water-depressed microenvironments of Western Chaco (Mendoza 2003). As population increased, new groups formed, reducing the subsistence area used by any given group and resulting in increasingly packed ranges.

As a reasonable response to increased regional packing, Chacoan hunter-gatherers began to use aquatic resources more extensively and started practicing some horticulture. They also began to keep sheep and goats, probably as early as the sixteenth century. Using the resources more intensively, the social units augmented their dependence on food storage and developed some kind of "ownership" (in the sense of excluding or limiting the use of resources by other social units) over the best fishing spots and the most profitable patches in their home ranges. Nevertheless, the bands did not hold exclusive rights over the land where they commonly trekked and could not deny others access to the resources. The notion of ownership in hunter-gatherer societies is sometimes construed by saying that others who want to exploit the resources must "ask permission," although "permission" cannot be denied to those who ask—the first campesino settlers who established their cattle ranches in the Toba home ranges actually asked permission of the leaders of the bands.

CAMPESINO SETTLEMENTS

The expansion of Europeans into the region drastically reduced the ranges of movement of the indigenous peoples and pressured their relocation to less productive areas, considered an out-of-limit frontier by the settlers. While other typical Chacoan societies living in Eastern Chaco adopted the horses brought in by European colonists and became equestrian foragers, most of the bands in Western Chaco remained nonequestrian. These foot foragers were familiar with horses, but they had domesticated a limited number of animals when the cattle ranchers began moving into their territories.

Several authors studied the hunter-gatherers' resistance to colonization in the Chaco region (Carrasco and Briones 1996; Gordillo 2001, 2002; Saeger 2000). Indigenous bands formed alliances to fight the settlers and the military of the Argentine, Bolivian, and Paraguayan states. In 1883, for example, the expedition commanded by Lieutenant Colonel Rudecindo Ibazeta fought a coalition of indigenous warriors along the banks of the Pilcomayo River. A coalition of Toba, Wichí, Orejudos, and a few Chiriguanos attacked the soldiers. According to Juan Baldrich (1889), the official reporter of Ibazeta's expedition, in the combat that took place on August 1, 1883, the indigenous coalition numbered more than 800 warriors, 152 of them on horseback. In 1903, in the same area, 60 Toba warriors approached the expedition of the Argentine colonist Domingo de Astrada and proposed a pact: the Toba war party would join the explorers to attack a Nivaclé village and take the possessions of the Nivaclé and divide the booty equally (Astrada 1906). In 1908, the ethnographer Erland Nordenskiöld arrived in a Tapiete-Guarayo village in the Bolivian Chaco shortly after they had looted some Tsirakua-Ayoreo huts. "The entire collection of loot was disposed of to me," said Nordenskiöld, "in exchange for some few trifling articles of barter goods" ([1930] 1979, 141). Nordenskiöld also recorded the following observation: "When the Nivaclé Indians were at war with the Toba, the children of the Nivaclé villages used to play war. I have also seen children splitting into two groups, one representing the Whites and the other representing the Indians" (1912, 60).

Campesino settlements had been limited to the borders of Western Chaco until the last quarter of the nineteenth century in Argentina and until the 1930s in Bolivia and Paraguay. Once the Western Chaco came under the control of these nation-states, cattle ranchers were able to spread through the plains—away from the watercourses—using pond and well technology. Extensive ranching favored continuous grazing of free-ranging mixed herds of cattle, goats, sheep, horses, and donkeys. Only the distance to artificially constructed ponds and wells limited the ranges of the herds during the dry season. Continuous use of the mixed herds' overlapping ranges led to severe overgrazing and rapid degradation of the pastoral cover. This once-rich landscape was severely degraded during the twentieth century (Bucher and Huszar 1999; Riveros 2003).

WARFARE AND COMPETITION OVER RESOURCES

Competition over diminishing resources has been identified as an important cause of aggression and deadly violence in hunter-gatherer societies (Gat 2000a, 2000b). According to a comparative study by Keeley (1996), territories changed hands among hunter-gatherers at a rate of 5 to 10 percent per generation—equivalent to the United States losing or gaining California, Oregon, and half of Washington every twenty-five years.

Aboriginal warfare in the Gran Chaco has been recorded since the mid sixteenth century. In a gradually more encroached-upon environment, Chacoan hunter-gatherer groups married each other, traded, and attacked their neighbors while adjusting their strategies of food procurement (foraging, fishing, horticulture, herding) to fit new modes of subsistence. In the last quarter of the nineteenth century, Western Chaco hunter-gatherers had just passed the demographic packing threshold, estimated by Lewis Binford (2001) at about nine persons per hundred square kilometers for small groups of mobile hunter-gatherers dependent upon terrestrial plants in similar environments. The mean value for each Western Toba band in the early twentieth century was seven persons per hundred square kilometers. However, the actual packing value was probably much higher because the bands' ranges overlapped extensively within the territory habitually trekked by the Toba (Mendoza 2002, 119, table 10).

Although the indigenous ethnic groups of Western Chaco may have trekked widespread and overlapping ranges in the past, by the nineteenth century they had come to occupy narrowed contiguous home ranges. As their home ranges were encroached on, the natural resources turned scarcer. In this situation, trespassing and unauthorized use of resources were immediate causes of retaliation and vendetta warfare. In 1911, ethnographer Rafael Karsten observed, "These limits are commonly recognized, and trespassing, when it is willfully done, may become cause of war" ([1932] 1979, 103).

Chacoan hunter-gatherers devised special weapons, apparel, and rituals to practice warfare, handle human trophies, and reward the most courageous warriors with social prestige and spiritual wisdom. Older warriors would tutor motivated young males in each of the bands to take the warpath. Warfare brought booty and captives to the groups, and also—equally important in a threatened territory—served as a deterrent for intruders. The leaders of the bands were courageous warriors who had killed enemies and could exhibit human trophies.

This "state of endemic warfare" (Renshaw 2002, 225) was over by the 1930s. As ranchers and colonists completely occupied the land and military expeditions defeated the indigenous resistance, those once-mobile hunting-and-gathering bands became increasingly sedentary. Young men in search of prestige and spiritual wisdom occasionally raided the ranches of campesino settlers in the early 1940s, but these attacks ceased as a result of the joint efforts of the local police officers and the settlers. The indigenous groups renounced those violent forms of resistance and developed new types of leadership (transitional leaders instead of warriors who had killed an enemy), native brokers who learned to compromise with the nation-state, while the people developed novel subsistence strategies to complement their foraging activities (including wage labor and craft production) during the second half of the twentieth century.

NOTES

1. Fieldwork 1984, 1985, 1987, and 1988 was supported by grants from the Argentine Council for Scientific Research (CONICET). In 1993–95, I received generous support from the Graduate College of the University of Iowa and CONICET.

2. In 1875, the Italian traveler Giovani Pelleschi ([1881] 1886) collected trophy heads and a scalp of Toba warriors killed by the Wichí-Damacapi. Pelleschi wrote that on one stormy night, while he was staying at a Wichí camp, a warrior approached him asking for the head of the Toba: "The Indian grabbed the skull with his left hand, and as though possessed, started to claw at it and to stick his fingers into the eye-sockets and gaping mouth and then into his own mouth as though to suck them, all the while jumping about and shouting confusedly." This paragraph of Pelleschi's writings was retrieved from the Human Relation Area Files (eHRF Collection of Ethnography) on September 23, 2003. Available in electronic format at *http://ets.umich.edu/cgi/e/ehraf*.

3. Retrieved from the Human Relation Area Files (eHRF Collection of Ethnography) on September 23, 2003. Available at *http://ets.umich.edu/cgi/e/ehraf*.

11 THE STRUGGLE FOR SOCIAL LIFE IN FUEGO-PATAGONIA

Alfredo Prieto and Rodrigo Cárdenas

Fuego-Patagonia is located between 39° and 55° latitude in South America. Archaeological evidence confirms the presence of human populations in this region as early as 11,000 BP (e.g., Massone 1987; Nami 1987; Prieto 1991). The ethnohistorical record describes at least five cultures that can be grouped into two kinds of economies:[1] the "canoe" economies of the Yámana and Káweskar cultures, and the "terrestrial" economies of the Aónikenk, Selk'nam and Haush cultures (fig. 11.1). In addition, canoe and terrestrial economies were also combined to form economies that were dependent on both maritime and land resources (Borrero 1997).

YÁMANA AND KÁWESKAR

The Yámana inhabited the southern coast of Tierra del Fuego, in the areas approximately between the Brecknock Peninsula and Sloggett Bay, on down to Cape Horn. The Káweskar occupied the western archipelagos of southern Chile, approximately from the Gulf of Peñas to the Brecknock Peninsula. Both populations are estimated to have reached about 2,500 individuals during pre-Columbian times (Cooper 1946a, 83).

Both Yámana and Káweskar were specialized in the exploitation of maritime resources. Their hunting technologies included harpoons, spears, wooden clubs, slings, bird snares, and to a lesser extent, the bow and arrow. For gathering activities, they made use of forked spears and developed a highly specialized form of basketry. Both groups used tree-bark canoes as a mode of transportation and for carrying out their economic activities.

The Yámana territory was divided into five areas, each with a distinctive linguistic dialect. Each of these five areas was subdivided into kinship-based groups, which had exclusive rights over the territory they occupied and its resources. The Káweskar society was also divided into small kinship-based groups; however, their territories were more loosely defined (Bird 1946).

SELK'NAM, HAUSH, AND AÓNIKENK

Tierra del Fuego was the homeland of the Selk'nam and the Haush. The Selk'nam were subdivided into a northern group that inhabited the northern steppes and a southern group that inhabited the area south of Río Grande. The Haush inhabited the southeastern region of Tierra del Fuego in the Mitre Peninsula. The Aónikenk, in contrast, occupied the continental territory south of the Santa Cruz River in Argentina down to the Straits of Magellan. During pre-Columbian times, the Selk'nam population is estimated to have consisted of about 3,000 individuals, the Haush population of less than 1,000 individuals, and the Aónikenk population of about 3,000 people (Gusinde 1982; Lothrop 1928; Martinić 1995).

Both the Selk'nam and the Aónikenk hunted land mammals, while the Haush depended upon maritime resources. The main hunting weapons of these three groups consisted of the bow and arrow, spears, slings, bolas, and occasionally clubs.

The Selk'nam were divided into kinship-based groups, with each group occupying its own territory and having exclusive rights over its resources. The land of Tierra del Fuego is estimated to have been divided into 82 territories: 69 Selk'nam, 11 Haush, and 2 Káweskar (Chapman 1982).

Although with different strengths, all Fuego-Patagonian societies had a gender-based division of labor. Men were dedicated mostly to hunting and fishing, as well as to the manufacture of weapons. Women, in contrast, were responsible for gathering, childcare, domestic activities, and the manufacture of domestic utensils.

Archaeological and ethnohistorical evidence indicates that violence has always been present in these societies. The numerous sources of social conflict include interethnic (e.g., ethnic conflict, colonization) and intraethnic (e.g., domestic violence, violation of property rights) factors, and several social institutions have been developed to regulate the use of violence. The specific dynamics of violence in pre-Columbian times can be inferred by focusing on the development of violence during European colonization. Ultimately, this review is intended to provide direction for future studies on how patterns of violence have shaped social life in Fuego-Patagonia.

EVIDENCE OF VIOLENCE IN THE ARCHAEOLOGICAL RECORD

Archaeological evidence of violence during prehistoric times in Fuego-Patagonia is scarce, which might partly be attributable to the lack of systematic studies in this regard. All of the archaeological remains that we discuss below were located in what historically has been known as Aónikenk territory.

René Verneau (1903) was the first to present archaeological evidence of violence in Fuego-Patagonia, in the form of a human sternum containing an arrowhead that had become lodged in the bone after penetrating the victim through the back, found in Chubut, in Argentinean Patagonia (fig. 11.2). A more recent study (Gomez-Otero and Dahinten 1999) describes a burial site located in Chubut that dates

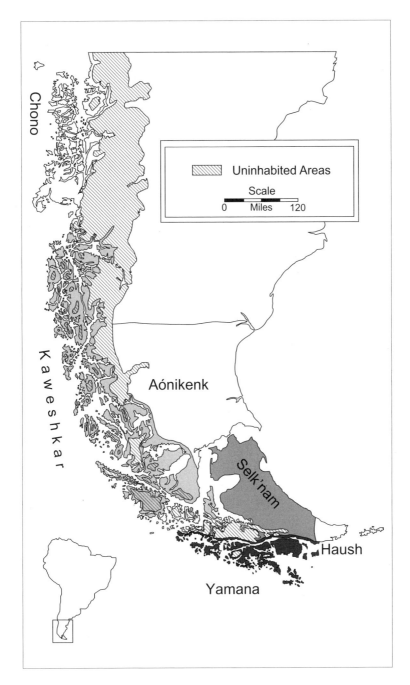

11.1　Fuego-Patagonia, indicating the location of the Indian groups. (Adapted from Butland 1957, fig. 11)

to the sixteenth century in which there is evidence of an exchange of high-status products, such as European glass beads, as well as metal artifacts. In this burial site, projectile points were found between the ribs and scapula of two adult men. Whether there was a relationship between the exchange of valuable goods and violence is unclear; however, the exchange of goods has been proposed as an aid in avoiding warfare (Clastres 1987).

A study conducted by Gustavo Barrientos and F. Gordon (2003) in Argentinean Patagonia presented evidence of traumatic injuries in 24 of 102 skulls. Two of the skulls contained fragments of arrowheads. Along the northeastern coast of the Straits of Magellan, an injured skull of an Aónikenk male aged forty to forty-five was discovered (Constantinescu 2003). The skull had two injuries that were produced by a sharp object in what appears to be the result of a close-contact fight. One of the injuries contained a fragment of green obsidian, but subsequent analyses have determined that the obsidian did not come from an arrowhead. In addition, this individual was able to recover from both injuries. The green obsidian source is probably located in the western region of the Straits of Magellan and was exploited by the canoe people (ancestors of the Káweskar) for at least 6,500 years. Green obsidian was considered very valuable, as indicated by its broad distribution throughout the region and its frequent use in the manufacture of lithic artifacts.

Although these studies provide valuable insight on violence in Fuego-Patagonia, they are still few in number, and researchers thus have difficulty in gaining an understanding of the global patterns of violence that existed in these societies. Many factors may have contributed to the low presence of violence in the archaeological record.

First, there are no systematic archaeological studies analyzing episodes of violence. The evidence documented so far is the by-product of research aimed at analyzing other archaeological problems (e.g., distribution of burial sites in a particular region).

Second, human burial sites are very difficult to find in Fuego-Patagonia because the native people lived and traveled in small groups, of at most twenty individuals, dispersed throughout an immensely broad region. As a result, burials occurred sporadically throughout the region, making the discovery and recovery of human remains arduous.

For instance, about half of the human skeletal collection housed at the Centro de Estudios del Hombre Austral in Punta Arenas has come from nonspecialists who accidentally discovered and donated the skeletons.

Additionally, most osteological collections have not been reliably dated. The information available for these skeletons is primarily in the form of estimates based on their association with other archaeological remains. Such estimates are inaccurate, as attested by the human remains obtained by Junius Bird in Cerro Sota in the 1930s (Bird 1988); these were considered the remains of the first human populations in the region (about 11,000 BP) but are much younger, dating only to 3900 BP with radiocarbon and accelerator mass spectrometry analysis.

The archaeological preservation of evidence of violence in human remains is also affected by the mortuary customs of Fuego-Patagonia, which varied temporally and geographically. Bodies may have been cremated, laid under a pile of stones or in a cave, buried in the ground, or simply left out in the open and exposed. Moreover, coastal and inland human remains have different taphonomical and archaeological characteristics (Guichon, Barberena, and Borrero 2001).

In the continental area of Fuego-Patagonia, the most visible mortuary structures are *chenques*: graves covered with piles of stones and generally placed on the tops of high hills. Customarily, after a body remained in the grave for a given period of time, the chenque was opened so that the bones could be defleshed and then put back in the grave. When chenques were located far from the coast, the bodies were transferred to a final grave close to the sea (Massone, Prieto, and Cárdenas 1985–86). On the Atlantic coast, enormous fields of chenques have been found, and some of the graves were found without human remains (Castro and Moreno 2000). The elevation of some graves is quite remarkable. The highest known burial site is located on Cerro Guido at the edge of a cliff, about one thousand meters above sea level.

The Káweskar placed cadavers in small caves. Corpses were often decorated with paint (Legoupil and Prieto 1991) and personal ornaments and were placed on structures made of painted sticks and animal skins. This type of mortuary practice usually resulted in natural mummification. The oldest burial site known of for the archipelago region dates to 4500 BP (Legoupil 2000).

11.2 A human sternum with an arrowhead penetrating it. (From Verneau 1903, plate XII)

Finally, we must consider the potentially damaging impact that scavenger animals have on human burial sites (see Martin 2003). Burial sites located in small caves have a greater chance of being destroyed by animals looking for food, and this is especially true for caves located in the steppe region; those in the archipelago region are for the most part left unharmed due to their isolation.

Thus, the lack of archaeological evidence of violence may not necessarily be because of low levels of violence in Fuego-Patagonia but instead may be attributable to the nature of the cultural and taphonomic processes affecting the formation of archaeological sites, and to the lack of systematic research exploring this issue. For a better understanding of the patterns of prehistoric violence in Fuego-Patagonia, the ethnohistorical record must therefore be analyzed as well.

ETHNOGRAPHIC EVIDENCE OF VIOLENCE

THE DEMOGRAPHY OF HOMICIDES

Probably the best-documented demography available of homicides is of the Káweskar. In 1948, Joseph Emperaire completed a demographic survey from which he constructed a genealogy that included 396 individuals and covered a period of about sixty to eighty years (at the time, only 61 of the individuals represented in this genealogy were alive). The demographic data describe homicidal deaths for 24 members, which is rather high for a society not regularly engaged in large-scale warfare; homicide was the cause of 13.5 percent of all adult deaths and 19 percent of all male adult deaths (Emperaire 1963, 82). Emperaire noted that these homicides were related predominantly to robbery and sexual affairs and that all lethal violence (either against women or against men) was carried out only by men. Finally, the data show that approximately half of all homicides were the result of intraethnic conflicts. Although these demographic data offer only a rough approximation of the levels of violence during prehistoric times, the survey does provide an idea of the frequency of such conflicts as well as of the most common causes that triggered violence.

Emperaire argued that the frequency of homicides among the Káweskar had declined rather than increased during the twentieth century. As he pointed out, the indigenous population in the region suffered a very steady and steep decline throughout the period of European colonization, and he concluded that this alone may have reduced the number of opportunities for engaging in violent conflicts (1963, 83). Martin Gusinde (1996) supported a similar idea with respect to Selk'nam violence during the beginning of twentieth century.

Gusinde also noted that indigenous territorial displacement produced by European colonization contributed to increasing conflicts in societies with strong institutions defining exclusive territorial rights, as with the Selk'nam. Trespassing on territories without authorization was the principal source of conflict. After Europeans began to territorially displace the Selk'nam from the north of Tierra del Fuego during the fourth quarter of the nineteenth century, conflict started to increase not only between the Selk'nam and the Europeans but also within Selk'nam society as a consequence of the displaced Selk'nam invading southern territories that were inhabited by other Selk'nam groups (Prieto 1994). However, because of the steady reduction of the Selk'nam population during that period, such temporary increases in violence among the Selk'nam most likely only reduced the amount of warfare over time.

Records dealing with homicidal behavior among the Yámana are also available. Between 1871 and 1884, the missionary Thomas Bridges registered twenty-two homicides among this group, which amounts to a homicide rate ten times that of the United States (Cooper 1946a, 95; Keeley 1996, 29). Gusinde, however, has argued that Bridges' report is an underrepresentation of Yámana homicides, because both indigenous and European informants told Gusinde that the number of murders was at least twice that amount (Gusinde 1961, 891).[2]

We can also get a sense of the frequency of violent acts by examining the oral traditions of these groups in a collection of Fueguian myths (Wilbert 1975, 1977). About 30 percent of the fifty-nine Selk'nam myths and about 27 percent of the sixty-six Yámana myths describe episodes of violence. Most of these myths describe homicides normally performed exclusively by male characters, which seems to be a defining characteristic of the patterns of violence among Fuego-Patagonian societies.

THE TECHNOLOGY OF VIOLENCE

Hannah Arendt (1969) argued that the patterns of violence within a society depend on the technological sophistication of weapons: technological revolutions lead to changes in violence. Therefore, a first step in understanding the social patterns of violence in Fuego-Patagonia is to identify the technology and the social distribution of weapons.

Ethnohistorical data suggest that the instruments used for hunting and gathering in Fuego-Patagonia were largely the same instruments employed for carrying out violent acts (e.g., the bow and arrow, slings, spears, and clubs). The data also show that only two artifacts were specially made or modified to be used as weapons for violence. Lucas Bridges (1950, 223), describing one such artifact, noted that Selk'nam men generally removed the barbs of their arrows when using these to punish their wives, a measure apparently taken to prevent the punishment from becoming lethal. Another such artifact, used by the Aónikenk, consisted of a thick armor and helmet, which were made of animal hides and used during combat for protection against arrows (Cooper 1946c; Martinić 1995).

As mentioned previously, in each ethnic group only men were responsible for hunting. This exposed men to the weapons that would eventually be used in combat: skill in the use of hunting weapons entailed skill in using weapons for violence. Because hunting weapons were more or less equally distributed among the male population, nearly every man could use them competently; in other words, there was a generalized capacity in the male population to perform deadly attacks on enemies. At the same time, because the division of labor entailed these kinds of weapons exclusively to men, the tools of violence, particularly long-range weapons such as the bow and arrow, were not equally accessible to women.

Correlated with the concentration of weapons in the male population is the fact that most documents describe men as the main agents and targets of lethal violence. This is not to say that homicide against women, or by women, did not occur; instead, violent behavior against women was nonlethal and punitive in nature, and lethal violence carried out by women was rare.

Intraethnic Violence

Marital violence   Almost every ethnographic account of Fuego-Patagonian societies noted the widely held belief of male authority over women. However, a closer look shows that the status of women varied between each society. For example, although the Yámana did not have a matriarchal society, the division of labor within this society gave equal importance to both sexes, and women were not excluded from central Yámanan ceremonies (Chapman 1997; Cooper 1917, 1946a; Gusinde 1961). This is not true, however, of the Selk'nam, who had a strong patriarchal society (Chapman 1982) and whose women were socially and economically subordinated to men. In fact, Selk'nam patriarchal ideology portrayed women as the enemies of men.[3] In addition, most high-status roles and important ceremonies were exclusively reserved for men, and women were severely humiliated in such ceremonies (Chapman 1982, 1997; Gusinde 1982).

The difference in the status of women in the Yámana and Selk'nam societies is also illustrated through the mythological origins of hunting weapons. For both cultures, women were considered the primary inventors of hunting weapons. However, for the Selk'nam, the woman responsible for creating hunting weapons was believed to have been an evil and selfish person and, as the myth goes, was later murdered by a male hero. In contrast, the Yámana creator of weapons was portrayed as a caring sister who only wanted to help her two brothers, the Yámana cultural heroes. There is no story of subsequent murder in the Yámana tradition.

Nevertheless, independent of the social status of women in these two societies, the ethnographic record indicates that male violence against women was much more common than female violence against men. Gusinde, who generally held an idyllic view of marital relations among the Fueguians, wrote the following about Selk'nam men: "He gets into a certain state of complete loss of judgment, and ridiculous trifles or his own bad mood may cause him to beat his wife with sticks, to wound her on the body with scratches of an arrow point, to abuse her with insulting reproaches, and, finally, to let her go hungry. She herself will never offer resistance; at most she crawls under the covers or holds her arms before her face and head, in order to ward off the blows" (Gusinde 1996, 513).[4]

One of the most frequent causes of marital violence was adultery. Written records indicate that adultery was common even though it was morally condemned. This is illustrated in several Yámana myths describing male punishment of an adulterous wife, which often resulted in the homicide of both the wife and her lover by her husband.[5] Violent punishment against adultery was more commonly inflicted on women than on men. The husband alone inflicted punishment against his wife; in contrast, the wife's relatives were the common agents for carrying out violent punishments on an adulterous husband. In Yámana society, an adulterous husband could have been murdered by his wives' relatives if he continued in his unfaithfulness (Gusinde 1961). Although qualitative accounts of these ethnic groups indicate that marital violence only rarely developed into homicide (e.g., Gusinde 1961), the scarce amount of quantitative data available places marital-related violence as one of the major causes of homicide, at least in Káweskar society (Emperaire 1963).[6]

In Selk'nam society, girls were taught to be obedient to their husbands, to be "attractive, busy and silent" (Chapman 1982, 89). A woman who did not follow the will of her husband would often suffer violent punishment. Lucas Bridges, for instance, described the case of Koiyot, a Selk'nam man who broke his wife's leg with a wooden club after she refused to go to work (1950, 382).

Spousal mistreatment could often lead to a situation in which the abused wife along with another man or her relatives would plan her abduction (or liberation), which often led to warfare (Gusinde 1996, 460). In Selk'nam as well as in Yámana society, family members would avenge abuses that were committed against a close relative. In other words, every person enjoyed, up to certain extent, the protection of blood-related kin. This may have prevented marital violence to escalate to homicide, but when lethal violence did occur, family members of the victim retaliated against the murderer, and subsequently the murderer's kin also became involved in the conflict.

Involuntary abductions also occurred. During warfare, the winning side would abduct the women and children of their defeated rivals. Gusinde (1996) argued that Selk'nam men did not regularly engage in warfare to obtain women. However, when abductions did occur, only an influential man, such as a powerful and feared shaman, benefited from such action. Bridges noted that women who were abducted involuntarily were very likely to suffer abuses:

When badly treated, women took the first opportunity to give their captors the slip, though, if they were caught by their new husbands before they could get back to their own people, they run the risk of being soundly beaten or arrowed through the legs with arrows from which the barbs have been removed—generally. A wife of long standing, if she obstinately refused to do her husband's will, was just as likely to be thrashed or arrowed. The clumsy, blundering Chalshoat shot his arrow a little too high when he once administered such punishment, and killed his wife. The women never forgave him for that. (Bridges 1950, 223)

CHILD HOMICIDE   Child homicide was rare but not absent. Among the Yámana, infanticide was practiced when the newborn was considered deformed.[7] As for the Selk'nam, most ethnographers agree that they did not regularly practice any form of infanticide (Bridges 1950; Gallardo 1910; Gusinde 1982). Gusinde expressed in the following terms the opinion of one of his informants: "If a [Selk'nam] baby perishes because of the carelessness or negligence of the mother, she is severely beaten, even though we all know that she did not want to murder her child" (Gusinde 1996, 553).[8]

Another rare instance of child homicide occurred during warfare. Sometimes, because of the institution of avenging the murder of kin members, a child may be murdered because of being the relative of a murderer. Bridges knew of only one such case among the Selk'nam, the killing of Shijyolh's two young sons, a situation that he described as "an unheard-of crime" (1950, 315).

INTRAETHNIC WARFARE   Among the ethnic groups inhabiting Tierra del Fuego, warfare consisted of small attacks involving about twenty men from each side (Cooper 1917, 1946a,b; Gusinde 1961, 1996). These conflicts were common, particularly among the Selk'nam, a circumstance that led some European travelers to state that "they lived in constant war" (see Gusinde 1996, 628). These conflicts did not involve fixed war tactics or strategies; rather, ambushes and surprise attacks were the most common form of assault (Gusinde 1996, 625). For this reason, the attacking group usually outnumbered the group being attacked.

Gusinde described the development of one of the last wars among the Selk'nam:

A final war in the old Indian way of fighting developed around the turn of 1900. . . . The cause was that a certain Felipe had murdered his opponent from the group on the Rio Irigoyen in the forest. The family of the dead man unjustly accused the kinfolk of Tenenesk, attacked them with a powerful force, raged very cruelly, and mercilessly strangled many women and children. On this occasion the two brothers of Tenenesk were killed and he himself received three arrows deep in his back. His group, which had been attacked, numbered only eleven men, whereas there were some 20 warriors on the opposing side. Seven months later, Tenenesk, with his own people and many helpers, set out for vengeance against the old enemy; a total of 30 persons were said to have been killed at that time. (1996, 632–33)

The Selk'nam very rarely took males captives; instead, wounded enemies were killed (Gusinde 1996, 128; Lothrop 1928, 88). However, as noted above, the Selk'nam did sometimes capture women, who were subsequently taken as wives (Bridges 1950, 295; Gallardo 1910). The Aónikenk have also been reported to have taken woman and child captives (Cooper 1946c; Fitz-Roy [1839] 1966, 166).

Usually only men participated in these combats, although women have occasionally aided a wounded relative by attacking the enemy (Bridges 1950; Chapman 1982). Bridges described a battle in which a Selk'nam warrior killed seven women after he discovered them cutting his uncle's body into pieces (Bridges 1950, 386; Gallardo 1910, 316).

As previously mentioned, revenge was one of the most common causes of conflict between groups. In Yámana and Selk'nam societies, blood revenge was institutionalized: the duty of the nearest kin member of a murdered victim was to avenge the death of his relative (Bridges 1950; Gallardo 1910; Gusinde 1961, 1996; Lothrop 1928). In this regard, Gusinde observed, "The desire and passion for revenge are extraordinarily emphasized among the Yámana" (1961, 406), a characteristic that he also found prevalent in Selk'nam society (1996, 624) and one that is commonly reported of the Káweskar (Emperaire 1963) and Aónikenk (Cooper 1946c; Martinić 1995). The amount of time that passed before revenge was sought was relative, with years sometimes elapsing before retaliation took place.

Insults could also trigger social conflict. Gusinde noted that the Yámana were continually preoccupied with monitoring the behavior of others as a way of detecting any possible offenses made against them. This peculiar behavior made social life very difficult in groups that were larger than the size of the nuclear family. In this regard, Samuel Lothrop noted that "when two [Yámana] groups camped together, trouble usually arose, and the weaker group moved away. This as well as the quest for food accounts for their frequent changes of residence" (1928, 164).

Insults and individual conflicts were also dealt with through duels. These duels involved the use of weapons, such as the bow and arrow among the Selk'nam (Gusinde 1996, 647) or bolas among the Aónikenk (Cooper 1946c, 152). A man known only as Montravel observed that among the Aónikenk, the wounded were buried without any type of ceremony, treated as cowards, while the victor was glorified (in Martinić 1995, 279). Duels were critical for social status, although apparently only men took part in them.

The infringement upon territorial rights also resulted in warfare (Cooper 1946c; Fitz-Roy [1839] 1966; Gusinde 1996; Martinić 1995; Viedma 1910). Each ethnic group had exclusive rights over the resources of the territory it occupied. Trespassing was forbidden to nonmembers unless the owners of the territory gave special authorization. Although war was not apparently utilized to acquire land (Gusinde 1996, 629), the ethnographic record describes a few cases of territorial expansion as a consequence of warfare (Chapman 1982).

A shaman may also be the cause or target of intergroup conflict. Of the Selk'nam, Bridges noted that the shaman (*xo'on*) was feared and respected by the rest of the community. The principal work of a xo'on was to cure illnesses by extracting objects (generally arrow points) believed to be the cause of the disease. More skillful and powerful shamans were believed to have the power not only to cure but also to inflict illness, even to the point of death. This is why shamans were the targets of violence in the event of a sudden death, especially when it happened under strange circumstances, because the victim's relatives might suspect that a shaman of a rival group used sorcery to murder their relative. For the same reason, shamans were also known to promote war against other groups or rival shamans by portraying their own enemies as dangerous. Shamans enjoyed prestige and some limited authority in these societies; however, because of the nature of their social role, as well as their highly visible social status, the cost of being a shaman was high. Bridges indicated that "frequently the chief object of a riding party, in the perpetual clans warfare of the Ona [Selk'nam], was to kill the medicine-man of an opposing group" (Bridges 1950, 264).

According to Montravel (in Martinić 1995, 305), circa 1840, twenty-one Aónikenk shamans were killed because they were believed to have supernaturally caused an epidemic that resulted in the deaths of more than two hundred individuals. By that time, the Aónikenk had come to live in big groups occupying a much larger territory, thanks to the introduction of the horse. The horse and the expansion of mobility, larger group size and hence the weakening of kinship ties, and the emergence of caciques were factors that created new socioeconomic and sociopolitical organization that consequently led to the development of new patterns of warfare.

Not all conflicts provoked by a homicide resulted in further homicides. For instance, among the Yámana, two opposing groups would conspicuously enact displays of rage and threaten each other with their weapons. The dispute would be over after a brief combat, resulting in a few injuries but no fatalities. The avengers would then solicit gifts in compensation for the loss of their relative (Bridges 1950; Gusinde 1961). Montravel described a similar situation for the Aónikenk, who would sometimes end an immense battle as soon as one person had died or had been seriously wounded (Martinić 1995). Bridges (1938, 1950) described a peacemaking ceremony practiced among the Selk'nam in which warriors would hand to members from the opposing side about five arrows with the arrowheads removed and replaced with a solid covering of thick hides. Afterwards, the warrior would move approximately sixty yards away from his enemy and begin to trot toward his opponent while dodging the arrows that his enemy vigorously attempted to shoot him with. This ceremony provided an opportunity to solve intraethnic conflicts through the display of each participant's athletic and hunting skills, an opportunity to gain social status or to lose face but without any lethal violence.

Direct interethnic contact was regulated by the geographical distribution of the ethnic groups. The Yámana engaged in interethnic relations with the Káweskar, Selk'nam, and Haush; the Selk'nam had direct contact with the Haush, Yámana, and Káweskar; the Káweskar with the Selk'nam, Yámana, Aónikenk, and Chonos; and the Aónikenk with the Káweskar and Mecharnúekenk.

The ethnohistorical record is not precise with respect to the frequency with which interethnic contact occurred. Gusinde (1961) argued that interethnic contact between Fueguians was only occasional, mainly because there were no demanding economic motivations to engage in such contact and because of the very arduous task of crossing the geographical obstacles that separated the regions the various groups occupied.

In any case, interethnic contact did occur, as indicated by the flux of primary sources and customs. For example, the Yámana and the Selk'nam shared some of the same myths and ceremonies (the *kina* ceremony and the *hain* ceremony, respectively). Ethnographers have also made note of the Haush influence on Selk'nam culture. For example, Gusinde discovered that the Selk'nam sang a war song whose lyrics were in Haush; Selk'nam men disclaimed knowing either the ethnic source of the song or the meaning of the lyrics (Gusinde 1982).

Because the frequency of intergroup contact is unknown, the frequency of violent conflicts between these groups is also unclear. John Cooper (1917) affirmed that interethnic contacts were "fairly peaceful"; however, the ethnographical record provides several indicators that such contacts were also violent. One such indicator is that the Káweskar, Yámana, and Haush have been described as being afraid of the Selk'nam (Bridges 1950; Gusinde 1961). Bridges, for instance, mentioned that the few Haush people he met told him that "[Selk'nam] were very bad men and had slaughtered many [H]aush" (Bridges 1950, 194). Another indicator is the description of latent interethnic conflicts by European explorers. For instance, during Pedro Sarmiento de Gamboa's expedition in 1580, three Káweskar men captured to be used as guides incited the Spaniards to kill the people of another ethnic group whom these three men accused of always being at war with them (Oyarzún 1976,

139). Robert Fitz-Roy also reported similar circumstances when two natives they brought with them on their expedition, York Minster and Jemmy Button, told them to open fire against men in Cabo Peñas, saying that "they were 'Oens-men' [Selk'nam] very bad men" ([1839] 1966, 119). Finally, Eugène Pertuiset (1877) reported that in the region around Useless Bay, an area of contact between Selk'nam and Káweskar, he observed the Selk'nam forcing the Káweskar to fish for them (Chapman 1982, 161).

A third indicator of interethnic conflict is the fact that the few Fueguian myths on interethnic relations narrate hostile encounters between ethnic groups. For example, two Selk'nam myths describe the homicide of a powerful Selk'nam shaman by Yámana people (Wilbert 1975, 89). In addition, Gusinde reported that the Yámana felt repugnancy toward the Káweskar because they thought the Káweskar were involved in cannibalism (1986, 237–38). This belief is expressed in two Yámana myths describing the journey of one Yámana group through Káweskar territory, and their discovery of the Káweskar's cannibalistic customs.[9]

The Aónikenk had little respect for the Káweskar, considering them to be inferior. Some Káweskar were reported to have lived as slaves among the Aónikenk. Curiously, several of the Káweskar who lived among the Aónikenk also became Aónikenk shamans (Martinić 1995), who, as previously mentioned, were frequent targets of violence.

UNDERSTANDING THE DIMENSIONS OF VIOLENCE

In human societies, violent behavior is a multidimensional phenomenon that involves factors such as rights and privileges over resources, religious beliefs, and class, gender, and ethnic conflicts. The materialization of such dimensions of violence can be identified by drawing on both archaeological and ethnographic data. Several questions for further research are evident. A first step for achieving a more integrated picture of prehistoric patterns of violence in Fuego-Patagonia is to implement more accurate human remains analyses. Such a task involves studying demographic aspects of human remains (e.g., sex, age, DNA, geographical distribution), typologies of injuries related to violent events, and paleodiet, as well as the development of a more precise record of the dates for sites from which such human remains have come. These analyses must, at the same time, be combined with taphonomic studies as well as studies of the formation of archaeological sites. Such analyses may show demographic patterns linked to episodes of violence, which ultimately will allow researchers to transcend the microphysics of individual cases and identify broad patterns of violence that can be generalized to the whole culture.

Another step is to understand not only violence per se but also the role that such patterns may have played in articulating social life. Fuego-Patagonian societies sustained a robust autarchy, which is evident in a number of social institutions and mechanisms that drove these ethnic groups to remain confined to a relatively small number of members. These social institutions and mechanisms weakened any possibility for the concentration of political authority and economic resources. One such social mechanism, for instance, was the practice of destroying valuable assets belonging to a recently deceased member of the ethnic group (e.g., horses were killed among the Aónikenk). Indeed, the patterns of violence in these societies seem tuned to the maintenance and pervasiveness of social autonomy: the more concentrated the resources or prestigious social status, the greater the likelihood of becoming a visible target of violence. Thus, for example, a group that acquired more land through warfare was also exposed to an increasing cost of defending its territory. A large territory meant the rise in violent pressures from neighboring groups, which may be one of the reasons why such expansions are rare in the ethnographic record. In this respect, it is essential to look for geographical areas that may have had a higher concentration of violence because of the presence of valuable resources, such as, for instance, obsidian. Similarly, those members who held positions of relative authority in these societies were more likely to be the target of violence. At one time, Lucas Bridges was invited by the Selk'nam to become a shaman, an invitation that he refused to accept in the face of the extreme dangers involved with holding such a position.

A final step is to evaluate these patterns of violence in an evolutionary framework. Most ethnographic reports of Fuego-Patagonian societies agree that lethal violence was selective. Aggression did not target blood-related kin, especially one's children, and indeed, vengeance by the victim's kin targeted the murderer's kinsmen, not just the murderer. Indeed, women (who according to the rules of exogamy tend not to be considered blood-related kin) often became targets of nonlethal violence. Additionally, domestic violence in the form of spousal homicide frequently developed from a conflict between a man and a woman with respect to the control over the woman's reproductive resources. In addition, commonly only men with high social prestige were able to capture women from other territories, a situation that also makes women more likely to suffer violence. Thus, the qualitative data on violence in Fuego-Patagonia can best be explained by the arguments made by Martin Daly and Margo Wilson (1988, 1999), who hold that aggression is based on males competing with other males for positions of high status, resources, and women. The fact that aggression in Fuego-Patagonia was selective, with raiders targeting non-blood-related kin for killing and taking women captives as mates whenever feasible, lends weight to this view. Indubitably, all these observations require a more precise evaluation through the analysis of future quantitative data gathered through archaeological research.

Are the patterns of violence observed in Fuego-Patagonia during the period of European contact the result of an adaptive process of human societies to the ecological conditions of life in the region? Is the social distribution of territories the result of a dynamic equilibrium, a regulated tension between the concentration of some resources and the dependency of others? These questions are an invitation for beginning to understand the fundamental dynamics of violence and its role in regulating the struggle for social life in Fuego-Patagonia.

Acknowledgments

We want to thank Karen Miller, Dominique Legoupil, Anne Chapman, Julieta Gomez-Otero, and Gustavo Barrientos for their invaluable assistance and, as always, useful comments.

Notes

1. This description is an oversimplification to introduce the reader to the

region's indigenous cultures during European contact. These kinds of simplifications have been recently challenged by archaeological research. For a discussion on the diversity of patterns of subsistence in Fuego-Patagonia, see Borrero 1997.

2. Informants might have reported some deaths as homicides when in fact they were natural deaths (e.g., attributable to disease). Shamans were often accused of murder when somebody died, even if the death was from natural causes. Thus, although the ethnographic reports seem reliable to some extent, they must be regarded with caution given the lack of precise descriptions of the homicides.

3. Formerly, according to the myth of the origin of Selk'nam patriarchal society, men were subordinated to women. Female supremacy was based on their enactment of powerful and terrible spirits that terrorized the men and forced males to do all of the domestic work. After men discovered the deceit, they killed all of the adult women but not the female children and institutionalized an identical custom, but this time of men terrorizing women.

4. Concerning Yámana marital violence, Gusinde wrote, "The excessive submissiveness of most of the women fosters among the men a consciousness of superior power not established by common law. If this is coupled with a nature given to violence and outbursts of rage among one or another of the men, the women must occasionally expect maltreatment. In his anger, usually caused by minor incidents, he beats her with any stick or scrap of leather he happens to have at hand. She ducks or bends sideways without crying out or weeping. It is all over in a few minutes, but for the woman it is accompanied by several hours or an entire night of suppressed pain. The deeply felt mortification pains her incomparably more than the blow or beating" (1961, 463–64).

5. For example, see myths 30 and 36 in Wilbert 1977.

6. Although Gusinde (1986, 958) did not provide any quantitative data, he believed that this was the case also for Yámana society.

7. For instance, Gusinde (1961, 531–32) narrated a disturbing story of infanticide told to him in which a woman murdered her child because, presumably, half of the child's body was covered with feathers.

8. Carlos Gallardo told of a woman, Cayeparr, who drowned her five-year-old daughter in a river (1910, 233). Gusinde's informants also told him about this case of infanticide (Gusinde 1996, 553).

9. Joseph Emperaire provided the following description of archaeological remains in Seno Skyring, an area of Káweskar population: "In the piles of

shells from the coasts and the islands of the Skyring Sound, we have found, among the mass of food remains, a certain amount of fractured human bones, dispersed, mixed with animal bones and, like these, with marks of intentional fractures. Certainly, these bones are small in number, because at the most they belonged to four different corpses. A skull of a woman, deprived of its jaw, had been opened by the use of a stone instrument. These few fragments of long bones and bones of the cranium would seem to indicate that the fueguian population that had their places of camping in a low terrace of the Skyring sound, two or three millennia ago, could be, at least occasionally, anthropophagous. From this distant period, no archaeological document formally proves that this tradition of anthropophagy, ritual or simply nutritional, has been continued" (1963, 203–4). However, the cannibalistic status of such remains is questionable. Emperaire did not base his observation on cut marks, and no further "evidence" has been found in the area (Dominique Legoupil, pers. comm. 2004).

12 ETHICAL CONSIDERATIONS AND CONCLUSIONS REGARDING INDIGENOUS WARFARE AND RITUAL VIOLENCE IN LATIN AMERICA

Richard J. Chacon and Rubén G. Mendoza

Despite the preponderance of evidence for conflict and violence in the precontact Americas, revisionist historians continue to argue that anthropologists and archaeologists have conspired to invent "bloody worlds" by exaggerating the scale of warfare and ritual violence identified with Amerindian societies (Montejo 1993). Some elements of this revisionist school of thought argue that scholarly misrepresentation is but one facet of a malicious colonialist legacy determined to denigrate and dehumanize indigenous cultures, societies, and histories (Deloria 1969, 1995; Hassler 1992a, 1992b, 1992c; Means and Wolf 1995; Montejo 1993, 1999a). The revisionists' argument is that European and American scholarship produced over the course of the past five centuries is dominated by racist, derogatory, and degrading colonialist representations of Amerindian communities from throughout the Americas.

For example, Peter Hassler argues that the conquistadors generated propaganda designed to offend the sensibilities of their Christian audience (1992). Kurly Tlapoyawa echoes this view by asserting that "the idea that our ancestors practiced human sacrifice is not only absurd, it is a calculated lie which was carried out and promoted by the Spanish propaganda machine" (2003, 1). Russell Means in turn holds that it is in fact a blatant Eurocentric lie that holds that the Aztec engaged in the practice of human sacrifice via human heart excision. Remarkably, he believes that ancient Mesoamerican artworks depicting human hearts held aloft over images of prostrate individuals with cleft torsos illustrates a form of precontact open-heart surgery (Means and Wolf 1995).

Such scholars assert that biased colonial histories have been manipulated for the sake of political and ideological ends to justify a five-hundred-year-old pattern of indigenous land expropriations, forced relocations, and the assimilationist political perspective to which indigenous peoples continue to be subjected to this day (Cojti Cuxil 1995; Cojti Ren 2004; Means and Wolf 1995; Montejo 1993, 1999a, 1999b). Arguing along these same lines, Vine Deloria contends that for indigenous peoples, "the struggle of this century has been to emerge from the heavy burden of anthropological definitions" (1995, 65). Furthermore, some revisionists argue that publishing data on Amerindian warfare and ritual violence only serves to justify further oppression of native peoples (Means and Wolf 1995; Montejo 1993, 1999a; cf. Cojti Ren 2004). A. Vexnim Cojti Ren (2004) contends that linking indigenous cultures to precontact warfare and ritual violence will "lead us to believe that in preconquest times our People were already in a state of oppression from our governors leading to the notion that our present situation as targets of violence and national policies is just the continuation of the past; we have just changed oppressors."

Latin Americans are justifiably proud of their Native American and their European ancestries alike. We nevertheless acknowledge that many early European colonists and conquerors bear responsibility for the killing and enslavement of indigenous peoples in the Americas through the course of the fifteenth through twentieth centuries. We similarly acknowledge that European colonialist powers have been less than forthcoming in accepting responsibility for the atrocities that were committed. We therefore concur with observations made by Russell Means and Marvin Wolf (1995) and Victor Montejo (1993, 1999a, 1999b) that assert that many ethnohistories produced by Europeans and their American colonial counterparts in the New World were inordinately based on racist assumptions formulated to legitimize the expansion of European empires in the Americas. One need only review Bernal Díaz del Castillo's accounts of the Cholula Massacre of 1519 to realize that such histories constitute both propaganda and a pattern of moral justification for the conquest and subjugation of Amerindians. Fray Diego Duran (1993) and a host of other religious in turn produced treatments clearly intended as derogatory and demeaning of Amerindian religious traditions and practice. Clearly, both religion and politics conspired to disinherit and disenfranchise indigenous culture and civilization by way of the Eurocentric frameworks of analysis prevalent in that time and place (see Petersen and Crock 2007).

We nevertheless acknowledge that Amerindian groups too have histories of predatory warfare, and many participated in the killing and enslavement of one another à la those motivations explored in this volume. As such, we are in accord with Montejo, who is on record as saying, "As a people, we do not deny the fact that warfare, violence and human sacrifice were practiced as this information is well documented by archaeology and epigraphy" (Montejo 1999a; cf. Cojti Ren 2004). However, we do not equate indigenous warfare and ritual violence with that pattern of wholesale genocide conducted by some European groups and their colonial counterparts throughout the course of their respective experience with New World culture history. To do so would constitute a misrepresentation of the facts and would therefore be yet another violation showing disregard for those millions of native peoples who have suffered unspeakable cruelties at the hands of Westerners during the past five hundred years.

We similarly concur with the accusation made by numerous revisionists (Cojti Cuxil 1995; Deloria 1969, 1995; Hassler 1992; Means and Wolf 1995; Montejo 1993, 1999a, 1999b; Tlapoyawa 2003) that the documentary record produced by Europeans in the Americas was often based on racist assumptions formulated to legitimize the expansion of European empires in the Americas. Nevertheless, we need only consider those chronicles produced by the likes of Peter Martyr, Bartolomé de Las Casas, Bernardino de Sahagún, Diego Duran, or Bernabe Cobo to appreciate the utility of these same European chronicles in reconstructing the Amerindian past, as well as for the purposes of documenting the catastrophic consequences of colonial culture contact. We therefore call for the judicious use and critical reassessment of these colonial-era sources, as assuming that such works are flawed in that they convey only half truths and propaganda would be a mistake.

In essence, we seek to address a troubling trend that clearly entails the agenda-driven acceptance or rejection of significant portions of the ethnohistorical record of the Americas. For some, the decision of whether or not to accept the historical veracity of the available ethnohistories is increasingly based on political and ideological leanings and preconceptions rather than on the analysis of the data as such. For instance, the revisionists summarily dismiss as unreliable the writings of Bernal Díaz del Castillo in large part because of an apparent bias in his efforts to account for the massacre of the Cholulteca in the incident of 1519. Nevertheless, said accounts also serve to recount the awesome grandeur of Mexico's native civilizations through the eyes of one of its *conquistadores*. According to Díaz del Castillo (1996, 190–91),

> when we saw so many cities and villages built in the water and other great towns on dry land and that straight and level Causeway going towards Mexico, we were amazed and said it was like the enchantments they tell of in the legend of Amadis, on account of the great towers and cues [temple-pyramids] and buildings rising from the water, and all built from masonry. And some of our soldiers even asked whether the things that we saw were not a dream. It is not to be wondered at that I here write it down in this manner, for there is so much to think over that I do not know how

to describe it, seeing things as we did that had never been heard of or seen before, not even dreamed about. . . . And then we entered the city of Iztapalapa, the appearance of the palaces in which they lodged us! How spacious and well built they were, of beautiful stone work and cedar wood, and the wood of other sweet scented trees, with great rooms and courts, wonderful to behold, covered with awnings of cotton cloth.

Díaz del Castillo continued, in apparent remorse, "I say again that I stood looking at it [México-Tenochtitlán] and thought that never in the world would there be discovered other lands such as these. . . . Of all these wonders that I then beheld today all is overthrown and lost, nothing left standing" (1996, 191).

Díaz del Castillo's (1996) glowing accounts of the magnificence of the capital of México-Tenochtitlán have been published and republished in countless other venues as though they were gospel. Yet no revisionist scholar to our knowledge has questioned the veracity or accuracy of the aforementioned passages by Díaz del Castillo, chronicled as recollections describing the magnificence of the Aztec capital. Ironically, however, this same man's accounts regarding Mesoamerican warfare, ritual human sacrifice, and cannibalism are nevertheless dismissed by the revisionist camp as representing little more than Spanish propaganda aimed at establishing a moral justification for the brutality of the conquest and colonization of the Americas. In short, Spanish colonial reports and conquest narratives are accepted as accurate sources of information so long as they speak to the grandeur of indigenous achievements or those perceptions deemed beneficial to bolstering indigenous self-determination and native self-esteem. By contrast, where armed conflict, ritual violence, or anthropophagi are concerned, these same documents are construed as biased and unreliable and therefore suspect by the revisionists. While we jointly support and encourage any and all community-level endeavors designed to bolster indigenous self-determination and native self-esteem, we do so only so long as such efforts are not promulgated on the basis of historical and cultural misrepresentations or, for that matter, at the expense of scholarly concerns with the integrity of such sources.

We contend that revisionist diatribes increasingly serve to shape and reshape the narrative of the past. As noted, the revisionists continue to argue that European colonial accounts are untrustworthy, as they constitute nothing more than elite and racist propaganda designed to denigrate and subordinate Amerindian peoples. By the same token, these ethnohistorical accounts are interpreted by the revisionists as having been designed to portray the Spanish colonizers and other European groups in the best possible light. Given the facts at hand, can the revisionist premise in question withstand critical scholarly scrutiny?

First, we contend that revisionist claims regarding colonial-era ethnohistorical accounts are invalidated as a result of the fact that Spanish documents contain highly critical and detailed descriptions of reprehensible Spanish and European behaviors inflicted upon the native peoples, as well as upon one another. We thus question the extent to which such information could have been used to promote the actions of the conquistadors in a heroic or "civilizing" light in the eyes of other European contemporaries.

We nevertheless acknowledge that the role of propaganda is to render political actions and reactions palatable to the victor and the vanquished. If anything, such firsthand accounts document the veracity of the ethnohistorical record precisely because they document how cowardly, cruel, and unscrupulous the Spanish conquistadors and other Europeans acted within the context of that time. After all, the Spanish chroniclers in particular documented countless atrocities and legally actionable offenses committed by their fellow countrymen to witness what they understood to represent the historic ramifications and achievements of their newfound conquests for both posterity and the bureaucracies of the day.

Furthermore, the Spaniards did not need to degrade indigenous peoples in order to exploit them. Christopher Columbus, in fact, extolled the beauty and nobility of the Taino people in his writings by acknowledging that "they are of simple manners and trustworthy, and very liberal with everything they have, refusing no one who asks for anything they may possess, and even themselves inviting us to ask for things. They show greater love for others than for themselves . . . for those people are very amiable and kind" (Columbus 1998). Yet the reported presence of such admirable qualities among Amerindians in no way precluded Columbus's actions in subjecting members of this group to the colonial onslaught of brutality, enslavement, and slaughter (Las Casas 1971). Simply put, given the colonial frontiers and predilections of the time, most Spanish and other European groups remained largely unmonitored beyond the scope of their own immediate communities. As such, they were essentially free to exploit and terrorize Amerindian peoples through three centuries of colonial domination.

Far from serving as that essential propaganda designed to promote notions of Eurocentric superiority and indigenous inferiority, colonial chronicles often provide scathing indictments of the European invaders and their invasions. We, of course, wish to clarify that we are not asserting that everything that the Spanish chroniclers recorded about the indigenous peoples they encountered was necessarily true or, for that matter, accurate. Bartolomé de Las Casas (1971), for example, was famed for his scathing exposé of the cruelty and deceit with which the conquistadors whitewashed their record of atrocities in the West Indies. Instead, we acknowledge that scholars need to maintain a cautious and healthy skepticism when weighing the relevance and veracity of colonial-era documents against the archaeological and other cultural evidence.

We believe that Thomas Biolsi and Larry Zimmerman (1997), Demetrio Cojti Cuxil (1995), Deloria (1969, 1995), Montejo (1993, 1999a, 199b), Means and Wolf (1995), Cojti Ren (2004), and Richard Wilson (1991) are essentially justified in asserting that many anthropologists and archaeologists have in the past acted with great insensitivity to and disregard for the rights of indigenous peoples. Indeed, we are deeply troubled by the reality that there can be no denial of the fact that some of our colleagues have not always conducted anthropological research with the best interests of native peoples in mind or at heart. The sad realization of this painful and shameful truth leads us to empathize with those who have been injured and/or exploited by members of our profession. Frankly, we are not at all surprised that native peoples, and their nonnative advocates, look at those of us within the ranks of the anthropological community with some degree of suspicion if not outright contempt. Amerindians have reason to be skeptical of scholarly evidence for that kind and scale of violence purportedly committed by the ancestors of their respective communities. Clearly, some anthropological findings have been exploited by outsiders hostile to the idea of indigenous self-determination and political and social empowerment. Indeed, we are in accord with Biolsi and Zimmerman (1997), Cojti Ren (2004), Paul General and Gary Warrick (2004), George Nicholas (2004), and Philip Walker (2000), who encourage anthropologists to forge constructive collaborations with indigenous communities to remedy or avert further transgressions (for examples of applications of this perspective, see chap. 7, this vol.; Dongoske, Aldenderfer, and Doehner 2000; Nicholas 1997; Swidler et al. 1997).

At the same time, we believe it is a mistake to deny that native peoples are equally capable of lethal engagements with one another and with outsiders. The failure to objectively report on the substantive defensive and offensive capabilities of Amerindian groups, even where motivated by the noblest of intentions, may exacerbate conditions in which violence may provide the only alternative as a form of self-defense, particularly where conflict entails engagements with outsiders (for the Catawba, see Heath 2004). As Keith Otterbein has acknowledged, "classifying peoples as nonviolent could position them to be victimized as easily as calling a people fierce could make them a target of attack" (2000a, 843). A tragic case study along these lines concerns how ancestral Waorani territory was overrun by land-hungry colonists in the 1990s. When outsiders and other potential interlopers became convinced that the Waorani were no longer warlike, non-Waorani moved into the region in unprecedented numbers, and a destructive pattern of conflict-ridden interactions soon ensued. According to Clayton Robarchek and Carol Robarchek (1998, 166), "From the moment word first reached surrounding groups that the Waorani were abandoning warfare, outsiders began encroaching on their land and resources." Therefore, characterizing traditional peoples as harmless, peace-loving children of the forest leaves them vulnerable to an aggressive pattern of trespass and violation by nonnative peoples. In this instance, outsiders were emboldened by the fact that they no longer feared the likelihood of Waorani retaliation for unauthorized intrusion into and usurpation of tribal territories. This well-intentioned, albeit paternalistic, view of the Waorani ultimately encouraged non-Waorani to disregard tribal sovereignty and other basic human rights. In sum, when the Waorani were no longer perceived as a potentially dangerous fighting force to be reckoned with, their territory was targeted for exploitation by the outsiders.

The failure to acknowledge and report the respective role that armed conflict and ritual violence plays in the lives of indigenous peoples is itself a vestige of colonial repression, as it denies native warriors their legacy of resistance. This denial minimizes how participation in acts of violence is perceived and/or justified from an emic perspective. For example, even the most cursory review of the literature will reveal that one of the most highly prized attributes that an Amerindian man could strive for was to be considered a fierce warrior who was ready and willing to courageously battle the enemy in the defense of his people.

However, some revisionists hold that the act of reporting data on Amerindian warfare and ritual violence only serves to justify further violence and oppression of indigenous peoples (Cojti Ren 2004). In response, we challenge the revisionists to explain comments made by Amazonian Jivaro warriors including "I was born to die fighting" (Harner 1972, 170) and "Only when I die, when I am mortally wounded, will I stop fighting" (Hendricks 1993, 39). Should scholars refrain from reporting such statements to placate the revisionists? What of the declaration made by a seven-year-old Amazonian Huambisa boy who boldly announced that "most of all I want to be a great warrior when I grow up so I can avenge my father's death and take many Aguaruna heads" (Cotlow 1953, 49)? Similarly, what are we to do with the words written by an ancient Aztec poet who wrote of the glory of dying for Huitzilopochtli's sake? This poet asserted that "there is nothing like death in war, nothing like the flowery death so precious to him who gives life: far off I see it: my heart yearns for it!" (Coe 2002, 204).

In well over a decade of research among the Achuar, Yora, and Yanomamö peoples of South America, Richard Chacon found that participation in battle constituted a paramount source of individual and collective pride (Chacon's field notes). In fact, one of the greatest compliments that one can pay an Amazonian male in each of the aforementioned groups is to refer to him as a fierce warrior. Among the

Achuar, the greatest honor that a man can achieve is the exalted status of *kakaram*, or "powerful warrior who has killed enemies in battle." Chacon conducted fieldwork in villages with several kakaram individuals in residence and has reported on the high status they enjoy and on the deferential treatment they receive from fellow tribesmen (Chacon 2004). This Amerindian ethos regarding lethal combat is illustrated by a statement made by an Achuar man who participated in various raids: "I am not afraid to fight. I do not fear death" (Chacon's field notes). This same individual later demonstrated courage by spearheading the defense of his village when it was attacked by raiders from a neighboring settlement (Chacon 2004).

Consequently, revisionist positions that dismiss the evidence for indigenous warfare and ritual violence are not only untenable but also clearly at odds with pan-Amerindian cosmology and belief. Amerindian cosmologies clearly assert the primacy of the warrior who courageously fights on behalf of his people.

The very survival and integrity of indigenous communities rest upon the courage and the tenacity of these combatants, and we believe that current efforts to silence the voice of the warrior tradition are at odds with the well-being of traditional tribal ideologies. For that reason, we argue in favor of the obligation to respectfully document and describe the dimension of the indigenous ethos that is concerned with warfare and ritual violence. We contend that to do otherwise promulgates a nonnative model in lieu of an indigenous worldview. The aversion to acknowledging participation in sanctioned acts of violence and organized conflict against outsiders only serves to cater to modern Western sensibilities. Such cultural representations invariably validate the voice of the outsider whose experience remains alien to that of the indigenous communities under consideration.

The very effort to negate the specter of violence in native society is patently Eurocentric in that it generally circumvents scholarly acknowledgment of the indigenous quest for self-determination and thereby the role of agency in the creation of native histories. The armed resistance of enemies (indigenous or nonindigenous) necessarily constitutes a key dimension of the Amerindian experience. Indigenous worldviews and cultural narratives centered on the need to justify armed conflict are dismissed by the revisionist camp as mythological constructs or as mere propaganda. Therefore, traditional and supernaturally sanctioned sources of cultural pride identified with the warrior theme are suppressed by outside agents of change. Denying Amerindian warriors a voice in this discourse necessarily results in native conflict being redefined via the prism of a nonnative value system.

Beth Conklin advocates the development of an engaged anthropology that empowers marginalized peoples. She nevertheless condemns the tailoring of research findings "to produce the images that certain activists or advocacy groups want" (2003, 5). She contends that the promotion of an idealized depiction of society, however well intended, will backfire when distorted claims made by scholars or community researchers are exposed or, as she aptly asserts, "when the gap between rhetoric and realty is revealed" (Conklin 2003, 5; see also Scheffel 2000; Stearman 1994). Indeed, Deloria captures the current state of affairs by asserting that "it becomes impossible to tell the truth from fiction or facts from mythology. Experts paint us [Native Americans] as they would like us to be . . . the American public feels most comfortable with the mythical Indian of Stereotypeland. . . . To be an Indian in modern American society is in a very real sense to be unreal and ahistorical" (1969, 9–10; see also Edgerton 1992; Krech 1999; Rothstein 2004; Vargas-Cetina 2003).

Given the many serious threats confronting indigenous peoples today, social scientists would do well to heed Conklin's assertion that idealized (mis)representations are shaky ground on which to stake out indigenous rights claims. Rather than distort our research to conform to the prevailing political and cultural agenda of the day, we should seek to enable native peoples to escape from the "noble savage slot trap" (Conklin 2003, 5). For that and related reasons, the promulgation of a politically expedient (i.e., nonviolent) aboriginal America hinders progress toward indigenous self-determination.

Heeding Conklin's admonition, in this volume we seek to dispassionately document the multidimensional sources and consequences of Amerindian warfare and ritual violence in a manner that is faithful to the facts and at the same time faithful to those indigenous traditions and beliefs that more cogently explain the phenomenon under study.

As Cojti Ren (2004) contends, human societies everywhere have had to cope with conflict emanating from within their own ranks, and the indigenous peoples of Latin America are no exception in this regard.

The conquistadors encountered many sophisticated indigenous societies with rich cultural traditions and remarkable technological achievements. However, the conquistadors confronted societies that were also in the throes of interminable and bloody conflicts. The Spaniards encountered native groups weary of harassment by or subjugation at the hands of more powerful traditional enemies and neighbors. Such societies were therefore willing to ally themselves with European invaders seeking to overthrow these same powerful and predatory enemies by way of armed conflict. Hernán Cortés, for example, successfully exploited prevailing interethnic animosities by recruiting Huastecan and Tlaxcaltecan allies who played pivotal roles in the defeat and subsequent destruction of the Mexica Empire (Smith 2003). Similarly, Francisco Pizarro in turn enlisted Huanca (Espinoza Soriano 1971) and Cañari (Cieza de Leon 1998) allies to the cause of toppling the Inca Empire.

There can be no doubt that early European colonials and their descendents committed untold atrocities against the native peoples of Latin America. However, given corollary indigenous examples cited in this volume, there can also be no question that deep-seated antagonisms and interethnic conflict existed between native groups long before the initial European landfall in the Americas. Violence, bloodshed, and the brutality of colonial campaigns, warfare, and subjugation were not entirely foreign concepts to Amerindian peoples prior to 1492. Richard Chacon and David Dye (2007), John Ewers (1975), Debra Martin and David Frayer (1997), and John Topic (1989) have published similar findings to that effect. We do not argue that precontact Amerindians were bloodthirsty predators, as frequently characterized by the Eurocentric and colonialist agendas of the day. Rather, we seek to establish that preconquest peoples of the Americas did not inhabit the "Paradise lost" that is often championed via revisionist critiques, as exemplified by one statement by Means and Wolf describing precontact life: "the Great Mystery had given us everything we need, a heaven on earth" (1995, 15).

We therefore reassert the need to more fully explore and understand Amerindian warfare and ritual violence via cross-cultural and interdisciplinary understandings and perspectives. We believe that such a call to action constitutes a more forthright, albeit challenging, alternative to that which currently seeks to deny or denounce anything that challenges the notion of the passive American Indian victim of Western imperialism. As social scientists, we feel an obligation to the profession and our respective communities to accurately, objectively, and faithfully convey our findings in a respectful and scholarly manner. As such, when we encounter evidence for warfare, human sacrifice, and cannibalism in the anthropological record, we believe that we are obliged to report such findings in a forthright manner. To do otherwise would constitute a violation of ethical protocols on our part. This objective is what we had in mind when we initially set about addressing that significant new body of research presented in this anthology devoted to the study of war and conflict in human societies.

This work has generated a multitude of new insights and observations regarding Amerindian warfare and ritual violence in Latin America. We believe that we have extended the scope of studies devoted to war and human conflict by way of our inclusion of corollary forms of civil and religious conflict seemingly reconciled by means of ritualized violence. What then can we conclude from those studies presented? We have identified warfare and ritual violence in terms of several idealized patterns and dynamics that include the following findings:

1. Warfare inherently has multiple causes. This anthology advances a variety of materialistic and nonmaterialistic explanations cited as the causal or primary motivations for warfare and other forms of human conflict. Furthermore, the authors hold that it is entirely reasonable to assume that human beings may be motivated to do battle as a consequence of multiple or conflicting factors, conditions, and variables (material and otherwise). (See also Chacon and Dye 2007.)

2. Tribal warfare can result in the significant loss of life. Clearly, a serious misconception is at play in presuming that tribal warfare was, or is, of little demographic consequence. Jeffrey Blick (1988) and Means and Wolf (1995) have nevertheless sought to minimize the demo-

graphic consequences of nonstate (or tribal) conflict and organized violence. Some of the contributions presented in this volume document the fact that tribal populations may be considerably diminished by way of "primitive" warfare (see chap. 8). Napoleon Chagnon (1988) and Lawrence Keeley (1996) have documented similar findings in other contexts. Moreover, John Verano (chap. 6, this vol.) clearly documents that the execution of Amerindian captives (on a significant scale) predated European contact in the Americas.

3. The reasons and rationale for fighting and the intensity of armed combat may vary through time. The contributions presented in this volume illustrate that the impetus for instigating warfare in the first instance may vary significantly from those reasons conjured to escalate or prolong its depth and magnitude (see chap. 1, this vol.).

4. Precontact patterns of indigenous warfare in the Neotropics are clearly substantiated. Some scholars have proposed that indigenous armed conflict in Amazonia is mostly attributable to conditions identified with Western contact (Ferguson 1990). However, Elsa Redmond (chap. 5, this vol.) documents the presence of warfare in the Neotropics prior to the first incursions of European colonials (see also Redmond 1994).

5. The intensity of indigenous warfare clearly varies with respect to the tribal group's articulation with state-level societies. Marcela Mendoza (see chap. 10, this vol.) demonstrates that the patterns of Chacoan warfare in the Tribal Zone are commensurate with those predicted by Brian Ferguson and Neil Whitehead (1992). Stephen Beckerman and James Yost (chap. 8, this vol.) in turn report that most Waorani raids cannot be attributed to competition over Western manufactures circulating in the Tribal Zone. Such findings demonstrate the complex nature of the sociopolitical and cultural nexus obtaining between state-level and tribal societies. This fact should serve as a cautionary tale to scholars regarding the sociopolitical dynamics of state-level societies with respect to the nature and intensity of native warfare in the Tribal Zone.

6. The relative utility and accuracy of the preponderance of Spanish colonial chronicles are corroborated by the available archaeological and forensic data. Despite revisionist claims that dismiss as mere propa-

ganda those ethnohistorical sources that report indigenous warfare and ritual violence and cannibalism (Montejo 1993, 1999a; see also Cojti Ren 2004; Means and Wolf 1995; Tlapoyawa 2003), many of the chapters presented here corroborate colonial-era narratives.

Our collective assessment and analysis thus acknowledges the fact that Spanish ethnohistorical accounts reporting armed conflict, ritual violence, and cannibalism in Latin America serve as relatively reliable sources for addressing the questions at hand. Many of the most contentious ethnohistorical details regarding human sacrifice and armed conflict have been corroborated in recent years by way of multiple lines of scientific evidence and analysis from archaeology and the forensic sciences. The recovery of modified and disarticulated human skeletal materials from a diversity of cultural contexts provides a significant new corpus of primary data substantiating Spanish descriptions of warfare, ritual violence, and cannibalism in the Americas (see chap. 2, this vol.). Kristen Romey (2004a, 2004b, 2005) and Mark Stevenson (2005) present additional archaeological evidence to corroborate ethnohistorical accounts of Mesoamerican ritual violence. Spanish accounts of ritual human sacrifice in the Andes now have the advantage of secondary corroboration via the archaeological recovery of in situ (mummified) human offerings (Ceruti 2003). Furthermore, we acknowledge that some of the bloody and often lethal native Andean rites mentioned in colonial era documents do in fact persist to the present day (chap. 7, this vol.).

Ultimately, we believe that this anthology devoted to the multidisciplinary and cross-cultural consideration of indigenous war and ritual violence in Latin America will reinvigorate extant theoretical frames of reference that seek to understand the global sources and consequences of human, not just Amerindian, conflict and violence.

References

Acosta, Jorge R. 1965. Preclassic and Classic Architecture of Oaxaca. In *Handbook of Middle American Indians*. Vol. 3: *Archaeology of Southern Mesoamerica, Part Two*, ed. R. Wauchope and G. Willey, 814–36. Austin: University of Texas Press.

Acosta, José de. [1590] 1962. *Historia natural y moral de las Indias*. 2nd ed. Mexico City: Fondo de Cultura Económica.

Adams, R. E. W., H. R. Robichaux, Fred Valdez Jr., Brett A. Houk, and Ruth Mathews. 2004. Transformations, Periodicity, and Urban Development in the Three Rivers Region. In *The Terminal Classic in the Maya Lowlands*, ed. Arthur A. Demarest, Prudence M. Rice, and Don S. Rice, 324–41. Boulder: University Press of Colorado.

Alencastre, Andres, and Georges Dumezil. 1953. Fétes et usages des Indiens de Langui (Province de Canas, Department du Cuzco). *Journal de la Sociéte des Américanistes* 42:1–118.

Algaze, Guillermo. 1993. Expansionary Dynamics of Some Early Pristine States. *American Anthropologist* 95:304–33.

Alva, Walter, and Christopher B. Donnan. 1993. *Royal Tombs of Sipan*. Los Angeles: Fowler Museum of Cultural History.

Alvarado Tezozómoc, Fernando. 1944. *Crónica Mexicana*. Mexico City: Secretaría de Educación Pública.

Ambrosino, James N., Traci Ardren, and Travis W. Stanton. 2003. The History of Warfare at Yaxuná. In *Ancient Mesoamerican Warfare*, ed. M. Kathryn Brown and Travis W. Stanton, 109–23. Walnut Creek, Calif.: AltaMira Press.

Anglería, Pedro Mártir de. 1964. *Décadas del Nuevo Mundo*. Mexico City: José Porrua e Hijos.

Arendt, Hannah. 1969. Reflections on Violence. *Journal of International Affairs* 23 (1): 1–35.

Arkush, Elizabeth, and Charles Stanish. 2005. Interpreting Conflict in the Ancient Andes: Implications for the Archaeology of Warfare. *Current Anthropology* 46 (1): 3–27.

Armillas, Pedro. 1951. Mesoamerican Fortifications. *Antiquity* 25:77–86.

Arrom, José Juan. 1975. *Mitología y artes prehispánicas de las Antillas*. Mexico City: Siglo Veintiuno Editores.

Astrada, Domingo de. 1906. *Expedición al Pilcomayo*. Buenos Aires: Robles y Cia.

Baker, Matthew J. 2003. An Equilibrium Conflict Model of Land Tenure in Hunter-Gatherer Societies. *Journal of Political Economy* 111:124–73.

Baldrich, Juan A. 1889. *Las Comarcas Vírgenes: El Chaco Central Norte*. Buenos Aires: Jacobo Peuser.

Balée, William. 1984. The Ecology of Ancient Tupi Warfare. In *Warfare, Culture, and Environment*, ed. R. Brian Ferguson, 241–65. Orlando, Fla.: Academic Press.

———. 1988. The Ka'apor Indian Wars of Lower Amazonia, ca. 1825–1928. In *Dialectics and Gender: Anthropological Approaches*, ed. Richard R. Randolph, David M. Schneider, and May N. Diaz, 155–69. Boulder, Colo.: Westview Press.

Balkansky, Andrew K. 1998. Origin and Collapse of Complex Societies in Oaxaca (Mexico): Evaluating the Era from 1965 to the Present. *Journal of World Prehistory* 12:451–93.

———. 2001. On Emerging Patterns in Oaxaca Archaeology. *Current Anthropology* 42:559–61.

———. 2002. *The Sola Valley and the Monte Albán State: A Study of Zapotec Imperial Expansion*. University of Michigan Museum of Anthropology Memoirs, no. 36. Ann Arbor.

Balkansky, Andrew K., Stephen A. Kowalewski, Verónica Pérez Rodríguez, Thomas J. Pluckhahn, Charlotte A. Smith, Laura R. Stiver, Dmitri Belieaev, John F. Chamblee, Verenice Y. Heredia Espinoza, and Roberto Santos Pérez. 2000. Archaeological Survey in the Mixteca Alta of Oaxaca, Mexico. *Journal of Field Archaeology* 27:365–89.

Ball, Joseph W. 1974. A Teotihuacan-style Cache from the Maya Lowlands. *Archaeology* 27 (1): 2–9.

Barrientos, Gustavo, and F. Gordon. 2003. Distribución temporal y espacial de señales de violencia interpersonal en muestras de cráneos del norte de Patagonia. Paper presented at the conference VI Jornadas de Antropología Biológica, San Fernando del valle de Catamarca.

Barrionuevo, Alfonsina. 1971. Chiarage. *Allpanchis* 3:79–84.

Bastien, Joseph W. 1978. *Mountain of the Condor: Metaphor and Ritual in an Andean Ayllu*. St. Paul, Minn.: West Publishing.

Benavente, Hernando. [1550] 1994. Relación de la conquista de Macas por el Capitán Hernando Benavente, 1550. In *Conquista de la region Jívaro (1550–1650): Relación documental*, ed. Anne Christine Taylor and Cristóbal Landázuri N. Quito: Marka.

Benson, Elizabeth P., and Anita G. Cook, eds. 2001. *Ritual Sacrifice in Ancient Peru*. Austin: University of Texas Press.

Benzoni, Girolamo. 2000. *La historia del Mondo Novo*. Guayaquil: Museo Antropologico, Banco Central del Ecuador.

Betanzos, Juan. 1996. *Narrative of the Incas*. Austin: University of Texas Press.

Billman, Brian R. 1996. *The Evolution of Prehistoric Political Organizations in the Moche Valley, Peru*. Doctoral dissertation, Department of Anthropology, University of California, Santa Barbara.

Binford, Lewis R. 2001. *Constructing Frames of Reference*. Berkeley: University of California Press.

Biolsi, Thomas, and Larry Zimmerman. 1997. *Indians and Anthropologists: Vine Deloria and the Critique of Anthropology*. Tucson: University of Arizona Press.

Bird, Junius. 1946. The Alacaluf. In *Handbook of South American Indians*. Vol. 1: *The Marginal Tribes*, ed. J. H. Steward, 17–24. Washington, D.C.: U.S. Government Printing Office.

———. 1988. *Travels and Archaeology in South Chile*, ed. John Hyslop. Iowa City: University of Iowa Press.

Blanton, Richard E. 1978. *Monte Albán: Settlement Patterns at the Ancient Zapotec Capital*. New York: Academic Press.

Blick, Jeffrey. 1988. Genocidal Warfare in Tribal Societies as a Result of European-Induced Culture Conflict. *Man* 23:654–70.

Blomberg, Rolf. 1957. *The Naked Aucas: An Account of the Indians of Ecuador*. London: Allen and Unwin.

Bolin, Inge. 1998. *Rituals of Respect: The Secret of Survival in the High Peruvian Andes*. Austin: University of Texas Press.

Boone, Elizabeth Hill. 1984. *Ritual Human Sacrifice in Mesoamerica: A Conference at Dumbarton Oaks, October 13th and 14th, 1979*. Washington, D.C.: Dumbarton Oaks Research Library and Collection.

Borrero, Alberto. 1997. The Origins of the Ethnographic Subsistence Patterns in Fuego-Patagonia. In *Patagonia: Natural History, Prehistory, and Ethnography at the Uttermost End of the Earth*, ed. C. McEwan, A. Borrero, and A. Prieto, 60–81. London: British Museum Press.

Boster, James, James Yost, and Catherine Peeke. 2004. Rage, Revenge and Religion: Honest Signaling of Aggression and Non-aggression in Waorani Coalitional Violence. *Ethos* 34 (4): 1–24.

Bourget, Steve. 1997. Las excavaciones en la Plaza 3a. In *Investigaciones en la Huaca de la Luna, 1995,* ed. S. Uceda, E. Mujica, and R. Morales, 51–59. Trujillo, Peru: Universidad Nacional de Trujillo.

———. 1998. Excavaciones en la Plaza 3a y en la Plataforma II de la Huaca de la Luna durante 1996. In *Investigaciones en la Huaca de la Luna, 1996,* ed. S. Uceda, E. Mujica, and R. Morales, 43–64. Trujillo, Peru: Universidad Nacional de Trujillo.

———. 2001. Children and Ancestors: Ritual Practices at the Moche Site of Huaca de la Luna, North Coast of Peru. In *Ritual Sacrifice in Ancient Peru,* ed. Elizabeth P. Benson and Anita G. Cook, 93–118. Austin: University of Texas Press.

Brachetti, Angela. 2001. La batalla de chiraje: Una pelea ritual en los Andes del sur de Peru. *Anales* 9:59–77.

Brady, James E., Ann Scott, Allen Cobb, Irma Rodas, John Fogarty, and Monica Urquizú Sanchez. 1997. Glimpses of the Dark Side of the Petexbatun Project: The Petexbatun Regional Cave Survey. *Ancient Mesoamerica* 8 (2): 353–64.

Braswell, Geoffrey E. 2003. Introduction: Reinterpreting Early Classic Interaction. In *The Maya and Teotihuacan: Reinterpreting Early Classic Interaction,* ed. Geoffrey E. Braswell, 1–44. Austin: University of Texas Press.

Braunstein, José, and Elmer S. Miller. 1999. Ethnohistorical Introduction. In *Peoples of the Gran Chaco,* ed. Elmer S. Miller, 1–22. Westport, Conn.: Bergin and Garvey.

Bremer, Catherine. 2006. Grisly Aztec Saga Reconstructed: Archaeologists Find Remains That Back Up Tale of Ritual Massacre. MSNBC, August 23, 2006. http://www.msnbc.msn.com/id/14485960/.

Bridges, Esteban L. 1938. Burying the Hatchet. *Man* 38 (2): 4–7.

———. 1950. *Uttermost Part of the Earth.* New York: E. P. Dutton.

Brochado, José Proenza. 1989. A expansão dos Tupi da cerâmica da Tradição Policrômica Amazônica. *Dédalo* 27:65–82.

Brockington, Donald L. 1973. *Archaeological Investigations at Miahuatlán, Oaxaca.* Vanderbilt University Publications in Anthropology, no. 7. Nashville.

Brown, M. Kathryn, and James F. Garber. 2003. Evidence of Conflict during the Middle Formative in the Maya Lowlands: A View from Blackman Eddy, Belize. In *Ancient Mesoamerican Warfare,* ed. M. Kathryn Brown and Travis W. Stanton, 91–108. Walnut Creek, Calif.: AltaMira Press.

Brown, M. Kathryn, and Travis W. Stanton, eds. 2003. *Ancient Mesoamerican Warfare.* Walnut Creek, Calif.: AltaMira Press.

Browne, David, Helaine Silverman, and Rubén García. 1993. A Cache of 48 Nasca Trophy Heads from Cerro Carapo, Peru. *Latin American Antiquity* 4 (3): 274–94.

Brownrigg, Leslie. 1972. El papel de rituos de pasaje en la integracion social de los Cañaris Quichuas del austral ecuatoriano. In *Actas y memorias del XXXIX Internacional de Americanistas,* vol. 6, ed. R. Avalos de Matos and Roger Ravines, 92–99. Lima: Sociedad Americanista.

Brundage, Burr. 1963. *Empire of the Inca.* Norman: University of Oklahoma Press.

Bucher, Enrique H., and P. C. Huszar. 1999. Sustainable Management of the Gran Chaco of South America: Ecological Promise and Economic Constraints. *Journal of Environmental Management* 57:99–108.

Burridge, Kenelm. 1973. *Encountering Aborigines—A Case Study: Anthropology and the Australian Aboriginal.* New York: Pergamon Press.

Butland, Gilbert J. 1957. *The Human Geography of Southern Chile*. Institute of British Geographers. London: George Philip and Son.

Cabodevilla, Miguel Angel. 1994. *Los Huaorani en la historia de los pueblos del Oriente*. Coca, Ecuador: Cicame.

Cabrera, Pablo. 1910. *Ensayos sobre etnología Argentina*. Córdoba, Argentina: Universidad Nacional de Córdoba.

Cachiguango, Luis Enrique. 2000. Wakcha Karai: Una praxis de la religiosidad andian en Cotama, Otavalo (Ecuador). In *Manos sabias para criar vida*, ed. Juan van Kassel and Horacio Larrain Barros, 301–11. Quito: Editorial Abya Yala.

———. 2001. *Experiencias de revitalizacion cultural en los simbolismos y praxis del Hutun Puncha Inti Raymi en Cotacachi*. Cotacachi: Reporte UNORCAC.

Caillavet, Chantal. 2000. *Etnias del norte: Etnohistoria e historia de Ecuador*. Quito: Abya-Yala.

Carder, Peter. 1906. *The Relations of Peter Carder of Saint Verian . . . Begun 1577*. Vol. 16: *Purchas His Pilgrimes*. 2nd ed. Glasgow: J. MacLehose and Sons.

Carmean, Kelli, Nicholas Dunning, and Jeff Karl Kowalski. 2004. High Times in the Hill Country: A Perspective from the Terminal Classic Puuc Region. In *The Terminal Classic in the Maya Lowlands*, ed. Arthur A. Demarest, Prudence M. Rice, and Don S. Rice, 424–49. Boulder: University Press of Colorado.

Carneiro, Robert L. 1970. A Theory of the Origin of the State. *Science* 169:733–38.

———. 1981. The Chiefdom: Precursor of the State. In *The Transition to Statehood in the New World*, ed. Grant D. Jones and Robert R. Kautz, 37–79. New York: Cambridge University Press.

———. 1990. Chiefdom-Level Warfare as Exemplified in Fiji and the Cauca Valley. In *The Anthropology of War*, ed. Jonathan Hass, 190–211. SAR Book. Cambridge, U.K.: Cambridge University Press.

———. 1998. What Happened at the Flashpoint? Conjectures on Chiefdom Formation at the Very Moment of Conception. In *Chiefdoms and Chieftaincy in the Americas*, ed. Elsa M. Redmond, 18–42. Tallahassee: University Press of Florida.

Carrasco, David. 1999. *City of Sacrifice: The Aztec Empire and the Role of Violence in Civilization*. Boston: Beacon Press.

Carrasco, Morita, and Claudia Briones. 1996. *La tierra que nos quitaron*. Documento IWGIA 18. Buenos Aires: LHAKA HONHAT-IWGIA.

Carvajal, Fray Gaspar de. [1542] 1934. *The Discovery of the Amazon According to the Account of Friar Gaspar de Carvajal and Other Documents*, introduction by José Toribio Medina, trans. Bertram T. Lee, ed. H. C. Heaton. American Geographical Society Special Publication no. 17. New York.

Cashdan, Elizabeth. 1983. Territoriality among Human Foragers: Ecological Models and an Application to Four Bushman Groups. *Current Anthropology* 24:47–66.

Caso, Alfonso. 1938. *Exploraciones en Oaxaca: Quinta y sexta temporadas, 1936–1937*. Instituto Panamericano de Geografía e Historia, Publicación 34. Mexico City.

———. 1947. Calendario y escritura de las antiguas culturas de Monte Albán. In *Obras completas de Miguel Othón de Mendizábal: Un homenaje*, vol. 1, 5–102. Mexico City: Talleres de la Nación.

Caso, Alfonso, Ignacio Bernal, and Jorge Acosta. 1967. *La cerámica de Monte Albán.* Memorias del Instituto Nacional de Antropología e Historia 13. Mexico City.

Castañeda, Quetzil E. 1996. *In the Museum of Maya Culture: Touring Chichén Itzá.* Minneapolis: University of Minnesota Press.

Castro, Alicia, and Julian Moreno. 2000. Noticia sobre enterratorios humanos en la costa norte de Santa Cruz–Patagonia Argentina. *Anales del Instituto de la Patagonia,* Ser. Cs. Ss., 28:225–31.

Centro de Cultura Pre Americana (Zemanahuak Tlamachtloyan). 2003. Sacrificios Humanos? Mexika Eagle Society website, http://www.mexika.org/ZemanSac.htm.

Ceruti, María Constanza. 2003. *Llullaillaco: Sacrificios y ofrendas en un santuario Inca de Alta Montaña.* Salta: Universidad Católica.

Chacon, Richard. 2004. Seeking the Headhunter's Power: The Quest for Arutam among the Achuar Indians of the Ecuadorian Amazon. Paper presented at the Society for American Archaeology Annual Meeting in Montreal, Canada, April.

Chacon, Richard, and David Dye. 2007. *The Taking and Displaying of Human Body Parts as Trophies by Amerindians.* New York: Springer.

Chagnon, Napoleon. 1988. Life Histories, Blood Revenge, and Warfare in a Tribal Population. *Science* 239:985–92.

Chapman, Anne M. 1982. *Drama and Power in a Hunting Society: The Selk'nam of Tierra del Fuego.* New York: Cambridge University Press.

———. 1997. The Great Ceremonies of the Selk'nam and the Yámana: A Comparative Analysis. In *Patagonia: Natural History, Prehistory, and Ethnography at the Uttermost End of the Earth*, ed. C. McEwan, A. Borrero, and A. Prieto, 82–109. London: British Museum Press.

Chase, Arlen F., and Diane Z. Chase. 1987. *Investigations at the Classic Maya City of Caracol, Belize, 1985–1987.* Pre-Columbian Art Research Institute, Monograph 3. San Francisco.

Chase, Arlen F., Nikolai K. Grube, and Diane Z. Chase. 1991. *Three Terminal Classic Monuments from Caracol, Belize.* Research Reports on Ancient Maya Writing, no. 36. Washington, D.C.: Center for Maya Research.

Chase, Diane Z., and Arlen F. Chase. 2003. Text and Context in Maya Warfare: A Brief Consideration of Epigraphy and Archaeology at Caracol, Belize. In *Ancient Mesoamerican Warfare*, ed. M. Kathryn Brown and Travis W. Stanton, 171–88. Walnut Creek, Calif.: AltaMira Press.

Cieza de León, Pedro. 1998. *The Discovery and Conquest of Peru.* Durham, N.C.: Duke University Press.

Clastres, Hélène. 1995. *The Land without Evil: Tupí-Guaraní Prophetism*, trans. Jacqueline Grenez Brovender. Urbana: University of Illinois Press.

Clastres, Pierre. 1987. *Investigaciones en antropología política.* Mexico City: Gédisa.

Clausewitz, Karl von. [1832] 1943. *On War*, trans. O. J. Matthijs Jolles. New York: Modern Library.

Cobo, Bernabe. 1979. *History of the Inca Empire.* Austin: University of Texas Press.

———. [1653] 1990. *Inca Religion and Customs*, trans. and ed. Ronald Hamilton. Austin: University of Texas Press.

―――. [1652] 1996. *History of the Inca Empire*, ed. Ronald Hamilton. Austin: University of Texas Press.

Cobos Palma, Rafael. 2004. Chichén Itzá: Settlement and Hegemony during the Terminal Classic Period. In *The Terminal Classic in the Maya Lowlands*, ed. Arthur A. Demarest, Prudence M. Rice, and Don S. Rice, 517–44. Boulder: University Press of Colorado.

Coe, Michael D. 1962. *Mexico*. New York: Praeger.

―――. 2002. *Mexico: From the Olmecs to the Aztecs*. London: Thames and Hudson.

Coggins, Clemency C. 1984. Murals in the Upper Temple of the Jaguars, Chichén Itzá. In *Cenote of Sacrifice: Maya Treasures from the Sacred Well at Chichén Itzá*, ed. Clemency C. Coggins and O. C. Shane III, 157–65. Austin: University of Texas Press.

Cohen, Roberta, and Francis M. Deng. 1998. *Masses in Flight: The Global Crisis of Internal Displacement*. Washington, D.C.: Brookings Institution Press.

Cojti Cuxil, Demetrio. 1995. *Configuracion del pensamiento politico del Pueblo Maya (2da. Parte)*. Guatemala City: Editorial Cholsamaj.

Cojti Ren, A. Vexnim. 2004. Maya Archaeology and the Political and Cultural Identity of Contemporary Maya in Guatemala. http://www.mayainfo.org.

Colin, Susi. 1999. The Wild Man and the Indian in Early 16th Century Book Illustration. In *Indians and Europe: An Interdisciplinary Collection of Essays*, ed. Christian F. Feest, 5–35. Lincoln: University of Nebraska Press.

Columbus, Christopher. 1998. The Columbus Letter to the King and Queen of Spain. http://www.usm.maine.edu/~maps/columbus/exit.html.

Conejo, Luis Alberto. 1995. La Fiesta de San Juan o Inti Raimi en la comunidad de La Bolsa. In *La fiesta religiosa indigena en el Ecuador*, 65–74. Quito: Editorial Abya Yala.

Conklin, Beth. 2003. Speaking Truth to Power. *Anthropology News* 44 (7): 5.

Constantinescu, Florence. 2003. Obsidiana verde incrustada en un cráneo Aónikenk: ¿tensión social intraétnica . . . o interétnica? "We'll never know!" *Magallania* 31:149–53.

Cooper, John M. 1917. *Analytical and Critical Bibliography of the Tribes of Tierra del Fuego and Adjacent Territory*. Bureau of American Ethnology Bulletin no. 63. Washington, D.C.: Smithsonian Institution.

―――. 1946a. The Yahgan. In *Handbook of South American Indians*. Vol. 1: *The Marginal Tribes*, ed. J. H. Steward, 81–106. Washington, D.C.: U.S. Government Printing Office.

―――. 1946b. The Ona. In *Handbook of South American Indians*. Vol. 1: *The Marginal Tribes*, ed. J. H. Steward, 107–25. Washington, D.C.: U.S. Government Printing Office.

―――. 1946c. The Patagonian and Pampean tribes. In *Handbook of South American Indians*. Vol. 1: *The Marginal Tribes*, ed. J. H. Steward, 127–68. Washington, D.C.: U.S. Government Printing Office.

Cooper Alarcón, Daniel. 1997. *The Aztec Palimpsest: Mexico in the Modern Imagination*. Tucson: University of Arizona Press.

Cortés, Hernán. 1967. *Cartas de relación*. 3rd ed. Mexico City: Editorial Porrúa.

Cotlow, Lewis. 1953. *Amazon Head-Hunters*. New York: Henry Holt.

Cowgill, George. 1979. Teotihuacan, Internal Militaristic Competition, and the Fall of the Classic Maya. In *Maya Archaeology and Ethnohistory*, ed. Norman Hammond and Gordon Willey, 51–62. Austin: University of Texas Press.

Crespi, Muriel. 1981. St John the Baptist: The Ritual Looking Glass of the Hacienda Indian Ethnic and Power Relations. In *Cultural Transformations and Ethnicity in Modern Ecuador*, ed. N. Whitten, 477–505. Urbana: University of Illinois Press.

Dahlin, Bruce H. 1984. A Colossus in Guatemala: The Preclassic Maya City of El Mirador. *Archaeology* 37:18–25.

Daly, Martin, and Margo Wilson. 1988. *Homicide*. New York: Aldine de Gruyter.

———. 1999. An Evolutionary Psychological Perspective on Homicide. In *Homicide Studies: A Sourcebook of Social Research*, ed. M. Dwayne Smith and Margaret A. Zahn, 58–71. Thousand Oaks, Calif.: Sage Publications.

Deagan, Kathleen A. 1989. The Search for La Navidad, Columbus's 1492 Settlement. In *First Encounters: Spanish Explorations in the Caribbean and the United States, 1492–1570*, ed. Jerald T. Milanich and Susan Milbrath, 41–54. Gainesville: University of Florida Press.

———. 2004. Reconsidering Taíno Social Dynamics after Spanish Conquest: Gender and Class in Culture Contact Studies. *Latin American Antiquity* 69 (4): 597–626.

Dean, Warren. 1984. Indigenous Populations of the São Paulo–Rio de Janeiro Coast: Trade, Aldeamento, Slavery and Extinction. *Revista de História* 117:3–26.

———. 1995. *With Broadax and Firebrand: The Destruction of the Brazilian Atlantic Forest*. Berkeley: University of California Press.

DeCicco, Gabriel, and Donald Brockington. 1956. *Reconocimiento arqueológico en el suroeste de Oaxaca*. Dirección de Monumentos Pre-Hispánicos, Instituto Nacional de Antropología e Historia, Informes 6. Mexico City.

de la Fuentes, Beatriz, ed. 1995. *La pintura mural prehispánica en México*, part 1, *Teotihuacán*. Vol. 1, *Catálogo*; vol. 2, *Estudios*. Mexico City: UNAM, Instituto de Investigaciones Estéticas.

———. 1998. *La pintura mural prehispánica en México*, part 2, *Área Maya: Bonampak*. Vol. 1, *Catálogo*; vol. 2, *Estudios*. Mexico City: UNAM, Instituto de Investigaciones Estéticas.

de la Torre, Segundo. 1995. La rama de gallos en la comunidad de Abatag. In *La fiesta religiosa indigena en el Ecuador*, 45–55. Quito: Editorial Abya Yala.

Deloria, Vine. 1969. *Custer Died for Your Sins: An Indian Manifesto*. New York: Avon.

———. 1995. *Red Earth, White Lies: Native Americans and the Myth of Scientific Fact*. New York: Scribner.

Demarchi, Darío A., Graciela M. Panzetta-Dutari, Christina C. Motran, María de los Angeles López de Basualdo, and Alberto J. Marcellino. 2001. Mitochondrial DNA Haplogroups in Haplogroups in Amerindian Populations from the Gran Chaco. *American Journal of Physical Anthropology* 115:119–203.

Demarest, Arthur A. 1978. Interregional Conflict and Situational Ethics in Classic Maya Warfare. In *Codex Wauchope: Festschrift in Honor of Robert Wauchope*, ed. Marco Giardino, Barbara Edmonson, and Winfred Creamer, 101–11. New Orleans: Tulane University.

———. 1992. Ideology in Ancient Maya Cultural Evolution: The Dynamics of Galactic Polities. In *Ideology and Pre-Columbian Civilizations*, ed. Arthur A. Demarest and Geoffrey Conrad, 135–57. Santa Fe, N.Mex.: School of American Research Press.

———. 1997. The Vanderbilt Petexbatun Regional Archaeological Project, 1989–1994: Overview, History, and Major Results of a Multidisciplinary Study of the Classic Maya Collapse. *Ancient Mesoamerica* 8 (2): 209–27.

———. 2004a. After the Maelstrom: Collapse of the Classic Maya Kingdoms and the Terminal Classic in Western Petén. In *The Terminal Classic in the Maya Lowlands: Collapse, Transition, and Transformation*, ed. Arthur A. Demarest, Prudence M. Rice, and Don S. Rice, 102–24. Boulder: University Press of Colorado.

———. 2004b. *Ancient Maya: The Rise and Fall of a Rain Forest Civilization*. Cambridge, U.K.: Cambridge University Press.

———. 2006. *The Petexbatun Regional Archaeological Project: A Multidisciplinary Study of the Maya Collapse*. Nashville: Vanderbilt University Press.

Demarest, Arthur A., Héctor Escobedo, and Matt O'Mansky, eds. 1996. *Proyecto Arqueológico Punta de Chimino, informe preliminar*. Guatemala City: Instituto de Antropología e Historia.

Demarest, Arthur A., and Federico Fahsen. 2003. Nuevos datos e interpretaciones de los Reinos Occidentales. In *XVI Simposio de Investigaciones Arqueológicas en Guatemala*, ed. Juan Pedro Laporte, Bárbara Arroyo, Héctor L. Escobedo, and Héctor Mejía, 159–74. Guatemala City: Instituto de Antropología e Historia.

Demarest, Arthur A., Nora María López, Robert Chatham, Kitty Emery, Joel Palka, Kim Morgan, and Héctor Escobedo. 1991. Operación DP28: Excavaciones en las murallas defensivas de Dos Pilas. In *Proyecto Arqueológico Regional Petexbatun, Informe Preliminar #3, Tercera Temporada*, ed. Arthur A. Demarest, Takeshi Inomata, Héctor Escobedo, and Joel Palka, 208–41. Guatemala City and Nashville: Instituto de Antropología e Historia de Guatemala and Vanderbilt University, Department of Anthropology.

Demarest, Arthur A., Matt O'Mansky, Claudia Wolley, Dirk Van Tuerenhout, Takeshi Inomata, Joel Palka, and Héctor Escobedo. 1997. Classic Maya Defensive Systems and Warfare in the Petexbatun Region: Archaeological Evidence and Interpretations. *Ancient Mesoamerica* 8 (2): 229–53.

Demarest, Arthur A., Prudence M. Rice, and Don S. Rice. 2004. The Terminal Classic in the Maya Lowlands: Assessing Collapses, Terminations, and Transformations. In *The Terminal Classic in the Maya Lowlands: Collapse, Transition, and Transformation*, ed. Arthur A. Demarest, Prudence M. Rice, and Don S. Rice, 545–72. Boulder: University Press of Colorado.

Diaz Cajas, Manuel. 1995. La Fiesta de San Juan en Iluman. In *La fiesta religiosa indigena en el Ecuador*, 75–98. Quito: Editorial Abya Yala.

Díaz del Castillo, Bernal. 1982. *Historia verdadera de la conquista de la Nueva España*, ed. C. Sáenz de Santamaría. Madrid: Instituto Gonzalo Fernández de Oviedo.

———. 1996. *The Discovery and Conquest of Mexico*. New York: De Capo Press.

Diehl, Richard A., and Janet Catherine Berlo, eds. 1989. *Mesoamerica after the Decline of Teotihuacan, A.D. 700–900*. Washington, D.C.: Dumbarton Oaks Research Library and Collection.

Dillehay, Tom D., ed. 1995. *Tombs for the Living: Andean Mortuary Practices*. Washington, D.C.: Dumbarton Oaks.

———. 2001. Town and Country in Late Moche Times: A View from Two Northern Valleys. In *Moche Art and Archaeology in Ancient Peru*, ed. J. Pillsbury, 259–84. Washington, D.C.: National Gallery of Art.

DiPeso, Charles C. 1974. *Casas Grandes: A Fallen Trading Center of the Gran Chichimeca*, vols. 1–8, ed. Gloria J. Fenner. Dragoon, Ariz.: Amerind Foundation.

Discovery Channel. 2002. *Unsolved History: Aztec Temple of Blood* (video). Silver Spring, Md.: Discovery Communications.

Dongoske, Kurt, Mark Aldenderfer, and Karen Doehner. 2000. *Working Together: Native Americans and Archaeologists*. Washington, D.C.: Society for American Archaeology.

Donnan, Christopher B. 1978. *Moche Art of Peru: Pre-Columbian Symbolic Communication*. Los Angeles: Museum of Cultural History, University of California.

———. 1997. Deer Hunting and Combat: Parallel Activities in the Moche World. In *The Spirit of Ancient Peru: Treasures from the Museo Arqueológico Rafael Larco Herrera*, ed. K. Berrin, 51–59. New York: Thames and Hudson.

Dortch, Charles E. 2002. Modeling Past Aboriginal Hunter-Gatherer Socio-Economic and Territorial Organisation in Western Australia's Lower South-West. *Archaeology in Oceania* 37:1–21.

Drennan, Robert D. 1976. *Fábrica San José and Middle Formative Society in the Valley of Oaxaca*. University of Michigan Museum of Anthropology Memoirs, no. 8. Ann Arbor.

———. 1989. The Mountains North of the Valley. In *Monte Albán's Hinterland, Part II: Prehispanic Settlement Patterns in Tlacolula, Etla, and Ocotlán, the Valley of Oaxaca, Mexico*, ed. S. A. Kowalewski, G. M. Feinman, L. Finsten, R. E. Blanton, and L. Nicholas, 367–84. University of Michigan Museum of Anthropology Memoirs, no. 23. Ann Arbor.

Dunn, Oliver, and James E. Kelley Jr., eds. 1989. *The Diario of Christopher Columbus's First Voyage to America*. Norman: University of Oklahoma Press.

Dunning, Nicholas P. 1992. *Lords of the Hills: Ancient Maya Settlement in the Puuc Region, Yucatán, Mexico*. Madison, Wisc.: Prehistory Press.

Dunning, Nicholas P., and Timothy Beach. 2007. *Ecology and Agriculture of the Petexbatun Region: An Ancient Perspective on Rainforest Adaptation*. Nashville: Vanderbilt University Press. Forthcoming.

Dunning, Nicholas P., Timothy Beach, and David Rue. 1997. The Paleoecology and Ancient Settlement of the Petexbatun Region, Guatemala. *Ancient Mesoamerica* 8 (2): 255–66.

Duran, Fray Diego. 1993. *The History of the Indies of New Spain*. Norman: Oklahoma University Press.

Duviols, Pierre. 1973. Huari and Llauaz: Agricultores y pastores, un dualismo prehispanico de opocision y complementaridad. *Revista del Museo Nacional* 39:153–91.

Earle, Timothy K. 1987. Chiefdoms in Archaeological and Ethnohistorical Perspective. *Annual Review of Anthropology* 16:279–308.

Edgerton, Robert. 1992. *Sick Societies*. New York: Free Press.

Eerkens, Jelmer W. 1999. Common Pool Resources, Buffer Zones, and Jointly Owned Territories: Hunter-Gatherer Land and Resource Tenure in Fort Irwin, Southeastern California. *Human Ecology* 27:297–312.

Ember, Melvin, and Carol R. Ember. 1994. Cross-Cultural Studies of War and Peace: Recent Achievements and Future Possibilities. In *Studying War: Anthropological Perspectives*, ed. S. P. Reyna and R. E. Downs, 185–208. Amsterdam: Gordon and Breach.

Emery, Kitty F. 2008. *Ancient Fauna, Bone Industries, and Subsistence History of the Petexbatun Region*. Nashville: Vanderbilt University Press. Forthcoming.

Emperaire, Joseph. 1963. *Los nómades del mar*. Santiago de Chile: Ediciones de la Universidad de Chile.

Erickson, Clark L. 2000. An Artificial Landscape Scale Fishery in the Bolivian Amazon. *Nature* 408:190–93.

Espinoza Soriano, Waldemar. 1971. *Los Huancas: Aliados de la conquista*. Lima: Universidad Nacional Central de Lima.

Evans, Clifford, and Betty J. Meggers. 1968. *Archaeological Investigations on the Río Napo, Eastern Ecuador*. Washington, D.C.: Smithsonian Institution Press.

Ewers, John. 1975. Intertribal Warfare as the Precursor of Indian-White Warfare on the Northern Great Plains. *Western Historical Quarterly* 6 (4): 397–410.

Fabbro, David. 1978. Peaceful Societies: An Introduction. *Journal of Peace Research* 15 (1): 67–83.

Faulkner, David K. 1986. The Mass Burial: An Entomological Perspective. In *The Pacatnamu Papers*, vol. 1, ed. C. Donnan and G. A. Cock. Los Angeles: Fowler Museum of Cultural History.

Fausto, Carlos. 1992. Fragmentos de história e cultura Tupinambá: Da etnologia como instrumento crítico de conhecimento etno-histórico. In *História dos Índios no Brasil*, ed. Manuela Carneiro da Cunha, 381–96. São Paulo: Editora Schwarcz.

———. 1997. *A dialética da predação e da familiarização entre os Parakanã da Amazônia oriental: Por uma teoria da guerra Ameríndia*. Ph.D. dissertation, Department of Anthropology, Universidade Federal do Rio de Janeiro.

———. 2000. Of Enemies and Pets: Warfare and Shamanism in Amazonia. *American Ethnologist* 26 (4): 933–56.

Feinman, Gary M. 1982. Patterns in Ceramic Production and Distribution, Periods Early I through V. In *Monte Albán's Hinterland, Part I: The Prehispanic Settlement Patterns of the Central and Southern Parts of the Valley of Oaxaca, Mexico*, ed. R. E. Blanton, S. A. Kowalewski, G. M. Feinman, and J. Appel, 181–206. University of Michigan Museum of Anthropology Memoirs, no. 15. Ann Arbor.

Feinman, Gary M., and Linda Nicholas. 1990. At the Margins of the Monte Albán State: Settlement Patterns in the Ejutla Valley, Oaxaca, Mexico. *Latin American Antiquity* 1:216–46.

Ferguson, R. Brian. 1990. Blood of the Leviathan: Western Contact and Warfare in Amazonia. *American Ethnologist* 17 (2): 237–57.

———. 1995. *Yanomami Warfare: A Political History.* Santa Fe, N.Mex.: School of American Research Press.

Ferguson, R. Brian, and Neil L. Whitehead. 1992. The Violent Edge of Empire. In *War in the Tribal Zone: Expanding States and Indigenous Warfare*, ed. B. Ferguson and N. Whitehead, 1–30. Santa Fe, N.Mex.: School of American Research Press.

Fernandes, Florestan. 1963. *Organização social dos Tupinambá.* 2nd ed. São Paulo: Difusão Européia do Livro.

Finsten, Laura. 1996. Periphery and Frontier in Southern Mexico: The Mixtec Sierra in Highland Oaxaca. In *Pre-Columbian World Systems*, ed. P. N. Peregrine and G. M. Feinman, 77–95. Monographs in World Archaeology, no. 26. Madison, Wisc.: Prehistory Press.

Fitz-Roy, Robert. [1839] 1966. *Narrative of the Surveying Voyages of His Majesty's Ships* Adventure *and Beagle between the years 1826 and 1836: Describing Their Examination of the Southern Shores of South America, and the Beagle's Circumnavigation of the Globe*, vol. 2. New York: AMS Press.

Flannery, Kent V. 1972. The Cultural Evolution of Civilizations. *Annual Review of Ecology and Systematics* 3:399–426.

———. 1998. The Ground Plans of Archaic States. In *Archaic States*, ed. G. M. Feinman and J. Marcus, 15–57. Santa Fe, N.Mex.: School of American Research Press.

———. 1999. Process and Agency in Early State Formation. *Cambridge Archaeology Journal* 9 (1): 3–21.

Flannery, Kent V., and Joyce Marcus. 1983. The Origins of the State in Oaxaca: Editors' Introduction. In *The Cloud People: Divergent Evolution of the Zapotec and Mixtec Civilizations*, ed. K. V. Flannery and J. Marcus, 79–83. New York: Academic Press.

———. 1990. Borrón y Cuenta Nueva: Setting Oaxaca's Archaeological Record Straight. In *Debating Oaxaca Archaeology*, ed. J. Marcus, 17–69. University of Michigan Museum of Anthropology Anthropological Papers, no. 84. Ann Arbor.

———. 1994. *Early Formative Pottery of the Valley of Oaxaca.* University of Michigan Museum of Anthropology Memoirs, no. 27. Ann Arbor.

———. 2003. The Origin of War: New ^{14}C Dates from Ancient Mexico. *Proceedings of the National Academy of Sciences* 100 (20): 11801–5.

Folan, William J., Joyce Marcus, Sophia Pincemin, Maria del Rosario Dominguez-Carrasco, and Laraine Fletcher. 1995. Calakmul: New Data from an Ancient Maya Capital in Campeche, Mexico. *Latin American Antiquity* 6 (4): 310–34.

Fox, John W., Garrett W. Cook, Arlen F. Chase, and Diane Z. Chase. 1996. Questions of Political and Economic Integration: Segmentary versus Centralized States among the Ancient Maya. *Current Anthropology* 37 (5): 795–801.

Freidel, David A. 1986. Maya Warfare: An Example of Peer Polity Interaction. In *Peer Polity Interaction and Socio-Political Change*, ed. Colin Renfrew and John F. Cherry, 93–108. Cambridge, U.K.: Cambridge University Press.

———. 1992. The Trees of Life: *Ahau* as Idea and Artifact in Classic Lowland Maya Civilization. In *Ideology and Pre-Columbian Civilizations*, ed. Arthur A. Demarest and Geoffrey W. Conrad, 115–33. Santa Fe, N.Mex.: School of American Research Press.

———. 1993. Flint-Shields and Battle Beasts: The Warrior Path of Kingship (as Told by David Freidel). In *Maya Cosmos: Three Thousand Years on the Shaman's Path*, ed. David Freidel, Linda Schele, and Jay Parker, 293–331. New York: William Morrow.

Freidel, David A., Barbara MacLeod, and Charles K. Suhler. 2003. Early Classic Maya Conquest in Words and Deeds. In *Ancient Mesoamerican Warfare*, ed. M. Kathryn Brown and Travis W. Stanton, 189–215. Walnut Creek, Calif.: AltaMira Press.

Freidel, David A., Kathryn Reece-Taylor, and David Mora-Marín. 2002. The Origins of Maya Civilization: The Old Shell Game, Commodity, Treasure, and Kingship. In *Ancient Maya Political Economies*, ed. Marilyn A. Masson and David A. Freidel, 41–86. Walnut Creek, Calif.: AltaMira Press.

Fried, Morton H. 1961. Warfare, Military Organization, and the Evolution of Society. *Anthropologica* 3:134–47.

Furst, Peter T. 1974. Morning Glory and Mother Goddess at Tepantitla, Teotihuacan: Iconography and Analogy in Pre-Columbian Art. In *Mesoamerican Archaeology: New Approaches*, ed. Norman Hammond, 187–215. Austin: University of Texas Press.

Gallardo, Carlos R. 1910. *Tierra del Fuego: Los Ona*. Buenos Aires: Cabaut y Cía.

García Cook, Angel. 1976. *El Proyecto Arqueológico Puebla-Tlaxcala*. Puebla, Mexico: Fundación Alemana Para la Investigación Científica.

———. 1994. Cantona. *Arqueología Mexicana* 2 (10): 60–65. Mexico City: Editorial Raíces.

Garcilasco de la Vega, Inca. 1966. *Royal Commentaries of the Yncas and General History of Peru, Part One*. Austin: University of Texas Press.

Gat, Azar. 2000a. The Human Motivational Complex: Evolutionary Theory and the Causes of Hunter-Gatherer Fighting, Part I: Primary Somatic and Reproductive Causes. *Anthropological Quarterly* 73:20–35.

———. 2000b. The Human Motivational Complex: Evolutionary Theory and the Causes of Hunter-Gatherer Fighting, Part II: Proximate, Subordinate, and Derivative Causes. *Anthropological Quarterly* 73:74–89.

General, Paul, and Gary Warrick. 2004. The Haudenosaunee (Six Nations) and Archaeology. *Society of American Archaeology* 5 (4): 29–30.

Gifford, Douglas, and Pauline Hoggarth. 1976. *Carnival and Coca Leaf: Some Traditions of the Peruvian Quechua Ayllu*. Edinburgh: Scottish Academic Press.

Gilt Contreras, Mario Alberto. 1955. Las guerrillas indigenas de Chiyaraque y Toqto. *Archivos Peruanos de Folklore* 1:110–19.

Goeje, Claudius H. de. 1943. Philosophy, Initiation and Myths of the Indians of Guiana and Adjacent Countries. *Internationales Archiv für Ethnographie* 44:1–136.

Gomez-Otero, Julieta, and Silvia Dahinten. 1999. Evidencias de contactos interetnicos en el siglo XVI en Patagonia. In *Actas del XII Congreso Nacional de Arqueología Argentina*, vol. 3, ed. Diez Martin, 44–45. La Plata, Argentina: Universidad Nacional de la Plata.

González, José R., Silvia Dahinten, and Miquel Hernández. 2001. The Settlement of Patagonia: A Matrix Correlation Study. *Human Biology* 73:233–48.

Gorbak, Celina, M. Lischetti, and C. Munoz. 1962. Batallas rituales de chiaraje y del tocto de la provincia de Kanas (Cusco-Peru). *Revista del Museo Nacional* 3:245–304.

Gordillo, Gastón. 2001. Un río tan salvaje e indómito como el indio Toba: Una historia antropológica de la frontera del Pilcomayo. *Desarrollo Económico* 162:261–80.

———. 2002. Remembering "The Ancient Ones": Memory, Hegemony, and the Shadows of State Terror in the Argentinean Chaco. In *Culture, Economy, Power: Anthropology as Critique, Anthropology as Praxis*, ed. Winnie Len and Belinda Leach, 177–90. Albany: SUNY Press.

Graham, Ian. 1965. *Tres Islas informe presentado al Museo Nacional de Arqueología y Etnología de Guatemala.* Guatemala City: Archivos del Museo de Guatemala.

———. 1967. *Archaeological Explorations of El Petén, Guatemala.* Middle American Research Institute Publication no. 33. New Orleans: Tulane University.

Guaman Poma de Ayala, Felipe. 1943. *Guaman Poma.* Buenos Aires: Editorial Nova.

———. [1615] 1987. *Nueva crónica y buen gobierno*, ed. John V. Murra. Madrid: Historia 16.

Guaña, Pablo. 1992. *Inti Raymi Cayambe.* Cayambe: CICAY–Museo de Cayambe.

Guandinango, Angel. 1995. Fiesta ritual de Inti Raimi y Fiesta de San Pedro. In *La fiesta religiosa indigena en el Ecuador*, 65–74. Quito: Editorial Abya Yala.

Guichon, R., R. Barberena, and L. Borrero. 2001. ¿Dónde y cómo aparecen los restos óseos humanos en Patagonia austral? *Anales del Instituto de la Patagonia*, Serie Cs. Hs., 29:103–18.

Guilliem Arroyo, Salvador. 1999. *Ofrendas a Ehécatl-Quetzalcóatl en México- Tlatelolco: Proyecto Tlatelolco, 1987–1996.* Mexico City: Instituto Nacional de Antropología e Historia.

Gusinde, Martin. 1961. *The Yamana: The Life and Thought of the Water Nomads of Cape Horn*, trans. Frieda Schütze. New Haven, Conn.: Human Relations Area Files.

———. 1982. *Los indios de Tierra del Fuego: Los Selk'nam.* 2 vols. Buenos Aires: Centro Argentino de Etnología Americana, Concejo Nacional de Investigaciones Científicas y Técnicas.

———. 1986. *Los indios de Tierra del Fuego: Los Yamana.* 3 vols. Buenos Aires: Centro Argentino de Etnología Americana, Concejo Nacional de Investigaciones Científicas y Técnicas.

———. 1991. *Los indios de Tierra del Fuego: Los Halakwulup.* 2 vols. Buenos Aires: Centro Argentino de Etnología Americana, Concejo Nacional de Investigaciones Científicas y Técnicas.

———. 1996. *The Fireland Indians.* Vol. 1: *The Selk'nam, on the Life and Thought of a Hunting People of the Great Island of Tierra del Fuego.* New Haven, Conn.: Human Relations Area Files.

Gutierrez, Pedro. 1905. *Historia de las guerras civiles del Peru.* Madrid: Libreria General de Victoriano.

Haas, Jonathan. 2003. The Archaeology of War. *Anthropology Newsletter* 44 (5): 7.

Hadingham, Evan. 1987. *Lines to the Mountain Gods.* New York: Random House.

Hakovirta, Harto. 1986. *Third World Conflicts and Refugeeism: Dimensions, Dynamics and Trends of the World Refugee Problem.* Helsinki: Finnish Society of Sciences and Letters.

Hansen, Richard D. 2001. The First Cities—The Beginnings of Urbanization and State Formation in the Maya Lowlands. In *Maya: Divine Kings of the Rainforest*, ed. Nikolai Grube, 50–65. Cologne, Germany: Kónemann.

Hardenburg, W. E. 1912. *The Putumayo: The Devil's Paradise*. London: T. Fisher Unwin.

Harner, Michael. 1972. *The Jivaro: People of the Sacred Waterfalls*. Garden City, N.J.: Doubleday/Natural History Press.

———. 1977. The Enigma of Aztec Sacrifice. *Natural History* 86 (4):46–51.

Hartmann, Roswith. 1972. Otros datos sobre las llamadas batallas rituals. In *Proceedings of the 29th and 30th International Congress of Americanistas*, vol. 6, 125–35. Lima: Instituto de Estudios Peruanos.

Hassig, Ross. 1992. *War and Society in Ancient Mesoamerica*. Berkeley: University of California Press.

Hassler, Peter. 1992a. *Menschenopfer bei den Azteken? Eine Quellen- und Ideologiekritische Studie*. New York: P. Lang.

———. 1992b. Human Sacrifice among the Aztecs? (Reprinted from *Die Zeit*, Hamburg, Germany; copyright World Press Review, 1992.) Mexika Eagle Society website, http://www.mexika.org/Sacrifice.html.

———. 1992c. Sacrificios humanos entre Los Mexicas y otros pueblos Indios: Realidad o fantasia? Mexika Eagle Society website, http://www.mexika.org/HasslerSac.htm.

Hastorf, Christine. 1993. *Agriculture and the Onset of Political Inequality before the Inka*. Cambridge, U.K.: Cambridge University Press.

Headrick, Annabeth. 2003. Butterfly War at Teotihuacan. In *Ancient Mesoamerican Warfare*, ed. Kathryn M. Brown and Travis W. Stanton, 149-170. Walnut Grove, Calif.: AltaMira Press.

Heath, Charles. 2004. Catawba Militarism: Ethnohistorical and Archaeological Overviews. *North Carolina Archaeology* 53:80–120.

Heckenberger, Michael J., Afukaka Kuikuro, Urissapá Tabata Kuikuro, J. Christian Russell, Morgan Schmidt, Carlos Fausto, and Bruna Franchetto. 2003. Amazonia 1492: Pristine Forest or Cultural Parkland? *Science* 301:1710–13.

Hemming, John. 1970. *The Conquest of the Incas*. New York: Harcourt Brace Jovanovich.

———. 1978. *Red Gold: The Conquest of the Brazilian Indians, 1500–1760*. Cambridge, Mass.: Harvard University Press.

———. 1987. *Amazon Frontier: The Defeat of the Brazilian Indians*. London: MacMillan.

Hendricks, Janet. 1993. *To Drink of Death: The Narrative of a Shuar Warrior*. Tucson: University of Arizona Press.

Hill, Jonathan, and Fernando Santos-Granero, eds. 2001. *Comparative Arawak Histories: Rethinking Culture Area and Language Group*. Urbana: University of Illinois Press.

Hopkins, Diane. 1982. Juego de Enemigos. *Allpanchis* 20:167–87.

Hrdlička, Aleš. 1914. *Anthropological Work in Peru, in 1913, with Notes on the Pathology of the Ancient Peruvians*, with twenty-six plates. Smithsonian Miscellaneous Collections, vol. 61, no. 18. Washington, D.C.: Smithsonian Institution.

Hulme, Peter. 1994. Tales of Distinction: European Ethnography and the Caribbean. In *Implicit Understandings: Observing, Reporting, and Reflecting on the Encounters between Europeans and Other Peoples in the Early Modern Era*, ed. Stuart B. Schwartz, 157–97. Cambridge, U.K.: Cambridge University Press.

Humes, Edward. 1991. *Buried Secrets: A True Story of Serial Murder, Black Magic, and Drug-Running on the U.S. Border*. New York: Dutton, Penguin Books.

Inomata, Takeshi. 2003. War, Destruction, and Abandonment: The Fall of the Classic Maya Center of Aguateca, Guatemala. In *The Archaeology of Settlement Abandonment in Middle America*, ed. Takeshi Inomata and Ronald W. Webb, 43–60. Salt Lake City: University of Utah Press.

———. 2006. *Warfare and the Fall of a Fortified Center: Archaeological Investigations at Aguateca*. Nashville: Vanderbilt University Press.

Isbell, William H., and G. F. McEwan, eds. 1991. *Huari Administrative Structure: Prehistoric Monumental Architecture and State Government*. Washington, D.C.: Dumbarton Oaks.

Jackson, M. A. 2004. The Chimu Sculptures of Huacas Tacaynamo and El Dragon, Moche Valley, Peru. *Latin American Antiquity* 15 (3): 298–322.

Joyce, Arthur A. 1991. Formative Period Social Change in the Lower Río Verde Valley. *Latin American Antiquity* 2:126–50.

———. 1994. Late Formative Community Organization and Social Complexity on the Oaxaca Coast. *Journal of Field Archaeology* 21:147–68.

Joyce, Arthur A., Marcus Winter, and Raymond G. Mueller. 1998. *Arqueología de la costa de Oaxaca*. Oaxaca: Centro INAH Oaxaca.

Joyce, Arthur A., Robert N. Zeitlin, Judith F. Zeitlin, and Javier Urcid. 2000. On Oaxaca Coast Archaeology: Setting the Record Straight. *Current Anthropology* 43:623–25.

Karsten, Rafael. [1932] 1979. *Indian Tribes of the Argentine and Bolivian Chaco*. New York: AMS Press.

Keegan, William F., Morgan Maclachlan, and Bryan Byrne. 1998. Social Foundations of Taino Caciques. In *Chiefdoms and Chieftaincy in the Americas*, ed. Elsa M. Redmond, 217–44. Gainesville: University Press of Florida.

Keeley, Lawrence H. 1980. *Experimental Determination of Stone Tool Uses: A Microwear Analysis*. Chicago: University of Chicago Press.

———. 1996. *War before Civilization*. New York: Oxford University Press.

Kelly, Raymond C. 2000. *Warless Societies and the Origin of War*. Ann Arbor: University of Michigan Press.

Kowalewski, Stephen A., Gary M. Feinman, Laura Finsten, Richard E. Blanton, and Linda Nicholas. 1989. *Monte Albán's Hinterland, Part II: Prehispanic Settlement Patterns in Tlacolula, Etla, and Ocotlán, the Valley of Oaxaca, Mexico*. University of Michigan Museum of Anthropology Memoirs, no. 23. Ann Arbor.

Krech, Shepard. 1999. *The Ecological Indian*. New York: W. W. Norton.

Kutscher, Gerdt. 1955. *Arte antiguo de la costa norte del Peru [Ancient art of the Peruvian North Coast]*. Berlin: Gebr. Mann.

Landa, Diego de. [1937] 1978. *Yucatan before and after the Conquest, 1524–1579*. New York: Dover Publications.

Lapiner, Alan C. 1976. *Pre-Columbian Art of South America*. New York: H. N. Abrams.

Larrick, James, James Yost, Jon Kaplan, Garland King, and John Mayall. 1979. Patterns of Health and Disease among the Waorani Indians of Eastern Ecuador. *Medical Anthropology* 3:147–89.

Las Casas, Fray Bartolomé de. 1951. *Historia de las Indias*. 2 vols. Mexico City: Fondo de Cultura Económica.

———. 1967. *Apologética historia sumaria*, ed. Edmundo O'Gorman. 2 vols. Mexico City: Universidad Nacional Autónoma de México, Instituto de Investigaciones Históricas.

Lathrap, Donald. 1970. *The Upper Amazon*. New York: Praeger.

———. 1971. *History of the Indies*. New York: Harper and Row.

LeBlanc, Steven A., and Katherine E. Register. 2003. *Constant Battles: The Myth of the Peaceful Noble Savage*. New York: St. Martin's.

Legoupil, Dominique. 2000. *Un premier bilan archaeologique tres positif*. Ecoussans, France: Ultima Patagonia 2000, Ed. Association Centre terre 33760.

Legoupil, Dominique, and Alfredo Prieto. 1991. Sepultura de niños canoeros en un abrigo pintado en Ultima Esperanza, Chile. *Anales del Instituto de la Patagonia*, Ser. Cs. Ss. 20:133–38.

Léry, Jean de. 1990. *History of a Voyage to the Land of Brazil, Otherwise Called America . . .* , trans. Janet Whatley. Los Angeles: University of California Press.

Lestringant, Frank. 1999. The Myth of the Indian Monarchy: An Aspect of the Controversy between Thevet and Lery (1575–1585). In *Indians and Europe: An Interdisciplinary Collection of Essays*, ed. Christian F. Feest, 37–60. Lincoln: University of Nebraska Press.

Lévi-Strauss, Claude. 1942. Guerra e comércio entre os índios da América do Sul. *Revista do Arquivo Municipal* 87:131–46.

Lopez, Juana. 2001. Primera victima en enfrentamientos en el Inti Raymi. *Periodico La Hora*, August 26.

López Alonso, Sergio, Zaíd Lagunas Rodríguez, and Carlos Serrano Sánchez. 2002. *Costumbres funerarias y sacrificio humano en Cholula prehispánica*. Mexico City: Universidad Nacional Autónoma de México, Instituto de Investigaciones Antropológicas.

López-Baralt, Mercedes. 1985. *El Mito Taíno: Lévi-Strauss en las Antillas*. Puerto Rico: Ediciones Huracán.

López de Gómara, Francisco, and Joaquín Ramírez Cabañas. 1943. *Historia de la conquista de México*. Mexico City: Editorial Pedro Robredo.

López Luján, Leonardo. 1994. *The Offerings of the Templo Mayor of Tenochtitlán*, trans. Bernardo R. Ortiz de Montellano and Thelma Ortiz de Montellano. Niwot: University Press of Colorado.

López Luján, Leonardo, and Vida Mercado. 1996. Dos esculturas de Mictlantecuhtli encontradas en el Recinto Sagrado de México-Tenochtitlan. *Estudios de Cultura Náhuatl*, vol. 26, 41–68. Mexico City: IIH-UNAM.

Lothrop, Samuel K. 1928. *The Indians of Tierra del Fuego*. New York: Museum of the American Indian, Heye Foundation.

Lovén, Sven. 1935. *Origins of the Tainan Culture, West Indies*. Göteborg: Elanders Bokfryckeri Akfiebolag.

Lundell, Cyrus L. 1933. The Agriculture of the Maya. *Southwest Review* 19:65–77.

Mackey, Carol J., and A. M. Ulana Klymyshyn. 1990. The Southern Frontier of the Chimu Empire. In *The Northern Dynasties: Kingship and Statecraft in Chimor*, ed. M. E. Moseley and A. Cordy-Collins, 195–226. Washington, D.C.: Dumbarton Oaks.

Marchant, Alexander. 1942. From Barter to Slavery: The Economic Relations of Portuguese and Indians in the Settlement of Brazil, 1500–1580. *Johns Hopkins University Studies in Historical and Political Science* 60 (1): 1–160. Baltimore: Johns Hopkins University Press.

Marcus, Joyce. 1974. The Iconography of Power among the Classic Maya. *World Archaeology* 6 (1): 83–94.

———. 1976. The Iconography of Militarism at Monte Albán and Neighboring Sites in the Valley of Oaxaca. In *The Origins of Religious Art and Iconography in Preclassic Mesoamerica*, ed. H. B. Nicholson, 123–39. Los Angeles: Latin American Center, University of California–Los Angeles.

———. 1980. Zapotec Writing. *Scientific American* 242:50–64.

———. 1983. The Conquest Slabs of Building J, Monte Albán. In *The Cloud People: Divergent Evolution of the Zapotec and Mixtec Civilizations*, ed. Kent V. Flannery and Joyce Marcus, 106–8. New York: Academic Press.

———. 1993. Ancient Maya Political Organization. In *Lowland Maya Civilization in the Eighth Century A.D.*, ed. Jeremy A. Sabloff and John S. Henderson, 111–84. Washington, D.C.: Dumbarton Oaks Research Library and Collection.

Marcus, Joyce, and Kent V. Flannery. 1996. *Zapotec Civilization: How Urban Society Evolved in Mexico's Oaxaca Valley*. London: Thames and Hudson.

Markman, Charles W. 1981. *Prehispanic Settlement Dynamics in Central Oaxaca, Mexico: A View from the Miahuatlán Valley*. Vanderbilt University Publications in Anthropology, no. 26. Nashville.

Martin, Debra, and David Frayer. 1997. *Troubled Times: Violence and Warfare in the Past*. Amsterdam: Gordon and Breach.

Martin, Fabiana. 2003. La marca del zorro: Cerro Johnny, un caso arqueológico de carroñeo sobre un esqueleto humano. *Anales del Instituto de la Patagonia*, Ser. Cs. Hs. 30:133–46.

Martin, Simon. 2000. Under a Deadly Star—Warfare among the Classic Maya. In *Maya: Divine Kings of the Rain Forest*, ed. Nikolai Grube, 175–85. Cologne, Germany: Kónemann.

Martin, Simon, and Nikolai Grube. 2000. *Chronicle of the Maya Kings and Queens: Deciphering the Dynasties of the Ancient Maya*. London: Thames and Hudson.

Martínez, Néstor. 2003. Contra la deformación histórica-cultural. Mexika Eagle Society website, http://www.mexika.org/NestorSac.htm.

Martinić, Mateo. 1995. *Los Aónikenk: Historia y cultura*. Punta Arenas, Chile: Ediciones de la Universidad de Magallanes.

———. 1999. Dawsonians o Selkkar: Otro caso de mestizaje aborigen histórico en Magallanes. *Anales del Instituto de la Patagonia*, Ser. Cs. Ss. 27:79–88.

Massone, M., A. Prieto, and P. Cárdenas. 1985–86. Contexto arqueológico de un enterratorio tehuelche excavado en la localidad de San Gregorio, Magallanes. *Anales del Instituto de la Patagonia*, Ser. Cs. Ss. 16:94–101.

Massone, Mauricio. 1987. Los cazadores paleoindios de Tres Arroyos. *Anales del Instituto de la Patagonia*, Ser. Cs. Ss. 17:43–60.

Matheny, Raymond T. 1987. Early States in the Maya Lowlands during the Late Preclassic Period: Edzna and El Mirador. In *City-States of the Maya: Art and Architecture*, ed. Elizabeth P. Benson, 1–44. Denver: Rocky Mountain Institute for Precolumbian Studies.

Matos Moctezuma, Eduardo. 1984. The Templo Mayor of Tenochtitlan: Economics and Ideology. In Boone 1984, 133–64.

McEwen, Colin, and Maria Silva. 1992. Que fueron a hacer los Incas en la costa central del Ecuador? In *5000 años de ocupacion*, ed. Presely Norton and Marco Garcia, 71–90. Quito: Editorial Abya Yala.

McGrane, Bernard. 1989. *Beyond Anthropology: Society and the Other*. New York: Columbia University Press.

McVicker, Donald. 1985. The "Mayanized" Mexicans. *American Antiquity* 50 (1): 82–101.

———. 1988. *Approaches to the Mural Art of Teotihuacan: Four Interpretive Essays*. Manuscript in the possession of the author.

Means, Russell, and Marvin J. Wolf. 1995. *Where White Men Fear to Tread: The Autobiography of Russell Means*. New York: St. Martin's Press.

Mendoza, Marcela. 2002. *Band Mobility and Leadership among the Western Toba Hunter-Gatherers of Gran Chaco in Argentina*. Lewiston, N.Y.: Edwin Mellen Press.

———. 2003. Range Area and Seasonal Campsites of Toba Bands in Western Chaco, Argentina. *Before Farming* 2:203–14.

Mendoza, Rubén G. 1992. *Conquest Polities of the Mesoamerican Epiclassic: Circum-Basin Regionalism, A.D. 550–850*. Ph.D. dissertation, University of Arizona, Tucson.

———. 1994. War Cult Caches of the Central Highland Oloman. Paper prepared for an edited volume on Mesoamerican dedicatory caches by Shirley Mock. Unpublished manuscript on file with the author.

———. 2001a. Book Review: *City of Sacrifice: The Aztec Empire and the Role of Violence in Civilization*, by David Carrasco. *Hispanic Outlook in Higher Education* 12 (1): 47.

———. 2001b. Lost Worlds and Forsaken Tribes: The Fantasy Heritage of Indian Identity and Mexican/Chicano Nationalism on the California Central Coast. Unpublished conference paper, American Anthropological Association, Washington, D.C., November.

———. 2003. Lords of the Medicine Bag: Medical Science and Traditional Practice in Ancient Peru and South America. In *Medicine across Cultures: History and Practice of Medicine in Non-Western Cultures*, ed. Helaine Selin, 225–257. London: Kluwer Academic Publishers.

———. 2004. The Divine Gourd Tree: Tzompantli Skull Racks, Decapitation Rituals, and Human Trophies in Ancient Mesoamerica. Invited symposium paper, Society for American Archaeology 69th Annual Meeting, Montreal, Canada, April 3, 2004.

———. 2007. The Divine Gourd Tree: Tzompantli Skull Racks, Decapitation Rituals, and Human Trophies in Ancient Mesoamerica. In Chacon and Dye 2007, 396–439.

Merino Carrión, Beatriz Leonor. 1989. *La Cultura Tlaxco*. Mexico City: Instituto Nacional de Antropología e Historia.

Métraux, Alfred. 1928. *La civilisation matérielle des tribus Tupi-Guarani*. Paris: P. Geuthner.

———. 1939. Myths and Tales of the Matako Indians (the Gran Chaco, Argentina). *Ethnological Studies* (Sweden) 9:1–127.

———. 1948. The Tupinambá. In *Handbook of South American Indians*, vol. 3, ed. Julian H. Steward, 95–133. Bureau of American Ethnology, Bulletin 143. Washington, D.C.: Smithsonian Institution.

———. [1950] 1979. *A religião dos Tupinambás e suas relações com a das demais tribus Tupi-Guaranis*. 2d ed. São Paulo: Companhia Editora Nacional.

Mexica Movement. 2005. There Is Only One Mexica Movement. http://Mexica-movement.org.

Miller, Arthur G. 1973. *The Mural Paintings of Teotihuacan*. Washington, D.C.: Dumbarton Oaks, Trustees for Harvard University.

Miller, Mary Ellen. 1986. *The Murals of Bonampak*. Princeton: Princeton Univ. Press.

———. 1993. On the Eve of the Collapse: Maya Art of the Eighth Century. In *Lowland Maya Civilization in the Eighth Century A.D.*, ed. J. A. Sabloff and J. S. Henderson, 355–413. Washington, D.C.: Dumbarton Oaks Research Library and Collection.

Miller, Mary, and Simon Martin, eds. 2004. *Courtly Art of the Ancient Maya*. San Francisco, Calif.: Fine Arts Museums of San Francisco.

Miller, Virginia E. 2003. Representaciones de sacrificios en Chichén Itzá. In *Antropología de la eternidad: La muerte en la cultura Maya*, ed. Andrés Cuidad Ruiz, M. H. Ruz Sosa y M.ª J. I. Ponce de León, 383–404. Publicaciones de la S.E.E.M., no. 7. Madrid: Sociedad Española de Estudios Mayas y Centro de Estudios Mayas.

Millon, Clara. 1988. A Reexamination of the Teotihuacan Tassel Headdress Insignia, "Coyote with Sacrificial Knife," "Coyote and Deer." In *Feathered Serpents and Flowering Trees: Reconstructing the Murals of Teotihuacan*, ed. Kathleen Berrin, 114–34, 207–17, 218–21. San Francisco, Calif.: Fine Arts Museums of San Francisco.

Millon, Rene. 1988. Where *Do* They All Come From?—The Provenance of the Wagner Murals from Teotihuacan. In *Feathered Serpents and Flowering Trees: Reconstructing the Murals of Teotihuacan*, ed. Kathleen Berrin, 78–113. San Francisco, Calif.: Fine Arts Museums of San Francisco.

Moffet, Barbara. 1999. Three Frozen Mummies Found on Peak in Argentina. (National Geographic press release, April 6, 1999.) http://www.nationalgeographic.com/events/releases/pr990406.html.

Molina, Cristobal. 1873. *Relacion de las fabulas y ritos de los Incas*. Santiago: Editorial Chilena!

Montaigne, Michel de. 1933. *The Essayes of Montaigne: John Florio's Translation*. New York: Modern Library.

Montandon, George. 1934. *Traite d'ethnologie cyclo-culturelle et d'ergologie systematique*. Paris: Payot.

Monteiro, John. 1992. Os Guarani e a história do Brasil Meridional, séculos XVI–XVII. In *História dos Índios no Brasil*, ed. Manuela Carneiro da Cunha, 475–98. São Paulo: Editora Schwarcz.

Montejo, Victor. 1993. In the Name of the Pot, the Sun, the Broken Spear, the Rock, the Stick, the Idol, Ad Infinitum, Ad Nauseam: An Exposé of Anglo Anthropologists' Obsessions with and Invention of Mayan Gods. *Wicazo SA Review* 9 (1): 12–16.

———. 1999a. Becoming Maya? Appropriation of the White Shaman. http://www2.hawaii.edu/~quetzil/uhm2001/Becoming_Maya.html.

———. 1999b. *Voices from Exile: Violence and Survival in Modern Maya History*. Norman: University of Oklahoma Press.

Moore, Alexander. 1978. *Cultural Anthropology*. New York: Harper and Row.

Moreno, Segundo, and Udo Oberem. 1981. *Contribucion a la etnia Ecuatoriana*. Otavalo, Ecuador: Instituto Otavaleño de Antropologia.

Morley, Sylvanus. 1946. *The Ancient Maya*. Stanford, Calif.: Stanford University Press.

Morote, Efrain. 1955. La Fiesta de San Juan, El Bautista. *Archivos Peruanos de Foklore* 1 (1): 160–200.

Morris, Ann Axtell. 1931. Murals from the Temple of the Warriors and Adjacent Structures. In *The Temple of the Warriors at Chichen Itzá, Yucatan*, ed. Earl H. Morris, Jean Charlot, and Ann Axtell Morris, vol. 1, 347–485, and vol. 2, plates 130–70. Carnegie Institution of Washington Publication no. 406. Washington, D.C.

Morris, Craig. 1998. Inka Strategies of Incorporation and Governance. In *Archaic States*, ed. Gary Feinman and Joyce Marcus, 293–309. Santa Fe, N.Mex.: School of American Research.

Muelle, Jorge. 1950. Pacarectambo. *Revista del Museo Nacional* (Peru) 14:153–60.

Murphy, Robert F. 1989. *Cultural and Social Anthropology: An Overture*. Englewood Cliffs, N.J.: Prentice-Hall.

Myers, Thomas. 1981. Aboriginal Trade Networks in Amazonia. In *Networks in the Past: Regional Interaction in Archaeology*, ed. P. Francis, F. Kense, and P. Duke, 19–30. Proceedings of the Twelfth Annual Congress of the Archaeological Association. Calgary: University of Calgary.

———. 1988. Vision de la prehistoria de la Amazonia superior. In *Primer seminario de investigaciones socials en la Amazonia*, ed. F. Santos, 37–87. Iquitos, Peru: Centro de Estudios Teológicos de la Amazonía.

Nami, Hugo. 1987. Cueva del medio: Perspectivas arqueológicas para la Patagonia austral. *Anales del Instituto de la Patagonia*, Ser. Cs. Ss. 17:73–106.

Neiderberger, B. C. 1987. *Paleopaysages et archaeologie pre-urbaine du Basin de México*, vol. 2. Mexico City: Centre d'Estudes Méxicaines et Centroamericaines.

Newson, Linda. 1995. *Life and Death in Early Colonial Ecuador*. Norman: University of Oklahoma Press.

———. 1996. The Population of the Amazon Basin in 1492: A View from the Ecuadorian Headwaters. *Transactions of the Institute of British Geographers*, n.s. 21 (1): 5–26.

Nicholas, George. 1997. Archaeology, Education and the Secwepemc. *SAA Bulletin* 15 (2): 9–11.

———. 2004. What Do I Really Want from a Relationship with Native Americans? *SAA Archaeological Record* 4 (3): 29–33.

Noelli, Francisco S. 1998. The Tupi: Explaining Origin and Expansions in Terms of Archaeology and of Historical Linguistics. *Antiquity* 277:648–63.

Nordenskiöld, Erland. 1912. Le vie des Indiens dans le Chaco (Amérique du Sud). *Revue de Géographie* 6, part 3.

————. [1930] 1979. *Modifications in Indian Culture through Inventions and Loans.* New York: AMS Press.

Nunes, Diogo. [1554?] 1924–26. Apontamentos de Diogo Nunes das suas viagems na America. In *História da colonização portuguesa do Brasil*, vol. 3, ed. Carlos Malheiro Dias, 367–68. Pôrto: Litografía Nacional.

Obando, Segundo. 1988. *Tradiciones de Imbabura.* Quito: Editorial Abya Yala.

Ogburn, Dennis. 2004. Dynamic Display, Propaganda, and the Reinforcement of Provincial Power in the Inca Empire. In *Foundations of Power in the Prehispanic Andes*, ed. Kevin Vaughn, Dennis Ogburn, and Christina Conlee, 225–39. Archaeological Papers, no. 14. Washington, D.C.: American Anthropological Association.

Ojeda Díaz, María. 1990. *Ritual de desmembramiento humano en Cholula.* Mexico City: INAH, Biblioteca Nacional de Antropología e Historia.

O'Mansky, Matt, and Nicholas P. Dunning. 2004. Settlement and Late Classic Political Disintegration in the Petexbatun Region, Guatemala. In *The Terminal Classic in the Maya Lowlands*, ed. Arthur A. Demarest, Prudence M. Rice, and Don S. Rice, 83–101. Boulder: University Press of Colorado.

Oramas, Luis R. 1916. *Materiales para el estudio de los dialectos Ayamán, Gayón, Jirajara, Ajagua.* Caracas: Litografía El Comercio.

Orbegoso, Clorinda. 1998. Excavaciones en la zona sureste de la Plaza 3c de la Huaca de la Luna durante 1996. In Uceda et al. 1998, 43–64.

Orlove, Benjamin. 1994. Sticks and Stones: Ritual Battle and Play in the Southern Peruvian Highlands. In *Unruly Order: Violence, Power, and Cultural Identity in the High Provinces of Southern Peru*, ed. D. Poole, 133–64. Boulder, Colo.: Westview Press.

Orozco y Berra, Manuel. 1877. El Cuauhxicalli de Tizoc. *Anales*, 3–36. Mexico City: Imprenta del Museo Nacional de Mexico.

Otterbein, Keith F. 1970. *The Evolution of War: A Cross-Cultural Study.* New Haven, Conn.: Human Relations Area Files.

————. 1997. The Origins of War. *Critical Review* 11 (2): 251–77.

————. 2000a. The Doves Have Been Heard from, Where Are the Hawks? *American Anthropologist* 102 (4): 841–44.

————. 2000b. Killing of Captured Enemies: A Cross-Cultural Study. *Current Anthropology* 41 (3): 439–43.

Oyarzún, Javier. 1976. *Expediciones españolas al estrecho de Magallanes.* Madrid: Ediciones de Cultura Hispánica.

Palka, Joel. 1997. Reconstructing Classic Maya Socioeconomic Differentiation and the Collapse at Dos Pilas, Peten, Guatemala. *Ancient Mesoamerica* 8 (2): 293–306.

Pané, Fray Ramón. [1498] 2001. *Relacíon acerca de las antigüedades de los Indios: Nueva versión con estudio preliminar, notas y apéndices por José Juan Arrom.* Mexico City: Siglo Veintiuno Editores.

Parsons, Elsie Clews. 1945. *Peguche: A Study of Andean Indians.* Chicago: University of Chicago Press.

Parsons, Jeffrey, Charles Hastings, and Ramiro Matos. 1997. Rebuilding the State in Highland Peru: Herder-Cultivator Interaction during the Late Intermediate Period in the Tarama-Chichaycocha Region. *Latin American Antiquity* 8 (4): 317–41.

———. 2000. *Prehispanic Settlement Patterns in the Upper Mantaro and Tarma Drainages, Junin, Peru*, vol. 1. Ann Arbor: Museum of Anthropology, University of Michigan.

Pasztory, Esther. 1988. A Reinterpretation of Teotihuacan and Its Mural Painting Tradition. In *Feathered Serpents and Flowering Trees: Reconstructing the Murals of Teotihuacan*, ed. Kathleen Berrin, 45–77. San Francisco, Calif.: Fine Arts Museums of San Francisco.

———. 1997. *Teotihuacan: An Experiment in Living*. Norman: University of Oklahoma Press.

Paz, Octavio. 1987. Food of the Gods. *New York Review*, February 26.

Pearsall, Deborah M. 1992. The Origins of Plant Cultivation in South America. In *The Origins of Agriculture*, ed. C. Wesley Cowan and Patty Jo Watson, 173–205. Washington, D.C.: Smithsonian Institution Press.

Pelleschi, Giovani. [1881] 1886. *Eight Months on the Gran Chaco of the Argentine Republic*. London: Sampson, Low, Marston, Searle and Rivington.

Pereira, Henrique M., Aviv Bergman, and Joan Roughgarden. 2003. Socially Stable Territories: The Negotiation of Space by Interacting Foragers. *American Naturalist* 161:143–52.

Pertuiset, Eugène. 1877. *Le tresor des Incas a la Terre de Feu: Aventures et voyages dans l'Amerique du Sud*. Paris: E. Dentu.

Petersen, James, and John Crock. 2007. Handsome Death: The Taking, Veneration, and Consumption of Human Remains in the Insular Caribbean and Greater Amazonia. In *The Taking and Displaying of Human Body Parts as Trophies by Amerindians*, ed. Richard J. Chacon and David H. Dye. New York: Springer. Forthcoming.

Pickering, Robert B. 1985. Human Osteological Remains from Alta Vista, Zacatecas: An Analysis of the Isolated Bone. In *The Archaeology of West and Northwest Mexico*, ed. Michael S. Foster and Phil C. Weigand, 289–326. Boulder, Colo.: Westview Press.

Pijoan Aguadé, Carmen María, and Josefina Mansilla Lory. 1997. Evidence for Human Sacrifice, Bone Modification and Cannibalism in Ancient México. In *Troubled Times: Violence and Warfare in the Past*, ed. Debra L. Martin and David W. Frayer, 217–39. Amsterdam: Gordon and Breach.

Pijoan, Carmen María, Josefina Mansilla, and Alejandro Pastrana. 1995. Un caso de desmembramiento, Tlatelolco, D.F. In *Estudios de antropología biológica*, vol. 5, ed. Rosa María Ramos Rodríguez and Sergio López Alonso, 81–90. Mexico City: Universidad Nacional Autónoma de México.

Pijoan, C. M., A. Pastrana, and C. Maquivar. 1989. El tzompantli de Tlatelolco: Una evidencia de sacrificio humano. In *Estudios de antropologia biológica*, vol. 4, ed. C. Serrano and M. Salas, 561–83. Mexico City: UNAM-INAH.

Piperno, Dolores R., and Deborah M. Pearsall. 1998. *The Origins of Agriculture in the Lowland Neotropics*. San Diego, Calif.: Academic Press.

Pittier, Henri. 1970. *Manual de las plantas usuales de Venezuela*. Caracas: Fundación Eugenio Mendoza.

Pizarro, Pedro. 1986. *Relacion del descubrimiento de los Reinos del Peru*. Lima: Fondo Editorial.

Platt, Tristan. 1986. Mirrors and Maize: The Concept of Yanantin among the Macha of Bolivia. In *Anthropological History of Andean Polities*, ed. J. Murra, N. Wachtel, and J. Revel, 228–59. Cambridge, U.K.: Cambridge University Press.

———. 1987. The Andean Soldiers of Christ, Confraternity Organization, the Mass of the Sun and Regenerative Warfare in Rural Potosi (18th–20th Centuries). *Journal de la Societe des Americanistes* 73:139–91.

Prescott, William H., and John Foster Kirk. 1873. *History of the Conquest of Mexico*. Philadelphia: J. B. Lippincott.

Prieto, Alfredo. 1991. Cazadores tempranos y tardíos en cueva del Lago Sofía. *Anales del Instituto de la Patagonia*, Ser. Cs. Ss. 20:75–99.

———. 1993–94. Algunos datos en torno a los enterratorios humanos de la región continental de Magallanes. *Anales del Instituto de la Patagonia*, Ser. Cs. Ss. 22:85–93.

———. 1994. *Arquería Selk'nam: La guerra y la paz en la Tierra del Fuego*. Punta Arenas, Chile: Ediciones Colegio Punta Arenas.

Proskouriakoff, Tatiana A. 1960. Historical Implications of a Pattern of Dates at Piedras Negras, Guatemala. *American Antiquity* 25 (4): 454–75.

Proulx, Donald A. 1985. *An Analysis of the Early Cultural Sequence in the Nepeña Valley, Peru*. Research Report no. 25. Amherst: Department of Anthropology, University of Massachusetts.

———. 2001. Ritual Uses of Trophy Heads in Ancient Nasca Society. In *Ritual Sacrifice in Ancient Peru*, ed. E. Benson and A. G. Cook, 119–36. Austin: University of Texas Press.

Puleston, Dennis E., and Donald W. Callendar. 1967. Defensive Earthworks at Tikal. *Expedition* 9:40–48.

Ramos Gavilán, Alonso. [1621] 1976. *Historia de Nuestra Señora de Copacabana*. La Paz: Universo.

Rands, Robert L. 1952. *Some Evidences of Warfare in Classic Maya Art*. Ph.D. dissertation, Columbia University, New York.

Rathje, William L. 1973. Classic Maya Development and Denouement: A Research Design. In *The Classic Maya Collapse*, ed. T. Patrick Culbert, 405–56. Albuquerque: University of New Mexico Press.

Rea, Amadeo M. 1986. Black Vultures and Human Victims: Archaeological Evidence from Pacatnamu. In *The Pacatnamu Papers*, vol. 1, ed. C. B. Donnan and G. A. Cock. Los Angeles: Museum of Cultural History.

Redmond, Elsa M. 1983. *A Fuego y Sangre: Early Zapotec Imperialism in the Cuicatlán Cañada, Oaxaca*. University of Michigan Museum of Anthropology Memoirs, no. 16. Ann Arbor.

———. 1994. *Tribal and Chiefly Warfare in South America*. Studies in Latin American Ethnohistory and Archaeology, ed. J. Marcus. University of Michigan Museum of Anthropology Memoirs, no. 28. Ann Arbor.

———. 1998. Introduction. In *Chiefdoms and Chieftaincy in the Americas*, ed. Elsa M. Redmond, 1–17. Tallahassee: University Press of Florida.

Redmond, Elsa M., Rafael A. Gassón, and Charles S. Spencer. 1999. A Macroregional View of Cycling Chiefdoms in the Western Venezuelan Llanos. In *Complex Polities in the Ancient Tropical World*, ed. Elisabeth A. Bacus and Lisa J. Lucero, 109–29. Archaeological Papers of the American Anthropological Association, no. 9. Arlington, Va.

Redmond, Elsa M., and Charles S. Spencer. 1994a. The Cacicazgo: An Indigenous Design. In *Caciques and Their People: A Volume in Honor of Ronald Spores*, ed. Joyce Marcus and Judith Francis Zeitlin, 189–225. University of Michigan Museum of Anthropology Anthropological Papers, no. 89. Ann Arbor.

———. 1994b. Savanna Chiefdoms of Venezuela. *National Geographic Research and Exploration* 10 (4): 422–39.

———. 1998. Introduction. In *Chiefdoms and Chieftaincy in the Americas*, ed. Elsa M. Redmond, 1–17. Tallahassee: University Press of Florida.

Renshaw, John. 2002. *The Indians of the Paraguayan Chaco*. Lincoln: University of Nebraska Press.

Rice, Don S., and Prudence M. Rice. 1981. Muralla de Leon: A Lowland Maya Fortification. *Journal of Field Archaeology* 8 (3): 271–88.

Rice, Prudence M., and Don S. Rice. 2004. Late Classic to Postclassic Transformations in the Petén Lakes Region, Guatemala. In *The Terminal Classic in the Maya Lowlands*, ed. Arthur A. Demarest, Prudence M. Rice, and Don S. Rice, 125–39. Boulder: University Press of Colorado.

Riches, David. 1995. Hunter-Gatherer Structural Transformations. In *Journal of the Royal Anthropological Institute* 1:679–702.

Ricketson, Oliver G., Jr., and Edith Bayles Ricketson. 1937. *Uaxactun, Guatemala, Group E, 1926–1931*. Carnegie Institution of Washington Publication no. 477. Washington, D.C.

Ringle, William H., George J. Bey III, Tara Bond Freeman, Craig A. Hanson, Charles W. Houck, and J. Gregory Smith. 2004. The Decline of the East: The Classic to Postclassic Transition at Ek Balam, Yucatán. In *The Terminal Classic in the Maya Lowlands*, ed. Arthur A. Demarest, Prudence M. Rice, and Don S. Rice, 485–516. Boulder: University Press of Colorado.

Rival, Laura M. 1999. The Huaorani. In *The Cambridge Encyclopedia of Hunters and Gatherers*, ed. Richard Lee and Richard Daly, 77–85. Cambridge, U.K.: Cambridge University Press.

———. 2002. *Trekking through History: The Huaorani of Amazonian Ecuador*. New York: Columbia University Press.

Rivero, Padre Juan. 1956. *Historia de las misiones de los Llanos de Casanare y los Ríos Orinoco y Meta*. Biblioteca de la Presidencia de Colombia 23. Bogotá: Empresa Nacional de Publicaciones.

Riveros, Fernando. 2003. *The Gran Chaco*. Rome, Italy: Food and Agriculture Organization of the United Nations (FAO). *www.fao.org/ag/agp/agpc/doc/Bulletin/GranChaco.html*.

Robarchek, Clayton, and Carol Robarchek. 1998. *Waorani: The Contexts of Violence and War*. New York: Harcourt Brace.

Robicsek, Francis, and Donald M. Hales. 1984. Maya Heart Sacrifice: Cultural Perspective and Surgical Technique. In *Ritual Human Sacrifice in Mesoamerica*, ed. Elizabeth H. Boone, 49–90. Washington, D.C.: Dumbarton Oaks Research Library and Collection.

Rodriguez, Ana Monica. 2006. Hallazgo arqueológico confirma sacrificios humanos prehispánicos. *La Jornada*, August 2. http://www.jornada.unam.mx/2006/08/02/a04n1cul.php.

Romey, Kristen. 2004a. Cenotes of Sacrifice. *Archaeology* 57 (3): 21–22.

———. 2004b. Diving in the Maya Underworld. *Archaeology* 57 (3): 16–19.

———. 2005. Watery Tombs. *Archaeology* 58 (4): 89.

Roosevelt, Anna C. 1989. Resource Management in Amazonia before the Conquest: Beyond Ethnographic Projection. In *Resource Management in Amazonia: Indigenous and Folk Strategies*, ed. Darrell A. Posey and William Balée, 30–62. Bronx: New York Botanical Garden.

Rosenberg, Annika. 1997. *Exhibiting the Arts of Human Sacrifice: A Critical Examination of the Exhibitions "AZTEC: The World of Moctezuma" and "Royal Tombs of Sipan."* M.A. thesis, University of California, Los Angeles.

Rostworowski de Diez Canseco, Maria. 1988. *Historia del Tahuantinsuyo.* Lima: Instituto de Estudios Peruanos.

———. 1999. *History of the Inca Realm.* Cambridge, U.K.: Cambridge University Press.

Roth, Walter E. 1915. An Inquiry into the Animism and Folk-Lore of the Guiana Indians. *Extract from the Thirtieth Annual Report of the Bureau of American Ethnology.* Washington, D.C.: Government Printing Office.

Rothstein, Edward. 2004. Who Should Tell History: The Tribes or the Museums? *New York Times*, Critics Notebook, December 21.

Rowe, John H. 1946. Inca Culture at the Time of the Spanish Conquest. In *Handbook of South American Indians*, vol. 2, ed. J. H. Steward, 183–330. Washington, D.C.: Bureau of American Ethnology.

———. 1948. The Kingdom of Chimor. *Acta Americana* 6 (1–2): 26–59.

Rubinstein, Robert A. 1994. Collective Violence and Common Security. In *Companion Encyclopedia of Anthropology*, ed. Tim Ingold, 983–1009. London: Routledge.

Ruedas, Javier. 2004. History, Ethnography, and Politics in Amazonia: Implications of Diachronic and Synchronic Variability in Marubo Politics. *Tipití: Journal of the Society for the Anthropology of Lowland South America* 2 (1): 23–64.

Ruppert, Karl, J. Eric S. Thompson, and Tatiana Proskouriakoff. 1955. *Bonampak, Chiapas, Mexico.* Carnegie Institution of Washington Publication no. 602. Washington, D.C.

Sabloff, Jeremy A., and William Rathje, eds. 1975. *A Study of Changing Pre-Columbian Commercial Systems: The 1972–1973 Seasons at Cozumel, Mexico.* Monographs of the Peabody Museum, no. 3. Cambridge, Mass.: Harvard University.

Sabloff, Jeremy A., and Gordon R. Willey. 1967. The Collapse of Maya Civilization in the Southern Lowlands: A Consideration of History and Process. *Southwestern Journal of Anthropology* 23:311–36.

Saeger, James Schofield. 2000. *The Chaco Mission Frontier: The Guaycuruan Experience.* Tucson: University of Arizona Press.

Sahagún, Fray Bernardino. 1905. *General History of the Things of New Spain*. Santa Fe, N.Mex.: School of American Research.

Salcamayhua, Juan de Santa Cruz. 1873. An Account of the Antiquities of Peru. In *Narratives in the Rites and Laws of the Yncas*, ed. Clements Markham, 100–115. London: Hakluyt Society.

Salinas Loyola, Juan de. [1571] 1965. Descubrimientos, conquistas y poblaciones de Juan de Salinas Loyola. In *Relaciones geográficas de Indias—Perú*, vol. 3, ed. Marcos Jiménez de la Espada, 197–214. Biblioteca de Autores Españoles 185. Madrid: Ediciones Atlas.

Sallnow, M. 1987. *Pilgrims of the Andes: Regional Cults in Cuzco*. Washington, D.C.: Smithsonian Institution Press.

Salzano, Francisco M., and Sidia M. Callegari-Jacques. 1988. *South American Indians: A Case Study in Evolution*. Oxford, U.K.: Oxford University Press.

Sánchez Saldaña, Patricia. 1972. El tzompantli de Tlatelolco. In *Religion en Mesoamerica, XII Mesa Redonda de la Sociedad Mexicana de Antropología*, ed. Jaime Litvak King and Noemi Castillo Tejero, 387–92. Mexico City.

San Martin, Juan. 2002. Ritual Conflict (Tinku) and Vindication of Indigenous Rights in Bolivia. *Mountain Research and Development* 22 (4): 394–96.

Santa Cruz Pachacuti, Juan de. [1571] 1968. *Relación de antiguedades deste reyno del Perú*. Madrid: Biblioteca de Autores Españoles.

Santos Granero, Fernando. 1992. *Etnohistoria de la Alta Amazonia: Siglo XV–XVIII*. Quito: Ediciones Abya-Yala.

———. 2000. The Sisyphus Syndrome, or the Struggle for Conviviality in Native Amazonia. In *The Anthropology of Love and Anger: The Aesthetics of Conviviality in Native Amazonia*, ed. Joanna Overing and Alan Passes, 268–87. New York: Routledge.

Scheffel, David. 2000. The Post-Anthropological Indian: Canada's New Image of Aboriginality in the Age of Repossession. *Anthropologica* 42:175–87.

Schele, Linda, and David Freidel. 1990. *A Forest of Kings: The Untold Story of the Ancient Maya*. New York: William Morrow.

Schele, Linda, and Peter Mathews. 1998. *The Code of Kings: The Language of Seven Sacred Maya Temples and Tombs*. New York: Scribner.

Schele, Linda, and Mary Ellen Miller. 1986. *The Blood of Kings: Dynasty and Ritual in Maya Art*. Fort Worth, Tex.: Kimbell Art Museum.

Schmidt, Bettina E., and Ingo W. Schroeder, eds. 2001. *Anthropology of Violence and Conflict*. London: Routledge, European Association of Social Anthropologists.

Sejourné, Laurette. 1978. *Burning Water: Thought and Religion in Ancient Mexico*. London: Thames and Hudson.

Sharer, Robert J. 2003. Founding Events and Teotihuacan Connections at Copán, Honduras. In *The Maya and Teotihuacan: Reinterpreting Early Classic Interaction*, ed. Geoffrey E. Braswell, 143–66. Austin: University of Texas Press.

Shimada, Izumi. 1994. *Pampa Grande and the Mochica Culture*. Austin: University of Texas Press.

Shook, Edwin M. 1952. Great Wall of Mayapan. *Carnegie Institution of Washington, Current Reports* 1 (2): 7–35.

Sikkink, Lynn. 1997. Water and Exchange: The Ritual of Yaku Cambio as Communal and Competitive Encounter. *American Ethnologist* 24 (1): 170–89.

Smith, Hallett. 1974. The Tempest. In *The Riverside Shakespeare*, ed. G. Blakemore Evans, 1606–10. Boston: Houghton Mifflin.

Smith, Michael. 2003. *The Aztecs*. Malden: Blackwell Publishing.

Soares de Sousa, Gabriel. [1587] 1948. *Notícia do Brasil*. Biblioteca Histórica Brasileira 16. São Paulo: Editora Martins.

Spencer, Charles S. 1982. *The Cuicatlán Cañada and Monte Albán: A Study of Primary State Formation*. New York: Academic Press.

———. 1990. On the Tempo and Mode of State Formation: Neoevolutionism Reconsidered. *Journal of Anthropological Archaeology* 9:1–30.

———. 1998a. Investigating the Development of Venezuelan Chiefdoms. In *Chiefdoms and Chieftaincy in the Americas*, ed. Elsa M. Redmond, 104–37. Gainesville: University Press of Florida.

———. 1998b. A Mathematical Model of Primary State Formation. *Cultural Dynamics* 10:5–20.

———. 2003. War and Early State Formation in Oaxaca, Mexico. *Proceedings of the National Academy of Sciences* 100 (20): 11185–87.

Spencer, Charles S., and Elsa M. Redmond. 1997. *Archaeology of the Cañada de Cuicatlán, Oaxaca*. American Museum of Natural History Anthropological Papers, no. 80. New York.

———. 1998. Prehispanic Causeways and Regional Politics in the Llanos of Barinas, Venezuela. *Latin American Antiquity* 9 (2): 95–110.

———. 2001a. Multilevel Selection and Political Evolution in the Valley of Oaxaca, 500–100 B.C. *Journal of Anthropological Archaeology* 20:195–229.

———. 2001b. The Chronology of Conquest: Implications of New Radiocarbon Analyses from the Cañada de Cuicatlán, Oaxaca. *Latin American Antiquity* 12:182–202.

———. 2003. Militarism, Resistance, and Early State Development in Oaxaca, Mexico. *Social Evolution and History* 2 (1): 25–70.

———. 2004a. A Late Monte Albán I Phase (300–100 B.C.) Palace in the Valley of Oaxaca. *Latin American Antiquity* 15:441–55.

———. 2004b. Primary State Formation in Mesoamerica. *Annual Review in Anthropology* 33:173–99.

Spencer, Charles S., Elsa M. Redmond, and Milagro Rinaldi. 1994. Drained Fields at La Tigra, Venezuelan Llanos: A Regional Perspective. *Latin American Antiquity* 5 (2): 119–43.

Staden, Hans. 1929. *Hans Staden: The True Story of His Captivity*, trans. M. Letts. New York: McBride.

Standen, Vivien G., and Bernardo T. Arriaza. 2000. Trauma in the Preceramic Coastal Populations of Northern Chile: Violence or Occupational Hazards? *American Journal of Physical Anthropology* 112:239–49.

Stearman, Allyn. 1994. Only Slaves Climb Trees: Revisiting the Myth of the Ecologically Noble Savage in Amazonia. *Human Nature* 5 (4): 339–56.

Sterpin, Adriana. 1993. L'Espace sociale de la prise de scalps chez les Nivacle du Gran Chaco. *Hacia una Nueva Carta Etnica del Gran Chaco* 5:129–92.

Stevenson, Mark. 2005. Mexican Archaeologists Find Rare Sacrifice. *Guardian Unlimited*, July 22. http://www.guardian.co.uk/worldlatest/story/0,1280,-5160615,00.html.

Steward, Julian, and L. Faron. 1959. *Native Peoples of South America*. New York: McGraw-Hill.

Stuart, David. 1995. *A Study of Maya Inscriptions*. Ph.D. dissertation, Department of Anthropology, Vanderbilt University, Nashville.

———. 2000. "The Arrival of the Strangers": Teotihuacan and Tollan in Classic Maya History. In *Mesoamerica's Classic Heritage: From Teotihuacan to the Aztecs*, ed. David Carrasco, Lindsay Jones, and Scott Sessions, 465–513. Boulder: University Press of Colorado.

Stuart, George E. 1992. Masterpieces of Ancient Cacaxtla. *National Geographic* 182 (3), September.

Sturtevant, William C. 1998. Tupinambá Chiefdoms? In *Chiefdoms and Chieftaincy in the Americas*, ed. Elsa M. Redmond, 138–49. Tallahassee: University Press of Florida.

Sugiyama, Saburo. 1992. Rulership, Warfare, and Human Sacrifice at the Ciudadela: An Iconographic Study of Feathered Serpent Representations. In *Art, Ideology, and the City of Teotihuacan*, ed. Janet Catherine Berlo, 205–30. Washington, D.C.: Dumbarton Oaks Research Library and Collection.

———. 1995. *Mass Human Sacrifice and Symbolism of the Feathered Serpent Pyramid in Teotihuacán, Mexico*. Ph.D. dissertation, Arizona State University, Tempe.

———. 2000. Teotihuacan as an Origin for Postclassic Feathered Serpent Symbolism. In *Mesoamerica's Classic Heritage: From Teotihuacan to the Aztecs*, ed. Davíd Carrasco, Lindsay Jones, and Scott Sessions, 117–43. Boulder: University Press of Colorado.

———. 2005. *Human Sacrifice, Militarism, and Rulership: Materialization of State Ideology at the Feathered Serpent Pyramid, Teotihuacan*. New Studies in Archaeology. Cambridge, U.K.: Cambridge University Press.

Sugiyama, Saburo, and Rubén Cabrera. 2003. Hallazgos reciente en la Pirámide de la Luna. *Arqueología* 11 (64): 42–49.

Suhler, Charles, Traci Ardren, David Freidel, and Dave Johnstone. 2004. The Rise and Fall of Terminal Classic Yaxuna, Yucatán, Mexico. In *The Terminal Classic in the Maya Lowlands*, ed. Arthur A. Demarest, Prudence M. Rice, and Don S. Rice, 450–84. Boulder: University Press of Colorado.

Susnik, Branislava. 1975. *Dispersión Tupí-Guaraní prehistórica: Ensayo analítico*. Asuncion, Paraguay: Museo Etnográfico Andres Barbero.

———. 1990. *Guerra, tránsito, subsistencia (ambito Americano)*. Asunción, Paraguay: Museo Etnográfico Andrés Barbero.

Swidler, Nina, Kurt Dongoske, Roger Ayon, and Allan Downer. 1997. *Native Americans and Archaeologists: Stepping Stones to Common Ground*. Walnut Creek, Calif.: AltaMira Press.

Talavera González, Jorge Arturo, Juan Martín Rojas, and Enrique Hugo García Valencia. 2001. *Modificaciones culturales en los restos óseos de Cantona, Puebla: Un análisis bioarqueológico*. Mexico City: Instituto Nacional de Antropología e Historia.

Taylor, Anne Christine. 1999. The Western Margins of Amazonia from the Early Sixteenth to the Early Nineteenth Century. In *The Cambridge History of the Native Peoples of the Americas*, vol. 3, part 2, ed. Frank Salomon and Stuart B. Schwarts, 188–256. Cambridge, U.K.: Cambridge University Press.

Taylor, Gerald. 1987. *Ritos y tradiciones de los Huarochiri*. Lima: Instituto de Estudios Peruanos.

Tebboth, Dora. 1989. *With Teb. among the Toba: Letters Written Home from the Mission Field*. Kent, U.K.: Lantern Press.

Tello, Julio C. 1913. Prehistoric Trephining among the Yauyos of Peru. *XVIII International Congress of Americanists* (London, 1912), vol. 1, 75–83.

Tessman, G. 1930. *Die Indianer Nordost-Perus: Grundlegende Forschungen fur eine systematische Kulturkunde*. Hamburg: Friederichsen, de Gruyter.

Thevet, André. 1944. *Singularidades da França Antarctica, a que outros chamam de América*. São Paulo: Companhia Editoria Nacional.

Thompson, J. Eric S. 1966. *The Rise and Fall of Maya Civilization*. Norman: University of Oklahoma Press (originally published, 1954).

Thorpe, I. J. N. 2003. Anthropology, Archaeology, and the Origin of Warfare. *World Archaeology* 35 (1): 145–65.

Tierney, Patrick. 1989. *The Highest Altar*. New York: Penguin Books.

Tlapoyawa, Kurly. 2002. *We Will Rise: Rebuilding the Mexikah Nation*. Victoria, B.C.: Trafford Publishing.

———. 2003. Did "Mexika Human Sacrifice" Exist? Mexika Eagle Society website. http://www.mexika.org/TlapoSac.htm.

Topic, John. 1989. The Ostra Site: The Earliest Fortified Site in the New World? In *Cultures in Conflict: Current Archaeological Perspectives*, ed. Diana Tkaczuk and Brian Vivian, 215–28. Calgary: University of Calgary Archaeology Association.

Topic, John R., and Theresa L. Topic. 1987. The Archaeological Study of Andean Militarism: Some Cautionary Observations. In *The Origins and Development of the Andean State*, ed. J. Haas, S. Pozorski, and T. Pozorski. Cambridge, U.K.: Cambridge University Press.

———. 1997. La Guerra Mochica. *Revista Arqueológica "SIAN"* (Universidad Nacional de Trujillo) 4:10–12.

Topic, Theresa Lange. 1990. Territorial Expansion and the Kingdom of Chimor. In *The Northern Dynasties: Kingship and Statecraft in Chimor*, ed. M. E. Moseley and A. Cordy-Collins, 177–94. Washington, D.C.: Dumbarton Oaks.

Tourtellot, Gair, and Jeremy Sabloff. 2004. Seibal Revisited: The Crown Jewel in the Regional Necklace? Paper presented at the 69th Annual Meeting of the Society for American Archaeology, Montreal.

Trejo, Silvia, ed. 2000. *La guerra entre los antiguos Mayas*. Memoria de la Primera Mesa Redonda de Palenque. Mexico City: Instituto Nacional de Antropología e Historia.

Ubelaker, Douglas H. 1992. Hyoid Fracture and Strangulation. *Journal of Forensic Sciences* 37 (5): 1216–22.

Uceda, Santiago. 1999. Esculturas en miniatura y una maqueta en madera: El culto a los muertos y a los ancestros en la época Chimú. *Beiträge zur Allgemeinen und Vergleichenden Archäologie* 19:259–311.

Uceda, Santiago, and Proyecto Arqueologico Huacas del Sol y de la Luna. 1998. *Investigaciones en la Huaca de la Luna, 1996*, ed. S. Uceda, E. Mujica, and R. Morales. Trujillo, Peru: Universidad Nacional de la Libertad Facultad de Ciencias Sociales.

Uhle, Max. 1903. *Pachacamac: Report of the William Pepper, M.D., LL.D., Peruvian Expedition of 1896*. Philadelphia: University of Pennsylvania.

Up de Graff, F. W. 1921. *Headhunters of the Amazon*. London: Herbert Jenkins.

Urton, Gary. 1993. Moieties and Ceremonialism in the Andes: The Ritual Battles of the Carnival Season in Southern Peru. In *El mundo ceremonial Andino*, ed. L. Millones and Y. Onuki, 117–42. Osaka, Japan: Museo Nacional de Etnologia.

Valdés, Juan Antonio. 1997. Tamarindito: Archaeology and Regional Politics in the Petexbatun Region. *Ancient Mesoamerica* 8 (2): 321–35.

Van Cleve, Janice. 2003. Who Was Eighteen Rabbit? A Life Revealed in Stone. Foundation for the Advancement of Mesoamerican Studies website. http://www.famsi.org/research/van_cleve/.

Van Tuerenhout, Dirk. 1996. *Rural Fortifications at Quim Chi Hilan, El Peten, Guatemala: Late Classic Maya Social Change Seen from a Small Site Perspective*. Ph.D. dissertation, Tulane University, New Orleans.

Vargas-Cetina, Gabriela. 2003. Representations of Indigenousness. *Anthropology News* 44 (5): 11–12.

Vasquez, Gerardo V. 1940. *Doctrinas y realidades en la legislacion para los Indios*. Mexico City: Departamento de Asuntos Indigenas.

Vega, Bernardo. 1980. *Los cacicazgos de la Hispaniola*. Investigaciones Antropológicas 13. Santo Domingo, Dominican Republic: Ediciones Museo del Hombre Dominicano.

Verano, John W. 1986. A Mass Burial of Mutilated Individuals at Pacatnamu. In *The Pacatnamu Papers*, vol. 1, ed. C. B. Donnan and G. A. Cock, 117–38. Los Angeles: Museum of Cultural History.

———. 1995. Where Do They Rest? The Treatment of Human Offerings and Trophies in Ancient Peru. In *Tombs for the Living: Andean Mortuary Practices*, ed. T. D. Dillehay, 189–227. Washington, D.C.: Dumbarton Oaks.

———. 1997. Physical Characteristics and Skeletal Biology of the Moche Population at Pacatnamu. In *The Pacatnamu Papers*. Vol. 2: *The Moche Occupation*, ed. C. B. Donnan and G. A. Cock, 189–214. Los Angeles: Fowler Museum of Cultural History.

———. 1998. Sacrificios humanos, desmembramientos y modificaciones culturales en restos osteológicos: Evidencias de las temporadas de investigación 1995–96 en la Huaca de la Luna. In *Investigaciones en la Huaca de la Luna 1996*, ed. S. Uceda, E. Mujica, and R. Morales, 159–71. Trujillo: Universidad Nacional de Trujillo.

———. 2001a. The Physical Evidence of Human Sacrifice in Ancient Peru. In *Ritual Sacrifice in Ancient Peru*, ed. E. Benson and A. Cook, 165–84. Austin: University of Texas Press.

———. 2001b. War and Death in the Moche World: Osteological Evidence and Visual Discourse. In *Moche Art and Archaeology in Ancient Peru*, ed. J. Pillsbury, 111–25. Washington, D.C.: National Gallery of Art.

———. 2003. Trepanation in Prehistoric South America: Geographic and Temporal

Trends over 2,000 Years. In *Trepanation: History, Discovery, Theory*, ed. R. Arnott, S. Finger, and C. U. M. Smith, 223–36. Lisse: Swets and Zeitlinger B.V.

Verano, John W., and Michael J. DeNiro. 1993. Locals or Foreigners? Morphological, Biometric and Isotopic Approaches to the Question of Group Affinity in Human Skeletal Remains Recovered from Unusual Archaeological Contexts. In *Investigations of Ancient Human Tissue: Chemical Analysis in Anthropology*, ed. M. K. Sandford, 361–86. Langhorne, Penn.: Gordon and Breach.

Verano, John W., and Héctor Walde. 2004. A Mass Human Sacrifice at Punta Lobos, Huarmey River Valley, Northern Coastal Peru. Paper read at 31st Annual Meeting of the Paleopathology Association, at Tampa, Florida, April 15.

Verneau, René. 1903. *Les ancient patagons*. Monaco: Imprimerie de Monaco.

Viedma, Antonio de. 1910. Descripción de la costa meridional del sur, llamada vulgarmente patagónica . . . In *Colección de obras y documentos relativos á la historia antigua y moderna de las provincias del Río de la Plata*, vol. 5, ed. Pedro de Angelis. 2nd ed. Buenos Aires: Librería Nacional J. LaJouane and Cía.

Viveiros de Castro, Eduardo. 1992. *From the Enemy's Point of View: Humanity and Divinity in an Amazonian Society*, trans. Catherine V. Howard. Chicago: University of Chicago Press.

———. 1998. Dravidian and Related Kinship Systems. In *Transformations of Kinship*, ed. Thomas Trautmann, Maurice Godelier, and Franklin E. Tjon Sie Fat, 332–85. Washington, D.C.: Smithsonian Institution Press.

Von Winning, Hasso. 1987. *La iconografía de Teotihuacan: Los dioses y los signos*, 2 vols. Mexico City: Universidad Nacional Autónoma de México.

Wahl, J., and H. Konig. 1987. Anthropologisch-Traumologische untersuchung der Menschlichen Sketettreste aus dem Bandkeramischen Massengrab bei Talheim, Kreis Heilbronn. *Fundberichte aus Baden-Wurtemberg* 12:65–193.

Walde, Héctor. 1998. *Informe final: Proyecto Arqueológico en Punta Lobos Puerto de Huarmey*. Lima: Submitted to the Instituto Nacional de Cultura, Lima.

Walker, Philip. 2000. Bioarchaeological Ethics: A Historical Perspective on the Value of Human Remains. In *Biological Anthropology of the Human Skeleton*, ed. M. Katzenberg and S. Saunders, 3–39. New York: Wiley-Liss.

Webster, David. 1976. *Defensive Earthworks at Becan, Campeche, Mexico: Implications for Maya Warfare*. Middle American Research Institute Publication no. 41. New Orleans: Tulane University.

———. 1977. Warfare and the Evolution of Maya Civilization. In *The Origins of Maya Civilization*, ed. Richard E. W. Adams, 335–72. Albuquerque: University of New Mexico Press.

———. 1978. Three Walled Sites of the Northern Maya Lowlands. *Journal of Field Archaeology* 5 (4): 375–90.

———. 1993. The Study of Maya Warfare: What It Tells Us about the Maya and What It Tells Us about Maya Archaeology. In *Lowland Maya Civilization in the Eighth Century A.D.*, ed. J. A. Sabloff and J. S. Henderson, 415–44. Washington, D.C.: Dumbarton Oaks Research Library.

Webster, David, Jay Silverstein, Timothy Murtha, Horacio Martínez, and Kirk Straight. 2004. *The Tikal Earthworks Revisited*. Occasional Papers in Anthropology, no. 28. University Park: Department of Anthropology, Pennsylvania State University.

Whatley, Janet. 1990. Introduction. In *History of a Voyage to the Land of Brazil, Otherwise Called America . . .* (by Jean de Léry), xv–xxxviii. Los Angeles: University of California Press.

White, Tim D. 1992. *Prehistoric Cannibalism at Mancos 5MTUMR-2346*. Princeton, N.J.: Princeton University Press.

Whitehead, Neil L. 1990. The Snake Warriors—Sons of the Tiger's Teeth: A Descriptive Analysis of Carib Warfare, ca. 1500–1820. In *The Anthropology of War*, ed. Jonathan Hass, 146–70. SAR Book. Cambridge, U.K.: Cambridge University Press.

Wibbelsman, Michelle. 2004. *Rimarishpa Kausanchik, Dialogical Encounters: Festive Ritual Practices and the Making of Otavalen Moral and Mythic Community*. Ph.D. dissertation in Anthropology, University of Illinois at Urbana-Champagne.

———. 2005. Otavalenos at the Crossroads: Physical and Metaphysical Coordinates of an Indigenous World. *Journal of Latin American Anthropology* 10 (1): 151–85.

Wilbert, Johannes, ed: 1975. *Folk Literature of the Selknam Indians: Martin Gusinde's Collection of Selknam Narratives*. Los Angeles: UCLA Latin American Center Publications, University of California.

———, ed. 1977. *Folk Literature of the Yamana Indians: Martin Gusinde's Collection of Yamana Narratives*. Berkeley and Los Angeles: University of California Press.

Willey, Gordon R. 1973. *The Altar de Sacrificios Excavations: General Summary and Conclusions*. Papers of the Peabody Museum of American Archaeology and Ethnology, vol. 64, no. 3. Cambridge, Mass.: Harvard University.

Willey, P. 1990. *Prehistoric Warfare on the Great Plains*. New York: Garland Press.

Williams, A. R., and Jesús Eduardo López Reyes. 2006. Pyramid of Death. *National Geographic* 210 (4): 144–53.

Wilson, David J. 1987. Reconstructing Patterns of Early Warfare in the Lower Santa Valley: New Data on the Role of Conflict in the Origins of Complex North-Coast Society. In *The Origins and Development of the Andean State*, ed. J. Haas, S. Pozorski, and T. Pozorski. Cambridge, U.K.: Cambridge University Press.

Wilson, Richard. 1991. Machine Guns and Mountain Spirits. *Critique of Anthropology* 11 (1): 33–61.

Workinger, Andrew G. 2002. *Coastal/Highland Interaction in Prehispanic Oaxaca, Mexico: The Perspective from San Francisco de Arriba*. Ph.D. dissertation, Vanderbilt University, Nashville.

Wright, Henry T. 1977. Recent Research on the Origin of the State. *Annual Review of Anthropology* 6:379–97.

Wright, Lori E. 2006. *Diet, Health, and Status among the Pasión Maya*. Nashville: Vanderbilt University Press.

Wright, Robin M., with Manuela Carneiro da Cunha. 1999. Destruction, Resistance and Transformation—Southern, Coastal, and Northern Brazil (1580–1890). In *The Cambridge History of the Native Peoples of the Americas*, vol. 3, part 2, ed. Frank Salomon and Stuart B. Schwarts, 287–381. Cambridge, U.K.: Cambridge University Press.

Yost, James. 1981. Twenty Years of Contact: The Mechanisms of Change in Huao ("Auca") Culture. In *Transformation and Ethnicity in Modern Ecuador*, ed. Norman Whitten, 677–704. Urbana: University of Illinois Press.

———. 1990. The Waorani. In *Encyclopedia of World Cultures*. Vol. 7: *South America*, ed. J. Wilbert, 351–53. Boston: G. K. Hall.

Zayas y Alfonso, Alfredo. 1931. *Lexicografía Antillana: Diccionario de voces usadas por los Aborígenes de las Antillas Mayores y de algunas de las Menores y consideraciones acerca de su significado y de su formación*, vol. 1. 2nd ed. Havana: Molina y Cia.

Zecenarro, Bernardino. 1992. De fiestas, rituos y batallas: Algunos comportamientos folk de la sociedad Andin de los Kanas y Chumpiwillcas. *Allpanchis* 40:147–72.

Zorn, Elayne. 2002. Dangerous Encounters: Ritual Battles in Andean Bolivia. In *Combat, Ritual and Performance*, ed. David Jones, 119–52. Westport, Conn.: Praeger.

Zuidema, R. Tom. 1991. Batallas rituales en el Cuzco colonial. In *Cultures et societes Andes et Meso-Amerique*, vol. 2. Provence, France: Publications de l'Universite de Provence.

———. 1992. Inca Cosmos in Andean Context. In *Andean Cosmologies through Time*, ed. R. Dover, K. Seibold, and J. McDowell, 17–45. Bloomington: Indiana University Press.

ABOUT THE CONTRIBUTORS

WILLIAM BALÉE is a professor of anthropology at Tulane University in New Orleans. He has conducted ethnographic fieldwork among the Tupian-speaking Ka'apor, Guajá, Araweté, Assurini do Xingu, and Tembé of eastern Amazonian Brazil in addition to work among the Sirionó of the eastern Bolivian lowlands. His research interests include ecological anthropology, ethnobotany, and the ethnohistory of lowland South America.

STEPHEN BECKERMAN is an associate professor of anthropology at Pennsylvania State University. He has conducted ethnographic fieldwork among the Barí of Colombia and the Waorani of Ecuador. His research interests include optimal foraging theory, indigenous subsistence patterns, conservation ecology, human reproductive strategies, and tribal warfare.

RODRIGO CÁRDENAS is an associate researcher at the Universidad de Magallanes, Chile. He has conducted archaeological excavations and ethnographic studies throughout Patagonia and Tierra del Fuego. His research interests include socioeconomic organization, the ethnohistory of hunter-gatherers, and the evolution of human cognition.

RICHARD J. CHACON is an assistant professor of anthropology at Winthrop University, South Carolina. He has conducted ethnographic fieldwork in Amazonia among the Yanomamö of Venezuela, the Yora of Peru, and the Achuar (Shiwiar) of Ecuador, and he has also worked in the Andes with the Otavalo and Cotacachi Indians of highland Ecuador. His research interests include optimal foraging theory, indigenous subsistence strategies, warfare, the evolution of complex societies, belief systems, ethnohistory, and the effects of globalization.

YAMILETTE CHACON is a graduate student in the Sociology Department at the University of South Carolina. She has conducted ethnographic fieldwork among the Otavalo and Cotacachi Indians of highland Ecuador. Her research interests include conflict and violence, the evolution of complex societies, social inequality, belief systems, gender issues, and globalization.

ARTHUR A. DEMAREST is a professor of anthropology at Vanderbilt University in Nashville, Tennessee. He has conducted archaeological fieldwork in El Salvador and Guatemala for over twenty-five years. His research interests include the archaeology and cultural evolution of Mesoamerica and South America.

ANGEL GUANDINANGO is a Cotacachi indigenous leader as well as a professor at the Escuela Maria Larea in Pinsaqui, Imbabura, in Ecuador. His research interests include Andean belief systems and ethnohistory.

DONALD MCVICKER is a professor emeritus of anthropology at North Central College, Chicago, and a research associate in anthropology at the Field Museum in Chicago. He has conducted archaeological excavations in the Southwest and Mexico. His research interests include the ancient civilizations of Mesoamerica and the history of archaeology.

MARCELA MENDOZA is an adjunct professor at the University of Oregon. She has conducted ethnographic fieldwork among the Western Toba of Argentina, and her research interests include the socioeconomic organization of lowland South American indigenous peoples.

RUBÉN G. MENDOZA is an archaeologist and professor of social and behavioral sciences at California State University–Monterey Bay. He has conducted archaeological excavations in California, Colorado, and Arizona and in Guanajuato and Puebla, Mexico. His research interests include Mesoamerican and South American civilizations and Hispanic, Native American, and mestizo traditional technologies and material cultures of the U.S. Southwest. He currently serves as the director for the California State University–Monterey Bay's Institute for Archaeological Science, Technology, and Visualization.

MATT O'MANSKY is an instructor at Youngstown State University in Ohio and a Ph.D. candidate at Vanderbilt University in Nashville, Tennessee. He has conducted archaeological field research in Guatemala, Belize, the United States, and France. His research interests include the archaeology of Mesoamerica, setttlement pattern research, warfare, and ethics in anthropology.

ALFREDO PRIETO is a professor of anthropology at the Universidad de Magallanes, Chile. He has conducted archaeological excavations throughout Patagonia and Tierra del Fuego. His research interests include the socioeconomic organization and ethnohistory of hunter-gatherers.

ELSA M. REDMOND is a research associate in the Division of Anthropology at the American Museum of Natural History. She has conducted archaeological investigations in Mexico and Venezuela. Her research interests center on the evolution of complex societies and include ethnohistory, warfare, and settlement patterns.

CHARLES S. SPENCER is the curator of Mesoamerican archaeology at the American Museum of Natural History. He has conducted archaeological excavations in Mexico and Venezuela. His research interests include the cultural evolution of social complexity in Mesoamerica.

JOHN W. VERANO is an associate professor of anthropology at Tulane University in New Orleans. He has conducted archaeological excavations in Peru since 1983. His research interests include Andean archaeology, physical anthropology, paleopathology, and forensics.

JAMES YOST, who now resides in Colorado, conducted ethnographic fieldwork among the Waorani of Ecuador between 1973 and 1982 and has made return trips there every year since. He has served as an anthropological consultant for various nongovernmental organizations and private industry throughout North and South America, India, New Guinea, and Africa. His primary research interests are warfare, cultural ecology, culture change, and cross-cultural communications. He continues to work extensively as a consultant to the Waorani.

INDEX